Convergence

Convergence

Essays on the Intersection
between Philosophy and Theology

Edited by DANIEL J. FICK
and JESSE K. MILEO

Foreword by R. J. SNELL

WIPF & STOCK · Eugene, Oregon

CONVERGENCE
Essays on the Intersection between Philosophy and Theology

Copyright © 2018 Wipf and Stock Publishers. All rights reserved. Except for brief quotations in critical publications or reviews, no part of this book may be reproduced in any manner without prior written permission from the publisher. Write: Permissions, Wipf and Stock Publishers, 199 W. 8th Ave., Suite 3, Eugene, OR 97401.

Wipf & Stock
An Imprint of Wipf and Stock Publishers
199 W. 8th Ave., Suite 3
Eugene, OR 97401

www.wipfandstock.com

PAPERBACK ISBN: 978-1-62564-717-7
HARDCOVER ISBN: 978-1-4982-8591-9
EBOOK ISBN: 978-1-5326-4640-9

Manufactured in the U.S.A.   01/02/18

All Scripture quotations, unless otherwise indicated, are taken from the Holy Bible, New International Version®, NIV®. Copyright ©1973, 1978, 1984, 2011 by Biblica, Inc.™ Used by permission of Zondervan. All rights reserved worldwide. www.zondervan.com The "NIV" and "New International Version" are trademarks registered in the United States Patent and Trademark Office by Biblica, Inc.™

Scripture quotations are from the ESV® Bible (The Holy Bible, English Standard Version®), copyright © 2001 by Crossway, a publishing ministry of Good News Publishers. Used by permission. All rights reserved.

For our Daughters:

To Isla Louise,
may you grow in the grace of God,
ever learning to plumb the depths of philosophy and theology.

To Rosalie Juliet, my "Little Precious Jewel,"
may you keep asking questions,
and may you always be a true philosopher,
a lover of God.

CONTENTS

Contributors | ix
Foreword by R. J. Snell | xi
Acknowledgements | xiii

    INTRODUCTION | 1
    —Daniel J. Fick

1 THE LOGIC OF THEOLOGY | 10
    —Douglas Groothuis

2 ARGUMENTS FOR THE EXISTENCE OF GOD AS A THEOLOGICAL FOUNDATION | 27
    —Robert O'Connor

3 EPISTEMOLOGICAL MATTERS MATTER FOR THEOLOGICAL UNDERSTANDING | 48
    —Joseph LaPorte

4 GOD AS THE INDISPENSABLE FOUNDATION FOR ETHICS | 62
    —Jesse K. Mileo

5 THE OLD TESTAMENT AND METAPHYSICS: A NEW GROUND FOR THEOLOGY? | 89
    —Jason Stanghelle

6 GOSPEL ETHICS | 111
    —Alan P. Stanley

7 THE LOGIC OF PAUL | 132
    —Philip D. Burggraff

8 PATRISTIC EPISTEMOLOGY | 155
    —Ryan M. Clevenger

CONTRIBUTORS

Philip D. Burggraff. PhD, McMaster Divinity College. Preaching and Teaching Pastor. Clearwater Community Church.

Ryan M. Clevenger. PhD Cand, Wheaton College.

Daniel J. Fick. MTS, Moody Theological Seminary. Adjunct Assistant Professor of Philosophy, Schoolcraft College.

Douglas Groothuis. PhD, University of Oregon. Professor of Philosophy, Denver Seminary.

Joseph LaPorte. PhD, University of Massachusetts. Professor of Philosophy, Hope College.

Jesse K. Mileo. MDiv, Moody Theological Seminary. MA, Wayne State University. Adjunct Assistant Professor of Philosophy, Schoolcraft College.

Robert O'Connor. PhD, University of Notre Dame. Associate Professor of Philosophy, Wheaton College.

Jason Stanghelle. PhD Cand, Trinity Evangelical Divinity School. Adjunct Faculty, Trinity College.

Alan P. Stanley. PhD, Dallas Theological Seminary. Lecturer in Bible and Christian Thought, Brisbane School of Theology.

FOREWORD

At the burning bush on Horeb, Moses is informed that the impending plagues will win the Israelites so much "favor in the sight of the Egyptians" that any request to "borrow" gold, silver, and clothing will be met with a generous response (Exod 3:20–22). So generous, in fact, as to despoil the Egyptians and fulfill God's promise to Abraham that his enslaved descendants would depart with "great possessions" (Gen 15:14).

"Borrow" is an odd term, especially if the people were departing for their own land and not merely worshiping God with embellishments "lent" for a few days before return, as some might suggest (Exod 10:24–26). "Ask" perhaps captures the tone more aptly than "borrow." On the other hand, very quickly the Israelites give away their new riches—first for the golden calf but also to furnish the tabernacle—and so the abundance of Egypt becomes, in part, the Lord's.

Christian theology has no particular philosophy of its own and demands allegiance to no one school or system, but we borrow knowledge whenever we need it. Plato, Aristotle, Plotinus, Kant, Reid, Wittgenstein, and many more, have favored us with their wealth, although we do, at times, argue on who is suitable for idolatrous calf or holy tent.

With real intelligence and care, the contributors to *Convergence* consider the ways theology borrows from philosophy, and how it benefits the church. Of course, as we know, the temptation to build calves persists, which is a good reason to think and discern carefully, a task made easier by this text.

R. J. Snell
Professor of Philosophy
Eastern University
St Davids, Penn.
5th Sunday of Lent, 2015

ACKNOWLEDGEMENTS

Philosophy and theology are not undertaken in a vacuum. As such, we have several to thank: To the distinguished scholars who contributed to this volume, we offer our sincere appreciation for both your scholastic proficiency and gifted writing. Any remaining errors, of course, belong to the editors. To R. J. Snell, we offer our thanks for your excitement about this volume and willingness to pen such an exemplary foreword. To Wipf & Stock, we offer our thanks for your willingness to accept projects based on *merit* rather than *marketability*, and for being an excellent collaborator and gracious host for this project. Lastly, but most importantly, we offer our thanks to Jesus the Christ, our Savior, Redeemer, and Friend, who purchased our redemption and called us into his marvelous light.

INTRODUCTION

Daniel J. Fick

What happens when affection for pop culture outweighs admiration for substance? That is, what happens when society is more interested in reading X's Twitter feed (where X is your favorite pop icon) than Descartes's *Meditations on First Philosophy*? In that instance, J. P. Moreland's concern rings true: "It doesn't take a rocket scientist to recognize that our entire culture is in trouble . . . [O]ur society has replaced heroes with celebrities, the quest for a well-informed character with the search for a flat stomach, substance and depth with image and personality."[1] This book was written in 1997! Our intellectual culture has sunk far lower over the last twenty years.

The Christian subculture has not been unaffected by this intellectual downgrade. And yet, a counterculture exists. This counterculture appreciates philosophy and theology, and desires to think deeply. A renaissance in Christian philosophy has taken place these past few decades through the thinking and writing of people like J. P. Moreland, Nancey Murphy, William Lane Craig, Elizabeth Burns, Alvin Plantinga, Lynne Rudder Baker, etc.[2] In fact, I implore my students every semester to realize the difficult truth of Moreland's claim and resist this intellectual downgrade, and, rather, embrace the life of the mind, reaching for substance and depth.

Grasping for substance and depth by exploring the life of the mind can be found in the disciplines of philosophy and theology. To be sure, these disciplines affect every aspect of life! This volume has two aims: (1) to demonstrate the importance of philosophy and theology, and (2) to highlight

---

1. Moreland, *Love Your God with All Your Mind*, 21.
2. See Moreland and Craig, *Philosophical Foundations*, 3.

why those two disciplines are interdependent. After defining some terms in philosophy and theology, I will briefly summarize each of the essays, followed by several reasons why the convergence between philosophy and theology matters. Let's start by defining some terms.

WHAT IS PHILOSOPHY?

Philosophy can be defined as "[t]he human attempt to systematically study the most fundamental structures of our entire experience in order to arrive at beliefs that are as conceptually clear, experientially confirmed, and rationally coherent as possible."[3] And who doesn't want to have clear concepts, not to mention beliefs, which are confirmed by our experiences, and deemed rational and coherent? Now, the word "philosophy" comes from the Greek words for "love" (*philos*) and "wisdom" (*sophia*). Seen in this light, we can also understand philosophy as the attempt to love wisdom. That is, people who think hard about the world around them, those asking questions and seeking knowledge about what matters most to them, should be considered students of philosophy.[4]

There are four main divisions within the discipline of philosophy (and many subdivisions thereafter). The intent of this volume is to track along these main divisions: logic, metaphysics, epistemology, and ethics.

Logic is the study of correct reasoning. It involves argumentation, both in formulation and evaluation. This oft-misunderstood discipline is the backbone of philosophy, for how can we argue for any philosophical position without being able to reason well? Therefore, we have two chapters that focus on logic: one identifying its importance for theology, and another interacting with, perhaps, the finest arguer in the biblical text, the Apostle Paul.

Metaphysics is, well, vast. It is the study of the nature of existence and asks questions like: What kinds of things exist? How is existence possible? What is space? What is time? What is spirit? What is soul? What is matter? It's a difficult division of philosophy. In fact, Immanuel Kant insists that "[m]etaphysics is a bottomless abyss . . . a dark and shoreless ocean marked by no beacons."[5] In other words, good luck not getting lost. That's why two chapters in this volume are dedicated to metaphysics: one interacting with

---

3. Lawhead, *A Historical Introduction to Philosophy*, 5.
4. See also Moreland and Craig, *Philosophical Foundations*, 13.
5. Kant, Walford, and Meerbote, *Theoretical Philosophy*, 111.

metaphysical claims about God's existence, and another arguing for greater metaphysical emphasis on Old Testament theology.

Epistemology is the study of knowledge. It's an attempt to "make sense out of knowledge, rationality and justified or unjustified belief."[6] Propositional knowledge (e.g., you know that *K*, where *K* is some proposition) is one type of knowledge that often reveals its importance in philosophical and theological inquiry. This volume has two chapters that interact with proper thinking regarding the claims of Christianity, as well as elucidating the epistemology of an early Christian thinker.

Ethics is the study of morality, which examines values in human behavior. When people talk about something being "right" or "wrong," they are often speaking ethically. And, although there are numerous ethical theories (e.g., deontological, egoism, utilitarianism, etc.), this discipline seems to be the most practical of all philosophical divisions, because it helps us consider situations and decisions we make every day. For this volume, we will look at the ethics of Jesus and a version of divine command theory.

WHAT IS THEOLOGY?

The simplest definition of theology is the study of God. It could also be understood as "[t]he science which treats God, His attributes, and His relations to the universe; the science or study of divine things or religious truth."[7] Theologizing, though, does not necessarily equate to Christian theology. Karl Barth rightly states that "there are many kinds of theologies. There is no man who does not have his own god or gods as the object of his highest desire and trust, or as the basis of his deepest loyalty and commitment."[8] This volume seeks to investigate the convergence of *Christian* philosophy and theology.

Now, Christian theology has its difficulties. An immediate concern is that of the chicken and the egg. Which comes first: our understanding of God or our understanding of Scripture? I agree with Kevin Vanhoozer when he says that, "our doctrine of God affects the way we interpret the Scriptures, while simultaneously acknowledging that our interpretation of

---

6. Moreland and Craig, *Philosophical Foundations*, 71.
7. Delbridge and Bernard, *The Compact Macquarie Dictionary*, 1045.
8. Barth, *Evangelical Theology*, 3.

Scripture affects our doctrine of God."[9] I will begin with bibliology, and, then, identify eight other theological categories.[10]

1. *Bibliology*: This category helps shape how and what we think about the Bible. It asks questions like: where does the Bible come from? Is it trustworthy? Is it authoritative? How do we interpret it? The Bible, and how we understand this comprehensive document, is the primary influence on the Christian understanding of the following theological topics.[11]

2. *Paterology*: We could also identify this category as Theology Proper. It investigates claims for the existence of God, as well as defining his nature, attributes, and works. Considering these concepts is essential to Christian theology. In fact, one philosophical theologian speculates that paterology "might even be thought of as supplying the whole framework within which one's theology is constructed, life is lived, and ministry is conducted."[12]

3. *Anthropology*: From a Christian perspective, anthropology is concerned with human nature, especially the *imago dei*. What does it mean for people to be made in the image of God? Are human beings made of two substances, namely material and immaterial (e.g., flesh and spirit)? What is God's purpose for humanity? Theological (and philosophical) inquiry helps solve these difficult questions.

4. *Hamartiology*: This category is the study of sin, which, simply put, is intrinsic rebellion against God. Along with examining sin's definition, this category also investigates concepts like: original sin, the pervasiveness of sin, and the temporal and eternal consequences of sin. Hamartiology has both affect and effect. That is, one's understanding of anthropology can affect one's understanding of hamartiology; or one's understanding of soteriology can be an effect of one's understanding of hamartiology.

---

9. Vanhoozer, *First Theology*, 10. See also 15–41.

10. According to Groothuis's chapter in this volume, there are at least thirteen categories of theology; although he claims that this is a non-exhaustive list. Also, for in-depth interaction with all thirteen categories, see the following: Bird, *Evangelical Theology*; Webster, *The Oxford Handbook of Systematic Theology*; Erickson, *Christian Theology*; and McGrath, *Christian Theology*.

11. Michael Bird is right, though, that other sources of theology include tradition, nature, experience, and culture. See *Evangelical Theology*, 62–76.

12. Erickson, *Christian Theology*, 234.

Introduction

5. *Christology*: So, Jesus is sort of central to Christian theology. Despite my blatant sarcasm, it should be noted that the pre-existence, birth, life, work, death, resurrection, and continued reign are of the utmost importance. This is the doctrine of Christology. The Apostle Paul gets it right when he says that our faith is in vain if not for the resurrection (1 Cor 15:14). And, although Paul is speaking singularly about the resurrection, you can't have the resurrection without the preceding events, nor can you have Jesus's continued reign without the resurrection.

6. *Soteriology*: Nobody likes bad news. There's not enough sauce on my pizza, my coffee is too sour, or the cat pooped on the carpet. Now, those menial problems normally have simple solutions. But what about when the bad news is really bad? Because of human sin (see *Hamartiology*), the cosmic bad news *is* really bad. If God is King, and if sin is rebellion against this King, then we've basically committed treason. Sometimes the punishment for treason was the death penalty. God's cosmic government seems to be no different. That is, both physical and eschatological death are consequences of our treason against God's kingdom. But the story does not end there. Soteriology demonstrates that, as an act of mercy, God delivered his own Son as a substitute sacrifice for the punishment our treason deserved *so that* we can be reconciled to God. Soteriology is about reconciliation.[13]

7. *Pneumatology*: The personhood and work of the Holy Spirit, or pneumatology, is deserving of its own theological inquiry. And yet, pneumatology regularly gets the table scraps of theological study. Perhaps it's because all of God's actions are, in effect, the work of the Holy Spirit; or, perhaps it's because the work of the Holy Spirit has been generally understood as embodying the practical effects of salvation.[14]

8. *Ecclesiology*: Flannelgraph Bible stories, potlucks, and doctrinal divisions have marked the Christian Church for centuries. But it's not all bad. Ecclesiology, otherwise known as the doctrine of the Church, "ensures the fidelity of the church to the gospel." The "articulation of its identity and mission" as the "visible representation and mediation

---

13. You can't go wrong reading both McKnight's *King Jesus Gospel* and Piper's *God is the Gospel*.

14. See Plantinga, *An Introduction to Christian Theology*, 284–285, for this postulation. Also, do yourself a favor and read Francis Chan's *Forgotten God*.

of the gospel" continues to promote the gathering of people from every tribe and tongue (Rev 7:9–12) to worship God and fulfill his Great Commission (Matt 28:19–20).[15] It tackles issues like baptism, the Lord's Supper, spiritual gifts, and the authority and government of the Church.

9. *Eschatology*: Throughout Christian tradition, eschatology has been understood as the study of "last things." These "last things" are, generally, based on biblical prophecies that have not yet been fulfilled. Richard Bauckham believes that eschatology is "founded on the promise of God . . . who created the world and who promises the redemption and completion of his creation."[16] Specific ideas within eschatology include the Rapture, the Millennium, and the Final Judgment. To be sure, though, eschatology is a highly debated category in Christian theology. For instance, is the Rapture prior to, in the middle of, or after the Tribulation?

BOOK OVERVIEW

This book has two parts. The former identifies how philosophy shapes theology. This shaping begins with Douglas Groothuis, Professor of Philosophy at Denver Seminary, who argues that logic is a necessary component for both philosophy and theology. And, logic can be used as a foundational tool for understanding the "logic of God." Next, Robert O'Connor, Associate Professor of Philosophy at Wheaton College, examines the intersection of philosophy and theology through the Design Argument, positing reasonable evidence for affirming God's existence. This consists of a critique and redesign of natural theology, as well as affirming the Bible's worth in providing a reasoned approach to believing God exists. Then, Joseph LaPorte, Professor of Philosophy at Hope College, provides an apt defense for a sensible Christian theology by arguing *why* Christian belief is rational or warranted, and, then, showing *how* belief can be known both experientially and propositionally. Lastly, Jesse K. Mileo, Adjunct Assistant Professor of Philosophy at Schoolcraft College, argues that God is the foundation for ethics against the Euthyphro dilemma, and that this is important for Christian theology because it preserves certain aspects of the gospel and gives proper glory to God.

---

15. Del Colle, *Oxford Handbook of Systematic Theology*, 249.
16. Bauckham, "Eschatology," 306–7.

Introduction

The latter part of this volume addresses philosophical issues that arise within the Bible and theology. Jason Stanghelle, PhD candidate at Trinity Evangelical Divinity School, attempts to triangulate Old Testament studies with philosophy and theology. He accomplishes this by investigating the metaphysical problem of space, identifying that theology, in general, and Old Testament studies, in particular, lack a well-grounded understanding of this concept. Next, Alan Stanley, Lecturer in Bible and Christian Thought at Brisbane School of Theology, explores Gospel ethics, observing that Jesus's ethic was related to the heart. That is, our outward actions are a commentary on the heart. Phillip Burggraff, Preaching and Teaching Pastor of Clearwater Community Church, then interacts with N. T. Wright's understanding of Paul and Logic, while explicating the argumentation of Galatians via discourse analysis. Lastly, Ryan Clevenger, PhD candidate at Wheaton College, invites us to enter into the theological and epistemological concerns of early Christianity through the lens of Gregory of Nazianzus, wherein he explores obstacles to, as well as a solution for, knowing God.

WHY IT ALL MATTERS

The hope is that this volume will catapult you into critical thinking, and create an appetite and appreciation for these disciplines. To be sure, a well-shaped theology can only be formed upon the bedrock of sound philosophy. To assist this process, I'd like to offer five reasons (amongst many others) why this convergence matters.

1. God's glory deserves it: Note that God's glory does not *need* it, but *deserves* it (Acts 17:24–25). So, although God does not need our help in anything, we ought to reciprocate to God by thinking through, living in, and declaring always the truth that has been revealed to us.

2. Everyone, in some sense, already does philosophy and theology: Have you ever made an argument? If so, you're doing logic (although you may commit lots of fallacies). Have you ever thought about existence? Then you're doing metaphysics. Have you ever believed something about God? Then you're doing theology. You get the point.[17] And yet, Douglas Groothuis proposes both necessary and sufficient conditions to claim the title philosopher (and, perhaps, theologian); namely, one must have a "strong and lived-out inclination to pursue truth about

---

17. Moreland and Craig, *Philosophical Foundations*, 11.

philosophical matters through the rigorous use of human reasoning, *and* to do so with some intellectual facility."[18] So, proceed with caution and rigor; you aren't a mechanic just because you work on a car.

3. We need both faith and reason: Christianity needs credibility, which can be provided by reason. Jonathan Edwards, an eighteenth-century Puritan, promoted his pietism with "a respectable philosophical structure, which would make it rationally credible and more enduring than it could be without the aid of philosophy."[19] That is, Edwards understood that a lasting and credible faith could profit from a robust philosophical influence. We should mimic this approach. And yet, this should not be seen as an attempt to discount the beauty, and the necessity, of faith. For faith is a necessary condition for salvation (Eph 2:8–9).[20] Far too often, Christian theists have "allowed themselves to be placed in the unfair position of having to 'prove' certain claims before their position will be admitted to the bar of rationality."[21] It's a both/and, not an either/or.

4. We need to fight against the culture of anti-intellectualism: One scourge of Christianity throughout the last century has been that of anti-intellectualism. Refer back to the J. P. Moreland quote that opened this introduction. What may have been addressed to general culture is also endemic within. It's not an anatomical muscle, but don't be afraid to exercise your brain. It is, arguably, God's greatest gift to your body.

5. These disciplines are often not converged: While securing contributors for this volume, many of the theologians (of course, not those who graciously agreed to contribute to this volume) expressed concern about their qualifications to write on theology *and* philosophy. This is problematic. More often than not, scholastic focus is either on philosophy *or* theology, rather than philosophy *and* theology.

So, with all that said, let's begin.

---

18. Groothuis, *On Jesus*, 5.

19. Fiering, *Jonathan Edwards's Moral Thought and Its British Context*, 60.

20. A necessary condition states: Without X, you won't have Y. So, without *faith*, you won't have *salvation*.

21. Ronald H. Nash, *Faith and Reason*, 105. See also Joseph LaPorte's chapter in this volume and Alvin Plantinga's *Warranted Christian Belief* or *Knowledge and Christian Belief*.

BIBLIOGRAPHY

Barth, Karl. *Evangelical Theology: An Introduction.* New York: Holt, Rinehart and Winston, 1963.
———. *The Epistle to the Romans.* Oxford: Oxford University Press, 1968.
Bauckham, Richard. "Eschatology." In *The Oxford Handbook of Systematic Theology*, edited by John Webster et al., 306–22. Oxford: Oxford University Press, 2010.
Bird, Michael F. *Evangelical Theology: A Biblical and Systematic Introduction.* Grand Rapids, MI: Zondervan, 2013.
Chan, Francis. *Forgotten God: Reversing Our Tragic Neglect of the Holy Spirit.* Colorado Springs, CO: David C. Cook, 2015.
Del Colle, Ralph. "The Church." In *The Oxford Handbook of Systematic Theology*, edited by John Webster et al., 249–66. Oxford: Oxford University Press, 2010.
Delbridge, Arthur, and J. R. L. Bernard. *The Compact Macquarie Dictionary.* Macquarie University, N.S.W.: Macquarie Library, 1994.
Erickson, Millard. *Christian Theology.* Grand Rapids, MI: Baker, 2013.
Fiering, Norman. *Jonathan Edwards's Moral Thought and Its British Context.* Eugene, Or: Wipf & Stock, 2006.
Groothuis, Douglas. *On Jesus.* Belmont, CA: Wadsworth, 2003.
Kant, Immanuel, David Walford, and Ralf Meerbote. *Theoretical Philosophy, 1755–1770.* Cambridge: Cambridge University Press, 2009.
Lawhead, William. *The Voyage of Discovery: A Historical Introduction to Philosophy.* Belmont, CA: Wadsworth/Thomson Learning, 2007.
McGrath, Alister E. *Christian Theology: An Introduction.* Oxford: Blackwell, 2001.
McKnight, Scot. *The King Jesus Gospel: The Original Good News Revisited.* Grand Rapids, MI: Zondervan, 2011.
Moltmann, Jürgen. *Theology of Hope.* London: SCM, 1967.
Moreland, James Porter. *Love Your God with All Your Mind: The Role of Reason in the Life of the Soul.* Colorado Springs, CO: NavPress, 1997.
Moreland, James Porter, and William Lane Craig. *Philosophical Foundations for a Christian Worldview.* Downers Grove, IL: InterVarsity, 2003.
Nash, Ronald H. *Faith & Reason: Searching for a Rational Faith.* Grand Rapids, MI: Zondervan, 1988.
Piper, John. *God Is the Gospel: Meditations on God's Love as the Gift of Himself.* Wheaton, IL: Crossway, 2011.
Plantinga, Alvin. *Knowledge and Christian Belief.* Grand Rapids, MI: Eerdmans, 2015.
———. *Warranted Christian Belief.* New York: Oxford University Press, 2000.
Plantinga, Richard J., Thomas R. Thompson, and Matthew D. Lundberg. *An Introduction to Christian Theology.* Cambridge, England: Cambridge University Press, 2010.
Vanhoozer, Kevin Jon. *First Theology: God, Scripture & Hermeneutics.* Downers Grove, IL: InterVarsity, 2002.
Webster, John, Kathryn Tanner, and Iain R. Torrance. *The Oxford Handbook of Systematic Theology.* Oxford: Oxford University Press, 2007.

1

THE LOGIC OF THEOLOGY

Douglas Groothuis

Much has been written about theological method, the means by which one goes about developing the various aspects of theology, such as the doctrine of God proper, soteriology, eschatology, and more. Then there is the theological prolegomena, which set forth preliminary considerations that form the framework for theological method. Let us start even further back, and dig for the most essential and foundational element of theology: logic itself.

Some will immediately protest that any such emphasis on logic exalts a merely human category and capacity above the being of God and his revelation to humanity. There are several different reasons why theologians make this sort of claim, usually focusing on the limitations of logic itself and the noetic effects of sin—the impairment to reason wrought by the fall. Instead of directly arguing against these protests, I will rather make the case that logic—as I stipulate its nature and domain—is necessary for theology. In so doing, I will also offer a theology of logic.

LOGIC PROPER

Without logic, philosophy and theology are impossible—not just difficult or obscure, but impossible. In fact, no intellectual or practical discipline is achievable without the use and recognition of logic. Sometimes the word "logic" is used in the sense of a rationale for action, however strange. So, one might speak of "the logic of Osama bin Laden"—meaning his worldview and reasons for terrorism. But this usage has nothing to do with logic proper. While the philosophy of logic is broad—involving predicate logic, modal logic, and more—this chapter addresses logic in the deepest sense as "laws of thought." These laws are not descriptive, but normative, as are moral laws. When we violate them, we are guilty of lawless thinking, of illogic. We break ourselves against their authority.

The first and perhaps most well-known law of logic is the law of noncontradiction. This concept was codified by Aristotle, but he did not invent it. This is akin to Newton discovering the law of gravity. He discerned something that was already there as a fact; he did not bring it into being. Rather, the theory reflected or stipulated the way the world works—with or without us observing it. That is, Newton discovered an objective reality, which he formulated into mathematics. In the same way, Aristotle stated this great law of logic, which I will state as follows: "Nothing can be both itself and not itself in the same way, at the same time, and in the same respect. More formally, A cannot be non-A. That is, nothing can possess incompatible properties." This law applies to statements as well as to states of affairs. Thus, I cannot be both fifty-seven years old on July twenty-seventh, 2014 (the truth) and fifty years old (the falsehood) on that same day. Both these states of affairs cannot be true as stipulated. The law holds even for imaginary states of affairs such as this: A unicorn (which has only one horn by definition) cannot both have a single horn and not have a single horn in the same way, at the same time, and in the same respect—even though there are (presumably) no unicorns.

Some, however, may object to this construction. First, one can be "in two minds" about a subject: say, whether or not to propose marriage. They find each possibility—propose or not to propose—equally appealing or equally uncertain. So, they hold two contradictory propositions. While this may cause psychological distress, it violates no law of logic. Thus, A and non-A are both affirmed, and with no fear of logical contradiction. But this example confuses the equiplausibility of two possible actions (which is an *epistemological* issue) with the logical relationship between two truth claims (which is a *metaphysical* issue). Thus, being "in two minds" indicates an indeterminacy of belief with respect to action: to propose or not (A or not-A). It has nothing to do with two incompatible states of affairs being actualized in the same way, at the same time, and in the same respect. One may be conflicted as to whether to study philosophy or to play video games, for example. But elements in *tension* with each other do not constitute logical contradictions "in which one and the same thing both is and is-not at the same time and in the same respect."[1]

Second, some argue that modern physics has showed that some physical states exhibit contradictory properties. Light has been disclosed to be both wave and a collection of particles. But a wave (which is a continuous state) is not a particle; and a collection of particles (which are discrete units) is not a wave. Notwithstanding, light possesses both these properties. Therefore, the law of noncontradiction has met its match. Some theologians have even used this example to justify the Bible's teaching that God is sovereign (A) and that humans have free will (not-A).[2] So, if light can do it, how much more God! And the poor old law of noncontradiction is worse off for it. On the contrary, the popular understanding of the nature of light is mistaken. Physicists rather speak of light as exhibiting wave-like properties and particle-like properties. That is, it can be *seen* as this or that; but it cannot be both this and that. The discovery of quantum electrodynamics (QED) near the turn of the century showed that

> light is essentially made up of particles but that all elementary particles are capable of "wave-like" behavior. By showing in a logically consistent manner how light was capable of behaving like a wave on some occasions and a particle on others, this breakthrough produced one self-consistent paradigm that satisfactorily resolved the confounding puzzle of "wave-particle duality."[3]

Thus, there is no justification from physics for the dismissal of the law of noncontradiction. In fact, the law is required for even rejecting the law—a fatal flaw pointed out centuries ago by Aristotle and Plato. Consider this conversation:

> John: The law of noncontradiction is false. Life is bigger than logic.
>
> Mary: Do you really believe that? Think about it.

---

1. Miller and Jensen, *Questions That Matter*, 33.

2. I heard this argument given by the President of a not insignificant evangelical seminary in the late 1970s.

3. Burson and Walls, *C. S. Lewis and Francis Schaeffer*, 86–87. The authors cite as their source: Feynman, *QED*, 37. For more on how modern physics (and science in general) does not refute the law of noncontradiction, see Sproul and Mathison, *Not a Chance*.

John: Yes, I do.

Mary: Let me restate this. You claim that the law of noncontradiction is false. That is, it is not true.

John: Yes. Why belabor the point?

Mary: Be patient and let me explain. By denying the law of noncontradiction you are saying that any claim that contradicts your claim is false. Is this correct?

John: Yes, that is what I mean by saying that the law of noncontradiction is false; that is, it is not true! What is the point?

Mary: John, you are affirming the law of noncontradiction even as you attempt to deny it.

John: No I am not.

Mary: Yes you are. In fact, for us to even disagree about your view of the law of noncontradiction presupposes the law of noncontradiction, since you say that my claim—which is contradictory to yours—is false.

John: (Long pause . . .)

Mary: But let me go back to your earlier statement. When you deny this great and fundamental law of logic, you implicitly claim that those who take the other side are wrong, precisely because their claim *contradicts* yours. You are, just like Aristotle, affirming A or non-A, but not both; and that *is* the law of noncontradiction.

John: So, you are saying that life is not bigger than logic?

Mary: What I am arguing is that the law of noncontradiction is true and has no exceptions. Much of life is mysterious, but it cannot contradict itself.

John: Well . . . Hmm.

This argument, put in dialogical form, is *transcendental*: it argues that the law of noncontradiction is a necessary assumption of all reasoning and of all reality.[4] If it is denied, we are left with no intelligible statements at all. As Gordon Clark pointed out, if the law of noncontradiction is false and is, thus, not applied to language, then any word (adjective, noun, verb, etc.) can mean anything.[5] For example, the word *saxophone* can mean a

---

4. Immanuel Kant used the term "transcendental" in a different, but related, manner in *The Critique of Pure Reason*. See Groothuis, "Kant's Transcendental Idealism."

5. Clark, *Thales to Dewey*, 88–89. Clark speaks of "the law of contradiction," but means the same thing as "the law of noncontradiction," which is how this idea is usually

curved reed instrument often used in jazz or it can mean trumpet or it can mean bicycle, and so on, *ad infinitum, ad absurdum*. Clark's argument is a *reductio ad absurdum*, meaning:

1. If the law of noncontradiction (P) is denied, then (Q) words become infinitely elastic in their meanings.

2. But (Q) is false and, in fact, absurd, since it would eliminate all coherent language in all of its functions: definition, reference, qualification, quantification, and all the rest. Only gibberish would remain. Thus: not-Q.

3. Therefore, the law of noncontradiction cannot be denied (not-P). This is concluded by using *modus ponens* in conjunction with *reductio ad absurdum*.

Despite the above argument, theologians and others often distinguish "human logic" from God's wisdom, often citing no less an authority than the apostle Paul:

> For the message of the cross is foolishness to those who are perishing, but to us who are being saved it is the power of God. For it is written:
>
> > "I will destroy the wisdom of the wise;
> > the intelligence of the intelligent I will frustrate."
>
> Where is the wise person? Where is the teacher of the law? Where is the philosopher of this age? Has not God made foolish the wisdom of the world? For since in the wisdom of God the world through its wisdom did not know him, God was pleased through the foolishness of what was preached to save those who believe. Jews demand signs and Greeks look for wisdom, but we preach Christ crucified: a stumbling block to Jews and foolishness to Gentiles, but to those whom God has called, both Jews and Greeks, Christ the power of God and the wisdom of God. For the foolishness of God is wiser than human wisdom, and the weakness of God is stronger than human strength. (1 Cor 1:18–25)[6]

Much can be said about this often-misunderstood passage,[7] but two points stand out.

---

put today.

6. Unless otherwise noted, all biblical quotations in this essay come from the NIV 2011.

7. See Piper, "In the Wisdom of God," 143–54; Moreland, *Love Your God with All*

First, Paul's words are God-inspired and thus, inerrant Scripture.[8] They are not, liberals or neo-orthodox theologians to the contrary, merely a human response to God's revelation or human speculation about the divine. The apostle Peter makes this clear:

> For we did not follow cleverly devised stories when we told you about the coming of our Lord Jesus Christ in power, but we were eyewitnesses of his majesty. He received honor and glory from God the Father when the voice came to him from the Majestic Glory, saying, "This is my Son, whom I love; with him I am well pleased." We ourselves heard this voice that came from heaven when we were with him on the sacred mountain.
>
> We also have the prophetic message as something completely reliable, and you will do well to pay attention to it, as to a light shining in a dark place, until the day dawns and the morning star rises in your hearts. Above all, you must understand that no prophecy of Scripture came about by the prophet's own interpretation of things. For prophecy never had its origin in the human will, but prophets, though human, spoke from God as they were carried along by the Holy Spirit. (2 Pet 1:16–21)

Since Peter regards his own writing as prophecy and refers to Paul's writings as Scripture (2 Pet 3:16), Paul's statement (1 Cor 1:18–25) must be taken as God's revelation—that is, as God's truth communicated to fallen mortals for their own eternal benefit. If this is true, then God's revelation cannot contain contradictions, since, as we argued above, the law of noncontradiction is a necessary assumption for all human language.

Thus, the argument comes to this:

1. Paul's words in 1 Cor 1:18–25 are the true, God-inspired, and inerrant revelation of God.

2. For God to communicate truly to humans in ways that humans can understand, that communication must abide by the law of noncontradiction.

Your Mind, 67–68.

8. For a short argument to this effect, see Groothuis, *Christian Apologetics*, 503–6. For the Chicago Statement on Biblical Inerrancy (1978), see Henry, *God, Revelation and Authority*, 4:211–19. For Henry's own treatment, see "Thesis Eleven: The Bible as the Authoritative Norm" in ibid., 4:7–128.

3. Therefore, we cannot put God's wisdom above or against the law of noncontradiction, however much it may differ from what Paul calls "human wisdom."

Second, it is very likely that Paul's disparagement of "human wisdom," rather than denying the law of noncontradiction, refers to poor reasoning used by fallen thinkers. Or perhaps it indicts those who claim that human reasoning is sufficient for life without the aid of knowledge given through biblical revelation. This kind of humanistic reason is sometimes called "unaided reason." Francis Schaeffer gets to the heart of this issue in how he defines humanism: "Humanism in the inclusive sense is the system whereby man, beginning absolutely by himself, tries rationally to build out from himself, having only man as his integration point, to find all knowledge, meaning and value."[9] In any event, it should be clear that Paul says nothing against reason proper, against the law of noncontradiction.

GOD AND LOGIC

One often hears and reads the claim that we must not limit God by our logic or human reasoning, since God is "above logic," or even that God is not subject to logical considerations at all. We just cannot "put God in a box." The claim is that if God is not the Lord over logic, then he is not Lord of all things. Put formally:

1. God is the Supreme Being in every way such that nothing is above him in value or power.
2. Making God subject to logic violates (1).
3. Therefore, God is not subject to logic.

Of course, this argument relies on logic for its cogency—as do all sound arguments. The argument, as such, is valid. This means that the conclusion follows logically from the premises, whether or not the premises are true. But let us consider whether premise (2) is true. If it is false, the argument fails.

One must first reckon with the fact that God cannot deny himself or lie. That is, for God to be God and reveal himself as God, he must be logically consistent. Consider Paul's words to Timothy: God "cannot deny

---

9. Schaeffer, *God Who Is There*, 17. Schaeffer defines the word "rationalism" in the same sense. See ibid., 179.

himself" (2 Tim 2:13; ESV). Paul again writes, "Paul, a servant of God and an apostle of Jesus Christ to further the faith of God's elect and their knowledge of the truth that leads to godliness—in the hope of eternal life, which God, who does not lie, promised before the beginning of time" (Titus 1:1–2).

The Book of Hebrews affirms:

> In the same way God, desiring even more to show to the heirs of the promise the unchangeableness of His purpose, interposed with an oath, so that by two unchangeable things in which it is impossible for God to lie, we who have taken refuge would have strong encouragement to take hold of the hope set before us. (Heb 6:17–18; NASB)

The very concept of lying, as opposed to telling the truth, is rooted in the law of noncontradiction. If God says the opposite of what is true he says of A that it is not-A. But God, as a Perfect Being, cannot do this—while humans may or may not lie.

The argument that human reason does not pertain to God rests on a category confusion related to God as the Creator of all things outside of himself. This argument would assert that God created logic in the same way that he created the universe. Therefore, logic is a category of the creation. Its existence is contingent, just like matter. Just as God is not subject to time or space or the will of angels or humans, God is not subject to the rules of logic. That would be beneath him, so to speak.

Despite its surface credibility, this argument is unsound. To understand why, consider another case of God's relationship to us. Not a few Christians say that God created morality in the same way that he created the universe. If so, then the truths of morality are contingent on God's will, and God could have created other moral truths, given his omnipotence. Just as God could have created a world without Douglas Groothuis or (more tragically) John Calvin, he might have created a world with different moral truths. But a few moments of reflection should bring this reasoning into question. A God who could make wanton killing or taking his name in vain would not be a God worth serving—outside of self-interest.

The better understanding of God in relation to moral truth is that the essence of morality rests in the eternal character of God (see Chapter 4 of this volume). We should not take his name in vain because God is worthy of reverence given his excellences (Exod 20; Isa 6:1–8). We should not murder because God made human beings in his image and likeness, thus making us the crown of creation (Gen 1:26; 9:1–7). In light of this reasoning concerning God and morality, we should affirm that moral truths flow from God's nature or essence. When he issues commands or makes moral promises, God is not issuing arbitrary memoranda, but, rather, expressing how his moral character bears on the human situation.

Mutatus mutandis, logic is not something God created, but issues from the nature of God as an omniscient, self-existent, and rational being. This captures part of the divine consciousness, but, of course, not all of it, since God responds affectively to states of affairs in a morally perfect way.[10] Logic and God are inseparable and his affective life is perfectly logical—that is, fitting for the situation, which God exhaustively knows.

I have saved what is perhaps the strongest case for the consonance of God and logic until now. This argument flows from the very character of God as revealed in the first few pages in the Gospel of John:

> In the beginning was the Word, and the Word was with God, and the Word was God. He was with God in the beginning. Through him all things were made; without him nothing was made that has been made. In him was life, and that life was the light of all mankind. The light shines in the darkness, and the darkness has not overcome it. (John 1:1–5)

The Greek term for "Word" in verse 1 is *Logos*. The semantic range of this word includes *logic*.[11] Thus, in the beginning was the rational communication who created all things. Unlike previous Greek concepts of Logos, John reveals that this Logos is personal and creative, making the entire world and giving light to all. The necessary implication is that the Logos made the world according to a rational plan and that the cosmos has a

---

10. This claim is somewhat controversial (since theologians often claim that God is impassible), but I will not defend it here, except to offer this brief argument:

It is virtuous to feel the proper emotion in any given setting (see Eccl 3:1–7).

The Scriptures report that God has a variety of emotions. Perhaps the most moving is this statement by God: "How can I give you up, Ephraim? How can I hand you over, Israel? How can I treat you like Admah? How can I make you like Zeboyim? My heart is changed within me; all my compassion is aroused" (Hos 11:8).

God is perfectly virtuous, because he is a perfect being.

Therefore, God feels the proper emotion in any given setting. That is, He has affective as well as cognitive experience.

11. For the semantic range and a general biblical theology of *logos*, see "Thesis Nine: The Mediating Logos" in Henry, *God, Revelation and Authority*, 3:164–247. See also Harris, *Jesus as God*, 54–55.

rational structure—one that is discernible to human beings, who are made in his image.[12] The great church historian, Jaroslav Pelikan, explains:

> "Logos of God" when applied to Jesus Christ means far more than "Word of God," more even than divine revelation; there were many other Greek vocables that would have sufficed to express that much and no more, and several of them were being used in the New Testament and in other early Christian literature. Employing the specific name Logos implied in addition to this that what had come in Jesus Christ was also the *Reason and Mind* of the cosmos.[13]

If God, the second person of the Trinity, is called the Logos in inspired Scripture, then we can find support for the reality and necessity of logic in the eternal and unchangeable character of God himself.

LOGIC, THEOLOGY, AND THEOLOGICAL METHOD

Given what has been argued thus far, we should consider briefly how logic bears on theological method, since these considerations are crucial for forming a biblically and logically faithful theology. The very word "theology" means "the logic of God." More broadly, theology concerns how God's revelation bears on all the great philosophical questions of life as well as all the particular topics raised in Scripture and in the history of the church. Of course, for theology to deliver truth to those to whom it is addressed, it cannot contain contradictions. The purpose of theology is not the mere accumulation or inventory of facts, but rather to bring God's truth to bear on the human condition in all its fullness.[14] Paul puts this concept powerfully with respect to the Hebrew Bible on which he and Timothy were educated:

> But as for you, continue in what you have learned and have become convinced of, because you know those from whom you learned it, and how from infancy you have known the Holy Scriptures, which are able to make you wise for salvation through faith in Christ Jesus. All Scripture is God-breathed and is useful for teaching, rebuking, correcting and training in righteousness, so

---

12. See Clark, "Logic and God."
13. Pelikan, *Jesus through the Centuries*, 62 (emphasis original).
14. For a more developed argument for theology as edification, see Frame, "What Is Theology?" 3–13.

that the servant of God may be thoroughly equipped for every good work. (2 Tim 3:14–17; see also Ps 119)

Paul's ringing affirmation applies, by extension, to the New Testament as well.[15]

If Scripture has this status, then theology must be true to Scripture as it organizes biblical truth concerning the standard categories or topics of theology:

1. Theology proper (Paterology)
2. Theology of Christ (Christology)
3. Theology of the Holy Spirit and His gifts (Pneumatology)
4. Theology of the church (Ecclesiology)
5. Theology of the nature of Scripture (Bibliology)
6. Theology of humanity (Anthropology)
7. Theology of angels (Angelology) and demons (Demonology)
8. Theology of sin (Hamartiology)
9. Theology of salvation (Soteriology)
10. Theology of last things (Eschatology)
11. Moral theology (how Scripture bears on ethics, personal and social)
12. Philosophical Theology (how Scriptural doctrines are justified and related to one another logically)
13. Theology of mission (missiology)[16]

I can only make a few comments on logic and theological method concerning these—and other—themes of theology.

First, all theologizing (and all exegesis) must aim for maximal consistency. Thus, something taught in one book of the Bible (which is discovered through proper interpretive method)[17] should not contradict something taught in another book of the Bible. If real contradictions exist, then three interrelated and terrible consequences follow: (1) The Bible could not be inerrant, since inerrancy requires the coherence of all biblical propositions

---

15. See Groothuis, *Christian Apologetics*, 503–6.
16. I do not claim that this list is exhaustive, but it represents key topics.
17. See Klein et al., *Introduction to Biblical Interpretation*; Fee and Stuart, *How to Read the Bible*.

and doctrines. (2) We cannot trust the Bible where it contradicts itself. (3) We lose some justification for trusting other parts of the Bible, if any contradictions are found, just as we question the truth of statements made by someone we know to be a liar.[18]

Some biblical scholars are content to write commentaries on individual books of the Bible without bringing this teaching into alignment with the rest of Scripture. Sadly, some exegetes even discount the need for such integration and systemization.[19] This ought not be, since God's nature is logical and his revelation is a true and logical expression of his nature as it bears on his creatures.

This call to consistency does not entail that one try to fudge biblical texts for the sake of fitting things together neatly. On the contrary, each text must be interpreted rigorously and then brought into systematic consistency with the rest of Scripture. This is no easy task, and the best theologian cannot hope to accomplish this with perfection. Nevertheless, the task is nonnegotiable, and it requires interdisciplinary conversations. Biblical critics and theologians need each other and should work together for the sake of offering to the world a true and rational account of the Christian worldview.[20]

But theology is more than merely grouping statements in coherent patterns. One must discern what is to be inferred from a proper theology. One may find that doctrine one, doctrine two, and doctrine three rationally imply a doctrine not specifically stated in the Bible. The Westminster Confession captures this cogently:

> The whole counsel of God, concerning all things necessary for his own glory, man's salvation, faith, and life, is either expressly set down in Scripture, or by good and necessary consequence may be deduced from Scripture: unto which nothing at any time is to be added, whether by new revelations of the Spirit, or traditions of men. (1:7)

"Good and necessary consequence" refers to the logical implications of what is laid down in Scripture. This cannot be accomplished without the

---

18. See Rom 3:4: "Let God be true, and every human being a liar. As it is written: 'So that you may be proved right when you speak and prevail when you judge.'"

19. Cf. Gundry, *Jesus the Word*.

20. See 1 Cor 12 on how each member of the body needs the other members. This should apply to academic pursuits as well. No Christian is an island.

aid of logic. B. B. Warfield's commentary on this section of the Confession is magisterial and deserves full quotation.

> It must be observed . . . that the teachings and prescriptions of Scripture are not confined by the Confession to what is "expressly set down in Scripture." Men are required to believe and obey not only what is "expressly set down in Scripture," but also what "by good and necessary consequence may be deduced from Scripture." This . . . involves a characteristic honoring of reason as the instrument for the ascertainment of truth. We must depend upon our human faculties to ascertain what Scripture says; we cannot suddenly abnegate them and refuse their guidance in determining what Scripture means. This is not, of course, to make reason the ground of the authority of inferred doctrines and duties. Reason is the instrument of discovery of all doctrines and duties, whether "expressly set down in Scripture" or "by good and necessary consequence deduced from Scripture": but their authority, when once discovered, is derived from God, who reveals them and prescribes them in Scripture, either by literal assertion or by necessary implication.[21]

For an example of reasoning from Scripture, consider the Trinity. The Bible teaches that there is but one God (Deut 6:4) and that the Father, the Son, and the Holy Spirit are all equally divine. However, the Bible does not tell us how to account for the oneness and threeness logically. Since God cannot contradict himself, the explanation must be, by "good and necessary consequent," a way of affirming monotheism *and* the deity of the Father, Son, and Holy Spirit. Given the declarations of Scripture, some formulations are logically ruled out, such as tri-theism and modalism (i.e., there are not three members of the Trinity, but three modes in which God reveals himself: Father, Son, and Holy Spirit). Nor can we confess that there is one and three gods, since this is illogical. The Athanasian Creed takes theological pains to stipulate what the Trinity is and is not. Part of it reads:

> Now this is the catholic faith:
>
> That we worship one God in trinity and the trinity in unity,
> neither blending their persons
> nor dividing their essence.
> For the person of the Father is a distinct person,
> the person of the Son is another,

---

21. Warfield, *Westminster Assembly*, 226–27, cited in Crampton, "*Westminster Confession of Faith* and Logic."

and that of the Holy Spirit still another.
But the divinity of the Father, Son, and Holy Spirit is one,
their glory equal, their majesty coeternal.

What quality the Father has, the Son has, and the Holy Spirit has.
The Father is uncreated,
the Son is uncreated,
the Holy Spirit is uncreated.

The Father is immeasurable,
the Son is immeasurable,
the Holy Spirit is immeasurable.

The Father is eternal,
the Son is eternal,
the Holy Spirit is eternal.

And yet there are not three eternal beings;
there is but one eternal being.
So too there are not three uncreated or immeasurable beings;
there is but one uncreated and immeasurable being.

The concern for maximal consistency is another way to emphasize the importance of Christianity as a *system* of doctrine, rather than an unrelated or loosely related collection of stories, parables, poems, letters, and so on. If theology is not systematic, it is not true to the Bible from which it ought to derive its content. This assumption and imperative for consistency is found near the conclusion of Ecclesiastes:

> Not only was the Teacher wise, but he also imparted knowledge to the people. He pondered and searched out and set in order many proverbs. The Teacher searched to find just the right words, and what he wrote was upright and true.
> The words of the wise are like goads, their collected sayings like firmly embedded nails—given by one shepherd. (Eccl 12:9–10)

While the Teacher did not have theology proper in mind, his emphasis was on choosing the right words, which fit together as coming from one consistent author. Such a sensibility should govern the conscience and intellect of contemporary theologians as well. Anyone engaging in theology is teaching doctrine to the church. Because of this, that person should heed the admonitions of Scripture on the seriousness of teaching. Here are just two:

> In your teaching show integrity, seriousness and soundness of speech that cannot be condemned, so that those who oppose you

> may be ashamed because they have nothing bad to say about us. (Titus 2:7b–8; see also Jas 3:1–3)

> Jesus replied, "And why do you break the command of God for the sake of your tradition? For God said, 'Honor your father and mother' and 'Anyone who curses their father or mother is to be put to death.' But you say that if anyone declares that what might have been used to help their father or mother is 'devoted to God,' they are not to 'honor their father or mother' with it. Thus you nullify the word of God for the sake of your tradition." (Matt 15:3–6; see also Mal 2:7–8)

In light of the arguments above, these exhortations to teach well and to avoid nullifying the Word of God will include the demand for rigorous reasoning.

The second point concerning logic and theological method pertains to philosophical theology, which is the philosophical assessment of theological claims.[22] The aim of a biblically faithful philosophical theology is to analyze key biblical doctrines—such as the Trinity, the Incarnation, and God's sovereignty with respect to human responsibility—in hopes of rendering them logically consistent and even compelling. This discipline relies on good exegesis and sound systematic theology to deliver the concepts needed for philosophical understanding. To refer to a stellar example, Millard Erickson's *The Word Became Flesh: An Incarnational Theology* carefully and thoroughly addresses the biblical sources for Christology, the biblical doctrine of Christ, and the philosophical understanding of Jesus as both divine and human.[23] Few works on Christology accomplish this much so clearly. Erickson's work wisely conjoins exegesis, systematic theology, and philosophical theology.

Not only must the texts of Scripture cohere with each other; the doctrines derived from Scripture must be noncontradictory as well. If one dispenses with logic for theology, one does a great disservice to God himself, since God's name (nature) is holy and must be hallowed. That is no small thing. One cannot count the contradictory holy or have any motivation to make it hallowed. "The fear of the Lord is the beginning of wisdom, and knowledge of the Holy One is understanding" (Prov 9:10). This is true in theology as well as in every other area of life and thought (1 Cor 10:31).

---

22. See Erickson, *Christian Theology*, 13–14.
23. Erickson, *Word Became Flesh*.

God will not violate his own nature; therefore, he is not illogical. Thus, theologians who try to articulate God's nature and attributes cannot wriggle free from logic's framework. Rather, good theology is rigorously logical to the end that the truths of Scripture may be known by God's redeemed and unredeemed creatures.[24]

BIBLIOGRAPHY

Burson, Scott R., and Jerry L. Walls. *C. S. Lewis and Francis Schaeffer: Lessons for a New Century from the Most Influential Apologists of Our Time*. Downers Grove, IL: InterVarsity, 1998.

Clark, Gordon H. *Thales to Dewey: A History of Philosophy*. 4th ed. N.p.: Trinity Foundation, 2000.

———. "Logic and God." *Trinity Review* (November–December 1980) 1–7. http://www.trinityfoundation.org/journal.php?id=16.

Crampton, W. Gary. "The *Westminster Confession of Faith* and Logic." *Trinity Review* 316 (February 2014) 1–4. http://www.trinityfoundation.org/journal.php?id=299.

Erickson, Millard J. *Christian Theology*. 3rd ed. Grand Rapids, MI: Baker Academic, 2013.

———. *The Word Became Flesh: An Incarnational Theology*. Grand Rapids, MI: Baker, 1992.

Fee, Gordon D., and Douglas Stuart. *How to Read the Bible for All Its Worth*. 3rd ed. Grand Rapids, MI: Zondervan, 2003.

Feynman, Richard P. *QED: The Strange Theory of Light and Matter*. Princeton: Princeton University Press, 1985.

Frame, John M. "What Is Theology?" In *Systematic Theology: An Introduction to Christian Belief*, 3–13. Phillipsburg, NJ: P&R Publishing, 2013.

Groothuis, Douglas. "Kant's Transcendental Idealism." *Academia*. http://www.academia.edu/8957234/Kants_Transcendental_Idealism.

———. *Christian Apologetics: A Comprehensive Case for Biblical Faith*. Downers Grove, IL: IVP Academic, 2011.

Gundry, Robert H. *Jesus the Word according to John the Sectarian: A Paleofundamentalist Manifesto for Contemporary Evangelicalism, Especially Its Elites, in North America*. Grand Rapids, MI: Eerdmans, 2001.

Harris, Murray J. *Jesus as God: The New Testament Use of* Theos *in Reference to Jesus*. 1992. Reprint, Eugene, OR: Wipf & Stock, 2008.

Henry, Carl F. H. *God, Revelation and Authority*. Vol. 3. God Who Speaks and Shows: Fifteen Theses, Part Two. Waco, TX: Word, 1979.

———. *God, Revelation and Authority*. Vol. 4. God Who Speaks and Shows: Fifteen Theses, Part Three. Waco, TX: Word, 1979.

Kant, Immanuel. *The Critique of Pure Reason*. Edited and translated by Norman Kemp Smith. New York: St. Martin's, 1965.

Klein, William W., Craig L. Blomberg, and Robert L. Hubbard Jr. *Introduction to Biblical Interpretation*. Rev. ed. Nashville: Thomas Nelson, 2004.

---

24. I thank Sarah Geis, Elizabeth Johnston, and a reviewer for their comments and corrections on this paper.

Miller, Ed L., and Jon Jensen. *Questions That Matter: An Invitation to Philosophy*. 5th ed. Boston: McGraw-Hill, 2004.

Moreland, J. P. *Love Your God with All Your Mind: The Role of Reason in the Life of the Soul*. 2nd ed. Colorado Springs, CO: NavPress, 2012.

Pelikan, Jaroslav. *Jesus through the Centuries: His Place in the History of Culture*. San Francisco: Harper & Row, 1987.

Piper, John. "In the Wisdom of God, the World Did Not Know God through Wisdom." In *Think: The Life of the Mind and the Love of God*, 143–54. Wheaton, IL: Crossway, 2011.

Schaeffer, Francis A. *The God Who Is There*. Downers Grove, IL: InterVarsity, 1976.

Sproul, R. C., and Keith Mathison. *Not a Chance: God, Science, and the Revolt against Reason*. Exp. ed. Grand Rapids, MI: Baker, 2014.

Warfield, Benjamin B. *The Westminster Assembly and Its Work*. N.p.: Still Waters Revival, 1991.

2

ARGUMENTS FOR THE EXISTENCE OF GOD AS A THEOLOGICAL FOUNDATION

Robert O'Connor

THE RELATION BETWEEN PHILOSOPHY AND THEOLOGY

This chapter explores the relationship between the disciplines of theology and philosophy specifically with respect to the traditional arguments for the existence of God. By traditional arguments, I mean those lines of reasoning widely regarded as justifying belief in God's existence such as the ontological, cosmological, teleological, and moral arguments. Were rational argumentation effective in establishing belief in God, philosophy might be thought to provide a useful, first step for coming to full faith. Many, however, hold that these arguments do not carry demonstrative weight and, as such, fail to provide reason to adopt belief in God. This essay will not proffer a definitive assessment as to the general success of natural theology. It speaks, rather, to the contribution that the Scriptures make to a full and proper understanding of one such argument, the argument from design. Rather than serving as a necessary propaedeutic to theological inquiry, it may turn out that natural theology depends upon insights drawn from a biblical theology for its success.

The point of departure is the curious observation that, although the Bible does make reference to the fact that natural phenomena provide grounds for belief in God, it does not articulate the particular lines of reasoning. Were these traditional arguments both successful and critical for belief, it would seem reasonable to expect that the biblical authors would explicate them for the reader. Psalm 19 makes reference to the course of the sun, speaking in no uncertain terms of the testimony of God's existence provided through this most universal of human experiences.[1] Similarly, Paul begins his letter to the church in Rome by calling attention to the fact that the world itself, quite apart from any special revelatory act of God, evidences not only God's existence but also his "invisible qualities—his eternal power and divine nature" (Rom 1:20). So confident is the Apostle of this that he insists that the knowledge available by this means provides sufficient grounds for universal moral accountability. Neither Paul nor the Psalmist, however, formulate the exact line of reasoning that presumably takes one from such experience of the world to belief.

There are a number of possible explanations for this lacuna. Perhaps God's existence is so evident that articulating these explicit lines of support would appear gratuitous. Science textbooks do not begin with arguments for the existence of the material world; similarly, special revelation takes as its point of departure the assumption of a divine reality. Or, perhaps the biblical authors take these lines of reasoning to be either unnecessary or inappropriate. They might regard it as unnecessary to delineate reasons for belief insofar as their immediate audience already affirms belief in spiritual realities. "So you are ignorant of the very thing you worship," Paul surmises from an Athenian alter to an unknown god. Given this affirmation, Paul proceeds by proclamation, explicating the nature and actions of the God of the Judeo-Christian tradition.[2] Perhaps, then, the biblical authors regard it as more important to delineate the nature of God rather than try to prove God's existence that appears, in any case, so widely accepted.

Alternatively, the biblical writers might have chosen not to articulate arguments for the existence of God based on the conviction that evidential support is not necessary for belief in any context. Perhaps, as a fideist might insist, belief should be predicated on a faith commitment rather

1. Ps 19:5–6.
2. Acts 17:23.

than the dictates of reason. Or perhaps belief is entirely appropriate in the same manner as is belief in the existence of that tree in one's yard or the self-conscious state of one's spouse. Rather than constructing arguments for belief, then, the biblical writers simply indicate the type of experiences upon which one might properly ground belief. This is not to say that such arguments fail to provide reasons for belief; rather, absent reasons to doubt, they are simply deemed unnecessary.

Of course, there remains the possibility that the biblical witness does not include arguments for the existence of God because of the abject failure of such arguments to justify belief. Contemporary philosophical analysis might lend credence to this view. In fact, rather than contributing to the project of belief, the current consensus insists that, when properly assessed, traditional arguments are antithetical to theology; their failure, which runs quite contrary to expectations, implies God's non-existence.[3] Even if this failure does not imply atheism, appeal to a faith that finds no support in reason might be taken to undermine the integrity of belief. Perhaps, then, the biblical authors deem it best not to call attention to the futility of reason in support of this foundational plank.

Now, one might agree that natural theology fails to prove God's existence while also insisting that they provide good reasons for belief. Although failing to establish belief, to render belief more reasonable than not, or to motivate the reasonable adoption of belief, they may, nonetheless, provide reasonable grounds for affirming belief. The biblical authors, then, might be gesturing in the direction of such grounds. Perhaps they simply intend to indicate the evidential support, albeit falling short of proof, for affirming belief in God. There is certainly value for believers in knowing that their position is not unreasonable. But, here again, one wonders why these authors wouldn't spell out those supporting reasons. Again, the fear may be that an explicit appeal to reason might prove counter-productive; although affirming the reasonableness of belief, the perceived failure of traditional arguments to establish theism might lend credence to atheism. If such constitute theism's best reasons for belief, the inability of these arguments to convince all rational subjects might suggest to some its fundamental

---

3. In the *Pensees* (IV, 242, 243; as quoted in Lewis, *The Problem of Pain*, 1) Blaise Pascal writes: "I wonder at the hardihood with which such persons undertake to talk about God. In a treatise addressed to infidels they begin with a chapter proving the existence of God from the works of Nature . . . this only gives their readers grounds for thinking that the proofs of our religion are very weak . . . It is a remarkable fact that no canonical writer has ever used Nature to prove God."

irrationality. Discretion being the better part of valor, then, the biblical authors make no attempt to offer what rational support is available for belief through discursive argumentation.

This chapter takes the position that, in fact, there is good evidence for belief, evidence that makes it more reasonable to accept belief in God than not. Additionally, this evidence is cited in Scripture. Evidence for belief includes the sort of natural properties to which natural theologians appeal—the order, grandeur, majesty, intricacy, and functional success of natural processes. However, it also includes non-natural properties such as the beauty and goodness of the natural order. The biblical text does not fully articulate the arguments for belief in the style of the philosopher. Even so, the biblical authors cite the evidence, insisting that it serve *as* evidence, thereby indicating that rational support for belief is readily available to all. For instance, in the seminal text of Romans 1, rather than explicitly articulating the premises of the argument, Paul maintains that knowledge of God's existence (and by extension, nature) is potentially available through experience to anyone, albeit lost to some. By this, Paul seems to suggest that at least one premise in an argument for God is subject to willful assent, a premise whose absence undermines the justification of belief. Specifically, refusal to affirm certain non-natural properties such as the beauty and goodness of the natural order functions as a defeater to the justification of belief and thus renders unavailable erstwhile knowledge of God.

If this is so, then, the apparent failure of traditional arguments does not entail the absence of reasons for belief nor betoken its irrationality. The arguments, as they stand, may fail to establish God's existence. Theological inquiry may, nevertheless, find rational support from general revelation. In fact, the biblical witness proclaims rational support for theological realism, not by articulating the full line of reasons for belief, but by indicating the critical components of successful endeavors. As such, whereas some traditions speak of philosophy as the handmaid of theology, this suggests that we should regard theology as having resources for substantively contributing to philosophy; a biblical theology, that is, substantively contributes to philosophical inquiry into God's existence. Thus, even if the philosophical consensus is largely correct about the failure of natural theology as traditionally construed, it is mistaken about the rational support reasoned arguments for God might provide. Support for this thesis comes from a careful assessment of the failure of natural theology, traditionally conceived (section 2), and then showing how input from the biblical witness can salvage that project (section 3).

Philosophy, of course, does not speak in a singular voice; some insist that design arguments, for instance, do provide evidence for belief in God. What is it that these advocates see that the broader philosophical community does not? We'll articulate a version of the design argument that draws upon a premise that is, first, rarely explicitly formulated and, secondly, drawn from, or at least consonant with, a biblical framework. That is, there is a pre-philosophical commitment that plays a critical role in the success of the design inference. Specifically, the teleological argument's success depends on recognizing, as the Scriptures insist, an inherent goodness in the world. Since one might, as Paul notes, refuse to acknowledge this premise, the resulting line of reasoning does not establish by proof God's existence. It does, nonetheless, provide reasons for belief from the evidence of general revelation.

THE FATAL WEAKNESS OF DESIGN ARGUMENTS

A careful, if also charitable, diagnosis of teleological arguments demonstrates the critical premise so often missing, or assumed without argument, in classical natural theology. For instance, Aquinas's "fifth way" offers a succinct version of the teleological argument:

> The fifth way is taken from the governance of the world. We see that things which lack intelligence, such as natural bodies, act for an end, and this is evident from their acting always, or nearly always, in the same way, so as to obtain the best result. Hence it is plain that not fortuitously, but designedly, do they achieve their end. Now whatever lacks intelligence cannot move toward an end, unless it is directed by some being endowed with knowledge and intelligence; as the arrow is shot to its mark by the archer. Therefore some intelligent being exists by whom all natural things are directed to their end; and this being we call God.[4]

This brief formulation presents the central line of support: 1) There are natural phenomena that consistently produce certain outcomes—"the best results." 2) That these phenomena consistently produce these outcomes suggests what we might call a "natural mode of operation," that is, that they are constituted in such a manner as to produce that outcome. 3) Lacking

4. Aquinas, *Summa Theologica*, Ia, Q. 2, Art. 3.

intelligence, that is, absent the ability to envision and choose a consequence of its movements, one can surmise that these modes of operation could not have directed themselves to that outcome. The analogue is the archer's arrow: although it strikes the bull's-eye, it lacks the capacity to envision or, even were it able to imagine and desire that outcome, to direct itself toward that end. 4) With respect to these natural phenomena, achieving the best result could not be a matter of luck. 5) Therefore, it stands to reason that, like the arrow, these natural processes have been directed toward that outcome by something else, viz., a being capable of envisioning, choosing, and directing the natural modes of operation toward the desired result.

Reference to the archer suggests that St. Thomas is invoking an analogical form of reasoning. It is more accurate to regard the archer as illustrating a principle that stands on its own accord: chance is insufficient to account for any phenomenon that is both sufficiently improbable and yet valuable. The notion that the arrow was launched by a random arrow-firing mechanism fails due to the exceeding improbability of consistently—"nearly always"—achieving a certain kind of result. No one questions the integrity of a lottery on the basis of a single winner; if a lottery continually picks the same winner, one then might suspect its having been fixed. By the look of things, some being endowed with understanding and intelligence has rigged the system.

Aquinas claims that there are natural phenomena that consistently "obtain the best result." The archery example illustrates the principle of reasoning, while also revealing a crucial assumption. Were one to find an arrow marking the bull's-eye, one would readily draw upon his or her understanding of the composition of the arrow, the mechanics of the bow, and so realize (let's suppose) the exceeding improbability that the flight of the arrow would hit the bull's-eye by sheer luck. Based on these considerations, one would rightly infer that it was directed toward that end by a skilled archer. However, although this inference appears relatively straightforward, certain further assumptions are required for support. First, one must assume that the target existed, as the target, prior to the release of the arrow. The discovery of the arrow would not elicit wonder if one thought that the archer, or some other interested party, had circumscribed the arrow with a "target" after the fact. Further, this argument rests on a prior or independent belief that striking the bull's-eye is a good outcome—"the best result." That the arrow (also) struck a particular knot in the wooden surface may be equally improbable but utterly incidental; it would not elicit a call for explanation. One's inference to the archer requires belief that striking that bull's-eye is the very point of the activity.

The difficulty with Aquinas's argument lies in the notion that this particular outcome was intended before the process commenced. Where other scenarios might account equally well for one's observations, something distinctive about this outcome must favor appeal to mind. Specifically, its improbability must be accompanied by its desirability, that is, the desirability of that outcome to someone or other. This is easily seen in a game of cards; any hand, randomly dealt, is equally improbable, and yet suspicion of cheating arises only when the deal always, "or nearly always," produces "the best result." What constitutes the best result? That depends on the game being played. Indeed, it depends upon prior and independent knowledge that there is a game, with a specific goal, in progress.

What are the assumptions, then, that must be granted in order for the inference to "this being we call God"? First, one must assume a prior or independent understanding of the point of existence—what counts as "winning" the cosmic game. Of course, full articulation of the argument typically makes reference to life or human flourishing or some such. But this supposes that life or human flourishing or some such outcome is *known* to be the target—the "best result"—*independently* of the observation that life or human flourishing are among the results of the process. Perhaps, the critic suspects, having discovered the existence of life, or having discovered that there are certain unlikely, natural phenomena conducive to human flourishing, we have simply circumscribed life, particularly human life, as the cosmic bull's-eye. Of course life, or human life, or human flourishing may well be the cosmic bull's-eye. That it is so, however, could only be known by means of an inference *from* the conclusion that God exists. Raw experience of the fact of existence lends no support to this crucial premise.

These concerns also dominate Hume's *Dialogues*. In Hume's hands, as articulated by in the character of Cleanthes, the argument receives a much more detailed and nuanced formulation:

> Look round the world: Contemplate the whole thing and every part of it: You will find it to be nothing but one great machine, subdivided into an infinite number of lesser machines, which again admit of subdivisions to a degree beyond what human senses and faculties can trace and explain. All these various machines, and even their most minute parts, are adjusted to each other with an accuracy which ravishes into admiration all men who have contemplated them. The curious adapting of means to ends,

> throughout all nature, resembles exactly, though it much exceeds, the production of human contrivance; of human design, thought, wisdom, and intelligence. Since therefore the effects resemble each other, we are led to infer, by all the rules of analogy, that the causes also resemble, and that the Author of Nature is somewhat similar to the mind of man, though possessed of much larger faculties, proportioned to the grandeur of the work he has executed. By this argument *a posteriori*, and by this argument alone, do we prove at once the existence of a Deity and his similarity to human mind and intelligence.[5]

Hume's Cleanthes adds several new elements to the earlier formulation, among which is his focus on natural phenomena at both the global ("the whole thing") and local levels ("every part of it"). Cleanthes classifies these phenomena as "machines," phenomena having some number of moving parts that both fit together and operate in concert in a manner that consistently produces, once again, a notable outcome. In this instance, the line of reasoning is, Cleanthes insists, straightforwardly analogical; it is predicated on a principle that similar effects have similar causes. The "world," in whole and in part, compares favorably with human artifacts. The similarity of these effects betokens a similarity in causes. Since we know that humans are intelligent agents, producing those artifacts by means of this faculty of mind or intelligence, it stands to reason that the cause of the world has utilized the same resource, but on a grander scale.

Cleanthes's argument elicits from Hume's Philo a flurry of criticisms. His first comments concern the weakness of the analogy: "But surely you won't say that the universe is so like a house that we can with the same certainty infer a similar cause or that the analogy here is entire and perfect?"[6] In response, Cleanthes affirms exactly that: "Steps of a stair are plainly contrived that human legs may use them in mounting . . . Human legs are also contrived for walking and mounting . . ." The inference to design, Cleanthes admits, "is not altogether so certain" in the latter case as the former, but it must be regarded as more than mere "presumption or conjecture."[7]

The weakness of this rejoinder suggests that Hume is not being quite fair to the strength of the argument. It is curious, for instance, that Hume completely ignores his own interlocutor's reference to machine-like natural phenomena, placing the focus, rather, on a static structure like the staircase

---

5. David Hume, *Dialogues Concerning Natural Religion*, 15.
6. Ibid., 16.
7. Ibid.

of a house (had he experience of escalators, for instance, the comparison might have been more apt). Even so, the central concern, once again, is in the ability to identify, by simple observation, purposiveness in a phenomenon. "These legs are made for walking, and that's just what they'll do," we might hear Cleanthes intone. Indeed, since that is what they do, we can rightly infer that this activity constitutes their function. Better yet, since this is their primary or certainly most notable function, we can cite this as support for purposiveness. Here, again, the argument is vulnerable: perhaps Cleanthes is correct to point out that this move does not constitute a *mere* presumption or conjecture; it is not unreasonable to suppose that, since this is at least one of the things legs do (along with, for instance, taking penalty kicks, applying a car's brakes, or attracting members of the opposite sex), that a creator had precisely *this* in mind when producing them. However, applying the brakes is a function of legs (and feet and hips, etc.), yet this use comes after the fact. After what fact, one might ask? Having legs, one designs brakes that can be depressed through leg action. But then, having legs, the child then uses them to walk and climb. Why suppose that one use, but not the other, constitutes *the* function. By what criterion does one render this judgment?

Imagine an architect who, unbeknownst to the casual observer, has two great loves: parkour, which involves bounding from the exterior of one building to another, and the slinky. Perhaps, then, that architect did not intend that grand staircase for ascending to the second floor after all. The suggestion is absurd: no architect we've ever known has designed a house with a staircase intended only for the amusement of the slinky enthusiast and of no particular relevance to the occupants' interest in occupying the second floor (one who prefers, that is, to bound up the exterior and through a second-floor window). But the absurdity follows, of course, only upon a contingent set of human-centered expectations.

"Were a man to abstract," Philo maintains, "from everything which he knows or has seen, he would be altogether incapable, merely from his own ideas, to determine what kind of scene the universe must be, or to give the preference to one state or situation of things above another."[8] Philo's point is that Cleanthes's argument depends on our experience of the kinds of things that produce the order and arrangement characteristic of the phenomena in question—such arise only from the operation of minds. As Philo develops his criticism, however, he makes clear that the inference from arrangement

---

8. Ibid., 17.

or order to mind is illicit: "Thought, design, intelligence, such as we discover in men and other animals, is no more than one of the springs and principles of the universe, as well as heat or cold, attraction or repulsion, and a hundred others which fall under daily observation."[9] Historically, appeal to the blind, unintended consequences of heat and cold, attraction and repulsion, has not presented a significant challenge to design. Appeals to the blind forces of evolutionary theory, however, have proven devastating. Why, Philo asks, would we suppose that this one type of cause, evident in those particular cases about which we are familiar, is responsible for the whole of the universe?

> What peculiar privilege has this little agitation of the brain which we call "thought," that we must thus make it the model of the whole universe? Our partiality in our own favor does indeed present it on all occasions, but sound philosophy ought carefully to guard against so natural an illusion.[10]

Again, there would seem to be a kind of presumptuous, self-serving, question-begging impulse that lies behind the notion that the universe was designed—as if it were all intended for producing life or human flourishing or some other highly valued—by human beings, that is—outcome. It is as if we recognized the precarious nature of our existence, naturally valued the fact, and decided to circumscribe the bull's-eye around ourselves: we are the reason, the very purpose, for all this. And so, we infer design.

There is a response available to this challenge of presuming to read purpose off of a state of affairs, a response evident in William Paley's iconic development of the argument. Paley takes the reader into the heath—the desolate, unpopulated space—and compares the experience of coming upon a watch and a stone.[11] His genius lies in articulating an argument that does not depend upon an analogical comparison (say between stairs and legs); rather, it rests upon a principle of inference one naturally draws from the existence of three, clearly delineated, abstract properties. Negatively—although the point is rather poorly developed—Paley recognizes that, in order for the inference from the watch to mirror the inference from natural, biological phenomena, it cannot depend upon the material out of which the watch was constructed (e.g., steel, brass, glass, etc.), or the form that it takes (e.g., rounded, having a fob, etc.), or any other feature we

9. Ibid., 19.
10. Ibid.
11. Paley, *Natural Theology*, 7.

might recognize as distinctively human in origin (e.g., markings, such as numbers, dials, springs, gears, and so forth). This is because the properties that design inferences depend upon must be such as are found in natural phenomena as well. The properties Paley explicitly identifies are these abstract features: (1) having many intricate, exquisitely minute and detailed parts, (2) having those parts fit together in such a manner that they move in concert, operating, that is, in a machinelike fashion, and (3) serving a specific purpose. Paley insists that these properties are always, and only, found together by design. As such, "[e]very operation which was made . . . concerning the watch, may be repeated with strict propriety concerning the eye; concerning animals; concerning plants; concerning, indeed, all the organized parts of the works of nature."[12] It is indisputable that the eye has (1) many parts that (2) fit together in order to (3) serve a purpose. This leads "inevitably" to an inference of design.

The explicit and largely exclusive reference to such local, rather than global phenomena, goes some ways toward addressing Hume's worry that the argument represents little more than the conceit that human life is the very purpose of the natural order. Paley largely resists extrapolating from such local phenomena as the eye to the whole of the cosmos: "Were there no example in the world of contrivance except that of the *eye*," he insists, "it would be alone sufficient to support the conclusion which we draw from it, as to the necessity of an intelligent creator."[13] Paley thereby avoids having to assign a purpose to the whole, instead cashing out the notion of "purpose" in terms of "function," where by "function" he means that which serves the interest of some larger entity or process of which the phenomenon in question is a component part. Paley does not presume that the world is all about human flourishing, the production and sustenance of life, or any such cosmic end. By that third feature, "for a purpose," he simply means the fact that the phenomenon in question serves some function, some use, in the particular context in which it is found. The eye, for instance, has an indisputable function, "the use to which it serves," in the context of the organism of which it is a part, viz., to allow for sight. This finesse allows Paley to avoid any taint of "presumption or conjecture"; the function of the eye (that is, the manner in which the organism utilizes the eye) is evident to anyone familiar with its role in the life of the organism. This allows Paley to reference its purpose as established fact. Thus, by placing the focus

12. Ibid., 35.
13. Ibid., 45 (emphasis original).

almost exclusively onto local phenomena, Paley avoids the need for prior or independent knowledge of the purpose of the cosmos. "If we perceive an useful end, and means adapted to that end, we perceive enough for our conclusion."[14] We know the purpose of the eye relative to the organism; that those many distinctive parts come together in so unlikely a manner as to fulfill that function is improbable in the extreme.

Paley's function finesse, however, fails. Appeal to intelligent agency is favored by its singular ability to explain the development of a phenomenon having the improbable features that either enable or facilitate the overall operations of the organism. So stated, the argument appears strong, for, in order for that organism to do what it does, the component part must take a specific, often very narrowly constrained, form. The inference from function to purposiveness, however, depends on a further assumption, namely, that the organism itself, whose operation is enabled or enhanced by that component, has "a function." In the context of biology, the operation of that larger organism concerns metabolism and successful reproduction—at a minimum, survival within the context of an ecosystem. One can rightly speak of the function of the component part in the context of the organism of which it is a part, but only on the assumption that the life of that organism represents its function vis-à-vis the greater whole. To suppose that the function of the part was intended so as to serve the function of the whole rests on the assumption that the function of the whole is itself evident. Only on the supposition that the organism is "supposed" to thrive within that ecosystem can one speak of *the* function of its component parts. Otherwise, one can only speak of the outcome it *happens* to facilitate.

Of the watch, Paley says, "if the several parts had been differently shaped from what they are, or of a different size from what they are, or placed after any other manner, or in any other order, than that in which they are placed, either no motion at all would have been carried on in the machine, or none which would have answered the use, that is now served by it."[15] It follows, then, that "the watch must have had a maker that there must have existed, at some time and at some place or other, an artificer or artificers who formed it for the purpose which we find it actually to answer; who comprehended its construction, and designed its use."[16] As we have seen, however, the inference presupposes that the purpose of the part is

---

14. Ibid., 43.
15. Ibid., 7.
16. Ibid., 8.

to fulfill "the use, that is now served by it," that is, the usefulness of the watch, and this inasmuch as it thereby positively contributes to the "purpose which we find it actually to answer." That is, implicit in the inference is the supposition that the designer constructed the parts in a very particular fashion in order to be useful to the broader system as it, in turn, fulfilled its purpose, i.e., the use that is now served by it. The watch, as is clear to anyone familiar with such devices, has a purpose, namely, the purpose that we find it actually to answer. What might one who has no experience with such devices conclude? Paley overlooks the fact that the ignorance of the man, "who, because [he] had never . . . seen watches, telescopes, stocking-mills, steam-engines, etc. made; knew not how they were made,"[17] extends also to his ignorance of their use. There is no reason to suppose that the purpose, or function, of such a device is evident simply upon observation. The purpose of the whole, let alone its parts, cannot be reliably discerned in its various doings. Watches, we might say, "do" any number of things; there is no reason to suppose that one of these was that doing intended by a designer.[18]

To put the point in other terms: "the use, that is now served by it" suggests a singularity of uses; that is, that the phenomenon only does one or, perhaps, only one notable, non-trivial, or unique thing. Notice that "use" is an intransitive verb, having no direct object (although one may use someone or something, having a use does not take a direct object) yet requiring an indirect object (having a use must always be taken as having a use *for* someone, *for* a particular purpose, *in order to achieve* some outcome or other, etc.). Something can have a use, be put to good use, be found useful to someone for some purpose. For the purposes of the argument, however, Paley needs "the use, that is now served by it," to signal a specific intention.

Paley implicitly acknowledges this crucial ambiguity in the notion of use when he says that "changes in the eye vary its power over the rays of light in such a manner and degree as to produce exactly the effect which is wanted."[19] "Wanted," in this context, is ambiguous in the same sense as is

---

17. Ibid., 40.

18. One thinks of the Kalahari Bushman first presented with a Coke bottle in *The Gods Must Be Crazy*. Having no experience of such a thing, they lacked any understanding of the intended purpose of the bottle and only assumed it had a purpose because it was sent from the gods. Indeed, they mistakenly imputed a specific intended purpose based on what the bottle did for them, creating chaos in their lives.

19. Paley, *Natural Theology*, 20.

use.[20] Similarly, when Paley refers to variations in the eye across species he observes that, "by different species of animals the faculty we are describing is possessed, in degrees suited to the different range of vision which their mode of life, and of procuring their food, requires."[21] In this instance, the use, what is wanted, is explicitly tied to what is *required* of each species, namely the ability to see well enough to acquire food and escape predation: "they require for their safety, as well as for assisting them in descrying their prey, a power of seeing at great distance."[22]

This is why the argument is so vulnerable to the Darwinian critique. Darwin's theory of evolution posits a mechanism for the development of the

---

20. Just as something might have a use (although not necessary a use for anyone) an effect can be wanted (although not wanted by anyone). The verb can occur with an object, as in *The house wants painting*, meaning thereby that the house lacks paint. Can a house also, then, want wings? It can also occur without an object, as in *All that wants is his signature*, in this instance meaning "to be lacking or absent, as a part or thing "necessary for completeness" ("Want," http://www.dictionary.com/browse/wanted?s=t). It is this latter sense that the argument demands so as to avoid implicitly begging the question as to whether these changes in the eye were intended or desired.

21. Paley, *Natural Theology*, 21.

22. Ibid., 21–22. One further example will suffice to show how Paley surreptitiously smuggles into his argument a specific, presumptive purpose, viz., the enabling and enhancing of life. "There may be also parts of plants and animals, as there were supposed to be of the watch, of which, in some instances, the operation, in others, the use is unknown. These form different cases; for the operation may be unknown, yet the use be certain," he says. Paley cites as an example the role of lungs in animals: "It does not, I think, appear, that we are acquainted with the action of the air upon the blood, or in what manner that action is communicated by the lungs," he admits. That is, we really don't know how the lungs operate in service of the broader system except insofar as they provide a supply of oxygen for the blood. How the air taken in by the lungs is utilized remains a mystery. "[Y]et," Paley insists, "we find that a very short suspension of their office destroys the life of the animal. In this case, therefore, we may be said to *know the use*, nay we experience the necessity, of the organ, though we are ignorant of its operation" (Paley, *Natural Theology*, 36, emphasis added). Lungs, it appears, are necessary for the life of the organ. Their purpose is the use to which they serve, even if we don't know exactly how it is they fulfill this service. No biologist would dispute this line of reasoning. But why suppose, as Paley clearly must, that sustaining the life of the animal is itself purposed. Water, we just as easily might observe, serves well to drown a mammal, that is, to end its life. Is the purpose of water, the use to which it serves, to end the life of animals? Air, on the other hand, appears to end the life of fish. Why not suppose that destroying rather than promoting life signals the purpose of these various natural phenomena? So, when Paley says, "[i]f we perceive an useful end . . . we perceive enough for our conclusion" (Paley, *Natural Theology*, 43), we have to ask, "useful to what end, or useful to whom?" In the absence of an answer to such questions, we cannot make the move from function or use to purpose.

very phenomena Paley had in mind, the eye. Arguments from evolution to design suggest that this is not the feature thought fatal to Paley's argument. It is, rather, with respect to that third, abstract property that Paley identifies that Darwin's proposal undermines the argument for design. Without the ability to objectively identify purpose, there can be no objective support for purposiveness. Darwin simply postulates that these phenomena have no purpose. Although they evidence a biological function, they remain, on the Darwinian schema, without purpose. The purpose of the eye is not to see (although it is among the many uses to which it serves) nor is it the purpose of the organism to find food and avoid prey so as to continue to live and perhaps flourish. The eye is useful for the furtherance of life, but there is no reason to suppose that the furtherance of life is distinctive relative to any other outcome, say to destroy life. If life is not an intended outcome, then there is no reason to regard the eye as having been carefully designed so as to enhance that outcome. Life happens—some organisms do survive and some do not. We can no more suppose that the eye is designed to serve this particular end than we can suppose that a maladapted "eye"—a defective eye, as we might say, that is incapable of sight—was intended to render that organism, and perhaps by extension the species, extinct.

The problem of the argument lies in the attempt to read intentionality off of a specific outcome. Appeal to mind arises on the supposition that some extant feature of the world was a feature that some agent had in mind prior to production. Something about that feature must support the supposition that an agent must have intended it. Being of some use seems most naturally to fit the bill. But being of some use means of some use *to* someone *for* something. But these are empty ciphers: anything might fill in these notions, for everything is useful for something or other. To indicate that something has a use—the use to which it serves—does nothing to distinguish that thing from any other feature of the world. The parochialism of the argument that so exercises Hume is not so much the appeal to a mechanism that is distinctively human, as the impulse to read into nature the sort of peculiar interest—an interest in life—that is so naturally and understandably of interest to the human mind. That inference makes perfect sense with regard to human artifacts such as stairs and watches for which specific human interests are known prior to and independently of the inference. However, to impute these kinds of specifically human interests onto the whole of the universe represents, in Hume's mind, an irrational illusion.

REDESIGNING DESIGN

Inferences to design appear to present a case of special pleading. We like life, we desire life, in particular we favor human life and its flourishing. Noting not only that we, and many other animals, live, and noticing the many parts that must fit together in just the right sort of manner so as to achieve that outcome, we draw the bull's-eye around ourselves and project mind upon the universe. Hume's criticism was devastating not for having anticipated the possibility of a Darwinian mechanism, an undirected "spring or force" capable of producing such complex phenomena as the eye, but for having noted the anthropocentric assumption of the argument.

So, if the argument from design fails to provide reason, quite apart from revelation, for belief in God, what are we to make of Paul's laudatory claims regarding our ability to know God on the basis of these natural phenomena? "Since what may be known about God is plain to them, because God has made it plain to them. For since the creation of the world" [that is, even prior to and quite independently of special revelation] "God's invisible qualities . . . have been clearly seen, being understood from what has been made . . ."[23] Was Paul simply mistaken to suppose that what has been made, the very sort of phenomena that Paley cites, evidences God's existence and nature? Perhaps we are wrong to interpret Paul as intimating the existence of a valid line of reasoning that leads from the world to the existence of God.

In fact, Paul indicates as grounds for belief a feature only vaguely intimated in the classical formulation. Elsewhere, while interacting with unbelievers, Paul insists that God will no longer tolerate disbelief, for "he has not left himself without testimony" of his existence and, indeed, moral attributes.[24] This reference to testimony is reminiscent of Psalm19: "The heavens declare . . . the skies proclaim . . . they pour forth speech . . . they display knowledge . . . Their voice goes out . . . their words to the end of the world."[25] What is that word, the testimony available to any who have ears to hear? According to Paul, "He has shown kindness by giving you rain from heaven and crops in their seasons; he provides you with plenty of food and fills your hearts with joy."[26] In this passage, Paul points not to the existence

---

23. Rom 1:19, 20.
24. Acts 14:17.
25. Ps 19:1–4.
26. Acts 14:17.

of life, and the sort of life-enabling processes highlighted by Paley. Rather, he calls attention to the exceeding goodness of the world. To reconstruct Paul's argument, the goods we enjoy, rather than simply the life we have, points toward a purposive agent.

In point of fact, it is failure to affirm this feature of the world that Paul cites in Romans 1 as solely responsible for humankind's culpable failure to find justification for belief in God: "For although they knew God, they neither glorified him as God nor gave thanks to him, but their thinking became futile and their foolish hearts were darkened."[27] They do not glorify him as God because they fail to recognize the tremendous gift, that good gift of life, that God provides. They do not thank him because they fail to recognize the tremendous favor, life in this world, that has been bestowed upon them. Had they but recognized the abundance of the life we enjoy, they would certainly have accredited it to divine agency. Is this line of reasoning any more successful than Paley's?

As we have indicated, the problem with Paley's invocation of function or use is the subjectivity and special pleading it introduces into the argument. The salient factor in Paul's suggestion is not so much the utility of these features of the world as it is their value. Surely, we have an interest in these outcomes: we value the rain and abundant crops, the plentiful harvest and the joy they bring. But these outcomes have an objective status impervious to Hume's accusation that in this we are simply projecting our peculiar interests or biases onto the cosmos. Paul indicates an objective, even if also non-natural, property upon which to construct the argument for design. Paley, albeit tacitly, concurs. With respect to the eye, Paley says:

> Besides that conformity to optical principles which its internal constitution displays, and which alone amounts to a manifestation of intelligence, having been exerted in its structure; besides this . . . there is to be seen, in every thing belonging to it and about it, an extraordinary degree of care, an anxiety for its preservation, due, if we may so speak, to its value and its tenderness.[28]

Due to its extraordinary functional complexity, Paley suggests, the eye has instrumental value for the furtherance of life. This, Paley supposes, is enough to infer design. "Besides this . . . if we may so speak," is its value, a value derivative of the intrinsic value of life itself.

---

27. Rom 1:21.
28. Paley, *Natural Theology*, 23.

CONVERGENCE

In this, Paley echoes Aristotle's reference to "the best result," revealing a supporting premise that might salvage his argument. Design is an inference not from the mere fact of life but rather from the intrinsic goodness of this phenomenon. To the extent that the structure of the eye, formed as it is according to the same optical principles by which human inventors have constructed the telescope, the eye in turn supports life. Such is its value, the instrumental value of the eye in service of life and the intrinsic value of life itself. As with the argument Paul offers, this formulation does not depend on a premise to the effect that some phenomenon serves human interests, that it serves our interest in life, or any other want or desire humans happen to harbor. Paul, with the Psalmist, does not presume that, since the world suits our purposes, its Creator must have purposed that outcome. Indeed, Scripture evidences a certain incredulity regarding our very existence: "What is mankind that you are mindful of them, human beings that you care for them?" The question is not rhetorical. The answer is in the objective value of human personhood: "You made him a little lower than the heavenly beings and crowned him with glory and honor."[29] The move, then, is from what is objectively the case to an explanation that rightly accounts for that phenomenon. The argument, that is, recognizes the value of certain phenomena, the occurrence of which remains exceedingly improbable, and yet characteristic of the world. This premise, from the goodness of the outcome to the intentionality of the cause, provides the requisite link with purposiveness.

The linking premise does not rest on speculation as to the Creator's specific intentions or desires. The link, rather, rests on the knowledge that rational, intentional agents act not merely for a reason but specifically for those reasons they regard as good, that is, productive of a good outcome. Perhaps, as is so often the case with fallible human agents, an agent is mistaken in judging the good. Even then, an agent will act for the sake of what he or she regards, even if mistakenly, as good. This is what it means to be an agent.[30] Even when acting in a manner producing non-goods, a rational agent will do so because he or she regards that act as, in some respect or other, good. Every activity, as Aristotle says, has a final cause, namely, the *good* at which it aims.[31] So, the argument goes, the fact that an exceedingly

---

29. Ps 8:4, 5.

30. With the exception of instances where an agent decides, *for some reason*, to act randomly.

31. See *The Basic Works of Aristotle*, specifically Aristotle's "Nichomechean Ethics,"

improbable outcome is good readily suggests that it did not happen randomly, but rather was the result of the choice of rational, intentional agency acting for the sake of that good.

Paley is not explicit in formulating this argument; he is not far off, however, for he does insist that the inference to design also constitutes a proof of divine goodness.[32] The features that Paley might have highlighted include, (1) many parts that (2) work together; rather than utility, he might have explicitly indicated the proclivity of such contrivances to (3) produce some good. This formulation avoids entirely Hume's worries about the subjectivity involved in the identification of purpose. Of course, the inference supports projection to an unknown agent only on the supposition of moral realism. Moral realism holds that the proposition proclaiming life to be good, for instance, is necessarily true. Is moral realism true? This is certainly the natural reading of the Scriptures: "God saw all that he had made," we are told of the original state of creation, "and it was very good" (Gen 1:31). And, in spite of sin and death and corruption, Paul affirms:

Book 1, Sec. 2: "If, then, there is some end of the things we do, which we desire for its own sake (everything else being desired for the sake of this), and if we do not choose everything for the sake of something else (for at that rate the process would go on to infinity, so that our desire would be empty and vain), clearly this must be the good and the chief good. Will not the knowledge of it, then, have a great influence on life? Shall we not, like archers who have a mark to aim at, be more likely to hit upon what is right?" (1094a17–25).

32. His argument rests on two premises: first, "that, in a vast plurality of instances in which contrivance is perceived, the design of the contrivance is *beneficial*," and second, "that the Deity has superadded *pleasure* to animal sensations, beyond what was necessary for any other purpose" (Paley, *Natural Theology*, 237, emphasis original). Undirected, natural processes like Darwinian evolution might explain the origins of life and survival and proliferation of species; it has no resources, however, to explain the sort of satisfaction we regularly experience in life. "In whichever way we consider the senses, they appear to be specific gifts, ministering, not only to preservation, but to pleasure" (Paley, *Natural Theology*, 253). When speaking of the causal source of this world, that designer Paley presumes to have established, he reasons: "'If he had been indifferent about our happiness or misery, we must impute to our good fortune . . . both the capacity of our senses to receive pleasure, and the supply of external objects fitted to produce it'" (Paley, *Natural Theology*, 242). Our actual experiences, however, counsel otherwise, for, "[i]t is," Paley insists in extraordinarily Pollyannaish terms, "a happy world after all" (Paley, *Natural Theology*, 238). "Nightly rest and daily bread, the ordinary use of our limbs, and senses, and understandings are gifts which admit of no comparison with any other" (Paley, *Natural Theology*, 241). Incorporating these premises into the main thread of argument would provide the necessary support for the inference from the characteristic, and objective, good of this world to the only source known to act always and only for the sake of the good.

"For everything God created is good" (1 Tim 4:4). If Scripture does not provide an argument for this thesis, at the very least it provides an account that renders plausible the objectivity of value. In any case, quite apart from special revelation, moral realism is by no means an unreasonable position. This premise may find support in Scripture, but is by no means dependent on affirming the truth of Scripture. Although Scripture suggests and supports this reformulation of the teleological argument, this line of reasoning is certainly available prior to and quite independent of special revelation.

IMPLICATIONS FOR THE RELATIONSHIP BETWEEN PHILOSOPHY AND THEOLOGY

The biblical witness does not explicitly articulate any of the traditional arguments for the existence of God. Indeed, the reality of a supernatural source of the world is largely assumed. There are gestures in Scripture, however, toward an argument that rests on premises available to all. Among these premises we find reference to the organizational structure of the world in which we live, but we also find acknowledgement of and appreciation for the evident goodness of that world. "Many are asking," implores the Psalmist, "'Who can show us any good?' Let the light of your face shine upon us, O Lord. You have filled my heart with greater joy than when their grain and new wine abound. I will lie down and sleep in peace, for you alone, O Lord, make me dwell in safety" (Ps 4:6–8). This passage carries a simple implication: joy is readily available to any who experience the fruits of the harvest. The fact that even greater joy is available in the presence of God does not diminish the goods we experience in the ordinary course of our existence. It is that goodness, improbable as it might be, that provides support for belief in intentional agency.

Of course, this fact raises the objection regarding those whose lives are not replete with such ordinary pleasures. Paley, based on a utilitarian calculus, contends that "throughout the whole of life, as it is diffused in nature, and as far as we are acquainted with it, looking to the average of sensations, the plurality and the preponderancy is in favor of happiness by a vast excess."[33] In this context, utility, for Paley, simply means happiness: "[H]appiness is the rule; misery, the exception."[34] It is, no doubt, a tough sell. He makes the claim, arguing for its truth; perhaps it is better

---

33. Paley, *Natural Theology*, 241.
34. Ibid.

to suppose that it reflects an affirmation of faith; or, perhaps, as Paul says elsewhere, the fact that, "[f]rom one man he made all the nations, that they should inhabit the whole earth; and he marked out their appointed times in history and the boundaries of their lands." That is, from the fact that the vicissitudes of history and natural processes are well suited for human flourishing throughout the whole earth, we might recognize the plausibility that this was intended, that "God did this," so that men and women everywhere would "seek him and perhaps reach out for him and find him, though he is not far from any one of us" (Acts 17:26–27). Cold and calculating reason, drawing from strictly natural features of the world, cannot establish belief in God. For anyone who is willing to acknowledge the goods we enjoy, on the other hand, the Scriptures offer good reason to accept and even pursue, with praise and thanksgiving, the designer of this world. If philosophy fails to prove the existence of God, it fails for its willful refusal to affirm with the Scriptures this reality: "It is," as Paley insists, "a happy world after all."[35]

BIBLIOGRAPHY

Aquinas, Thomas. *Summa Theologica*. Translated by Fathers of the English Domincan Province. 5 vols. Westminster, Md.: Christian Classics, 1948.

Aristotle. "Nicomachean Ethics," in *The Basic Works of Aristotle*. Edited by Richard McKeon. New York: Random House, 1941.

The Holy Bible, New International Version. Grand Rapids, MI: Zondervan, 1978.

Hume, David. *Dialogues Concerning Natural Religion and the Posthumous Essays*. Edited by Richard H. Popkin. Indianapolis: Hackett, 1982.

Lewis, C. S. *The Problem of Pain*. HarperCollins: San Francisco, 1940.

Paley, William. *Natural Theology, or Evidence of the Existence and Attributes of the Deity, Collected From the Appearances of Nature*. Edited by Matthew D. Eddy and David Knight. Oxford: Oxford University Press, 2006.

"Want." Dictionary.com. http://www.dictionary.com/browse/wanted?s=t.

---

35. Paley, *Natural Theology*, 238.

3

EPISTEMOLOGICAL MATTERS MATTER FOR THEOLOGICAL UNDERSTANDING[1]

JOSEPH LAPORTE

You could understand the philosophical discipline of epistemology to be the study of how to *think properly about the world*—as we typically take people to do when we say they are right-thinking, right-headed, or sensible. I'll survey a couple of important connections between this field of epistemology, on the one hand, and theology, on the other. The connections concern two discrete epistemological areas, whose distance from one another helps to indicate the great variety in areas of mutual interest for epistemologists and theologians. My goal is not to bridge the two discrete epistemological areas: each will have its own section. And I make no claims to comprehensiveness in discussing either area. My goal is just to fire the imagination, in order to draw readers more or less new to epistemology (or theology) into further study; but I hope that there will be matter here even for those who claim authority in both epistemology and theology.[2]

---

1. Thanks to Emily, Philip, and especially Michael, who keeps up the pressure. Thanks also to colleagues Curtis Gruenler and Andrew Dell'Olio.

2. I'll cite sparingly to two ends: both in order to (i) whet intuitions and pique interest by leading readers to see connections to traditions and literature with which they may be already familiar, and in order to (ii) show readers where to go to pursue a topic further.

The first topic concerns what it is for a belief to be rational or warranted, as opposed to irrational or otherwise epistemically wanting. The second topic concerns an interesting contrast between different ways one might know the same topic.

1. IS CHRISTIAN BELIEF GULLIBLE? THE PASTAFARIAN THREAT.

Perhaps you have heard of Pastafarianism. According to this silly farce, "The Flying Spaghetti Monster did come unto" the prophet Aunt Dee Dee, "waiting at the front of Fred's Italian Corner, for she was hungry and her wait did seem to be unending, and he filled her with His Heavenly Smells, and unto her He did speak."[3] If you believed that, you'd have a kooky belief. You should not believe kooky things. *Christian* belief is relevantly *similar*, with respect to evidence. So Christian belief is kooky, too. So you have every reason to reject Christian belief.

How convincing is this argument? Something along its lines is certainly widely popular. Wikipedia links several satirical parodies with a similar moral that have gone culturally viral. These include belief in a pink, invisible unicorn and belief in Bertrand Russell's teapot orbiting between Earth and Mars: Russell is quoted as proclaiming "the Christian God just as unlikely."[4] Similar polemic has since burgeoned, with "the New Atheism" that has made inroads into the culture, or at least brought the culture's latent sympathy into the open. The New Atheism marches under the banner of science and sophistication. Bigwigs and bestsellers of the movement (Dawkins, Harris, and so on) are well known and easily accessed. The main message of the New Atheistic group is that believing in the Gospel is fantastically *gullible*. So is believing in any religious revelation, perhaps even believing in God.

What well-known gullibility-chargers don't much acknowledge is that Christian epistemologists have articulated important *responses* to the charges. The conclusion of these responses, which are developed with great subtlety and power, is that the charges of gullibility are unconvincing. My purpose in this section is to introduce the reader to one Christian response

---

3. These are the first lines of the first page Google turns up today under "Pastafarianism": http://www.loose-canon.info/page53.htm.

4. The attribution is plausible and in the same spirit of Russell and the movement I now identify: http://en.wikipedia.org/wiki/Russell%27s_teapot#cite_note-garvey-2.

to the gullibility charge. This response seems promising and accessible, at least in its outlines, to the intelligent laity and professional academics of other fields. The response that I will distill from the literature seems to harmonize with all of the main lines of thinking on the issue in the Christian tradition of epistemology. The best spokesperson at present for the response is the distinguished epistemologist Alvin Plantinga, whose work I will quickly sketch. The reader will think of a number of objections to Plantinga's response quickly—too quickly. Most objections springing readily to mind are misunderstandings. I will address such misunderstandings, in an attempt to clarify the main idea. Then I'll situate the main epistemological idea with respect to familiar claims of a couple of venerable Christian traditions.

Plantinga's main point, which goes back to Thomas Reid and, arguably, to Aquinas and earlier, is that we *know* something to be so if and only if our *belief* that it is so, is produced in the manner in which it was *designed* to be produced. In that case, we don't merely *believe;* we really know. Our belief is *warranted*—or, alternatively: right-headed, sensible, respectable, rational in the sense of being a good assessment of reality by someone in his right mind, or whatnot. Our belief is not crackpot or kooky or gullible or such that anyone in his right mind would be ashamed to have it, because again (and somewhat roughly), it is properly produced by *an agent whose* cognitive *faculties are functioning as they are supposed to function.*

So consider your belief that your friend is looking at you over his cup of coffee, as you sit in a café. Do you *know* it? That depends. If your coffee has been spiked with a hallucinogen, and if the reason that you think you have a friend looking at you is because you're hallucinating that Ronald McDonald is winking and smiling at you, his friend, over a cup, then you don't really have warrant here—you don't *know* that your friend is looking at you over his cup of coffee. The problem is not that you *don't* really have any friend looking at you—i.e., the problem is not that your belief is *untrue.* You might really *have* an alarmed friend somewhere in the café, who has just noticed you staring off into space. But you don't *know* that you have a friend looking at you. Your belief is unwarranted.

In the normal case of forming such a belief ("my friend is looking my way over his cup"), you'd be fine. Your coffee would not be spiked. You'd just be enjoying yourself at a café, and you *would* know that your friend is looking at you. You'd be looking his way, the light would be entering your eyes, making the right impression on the right neurons, activating the right connections in your neural network, to form the belief that your friend is looking at you. This is how you're designed to take in information like this. You're forming this belief just the way you're supposed to. So you're rational, warranted, right-headed.

I've been talking in the abstract about what it *takes* in general for you to have knowledge or warrant, for you to be in your right mind instead of being out-of-it, irrational, wacky, kooky, etc. How does belief in the Gospel measure up, or belief in God? Well, let's *take for granted* at the moment that the Gospel is true. So we're supposing *God has created* you, in his own image, to have knowledge of him. And God has sent the Holy Spirit to move you to assent to the truth of the Gospel (by hypothesis) as you recite the Nicene Creed, say. *In that case*, you are *rational* in proclaiming the words of the Creed. You can even be said to have *knowledge*—you're operating just as you were made to operate, in these circumstances, by hypothesis. You're warranted. And your belief is not, after all, kooky, wacky, irrational, unwarranted. Something similar applies to your belief in God.

Fine, you say: maybe my beliefs are rational *if* the Christian story is true—my beliefs are rational by hypothesis. But that's taking a lot for granted! Can we just assume by hypothesis that we are made in God's image, as Christianity maintains? Isn't that begging the whole question? Isn't it trying to *prove* that Christianity is true by *assuming* it is true? Something like this objection will come to your mind soon after you've understood Plantinga's position, if you're typical. The objection has a satisfying answer.

The satisfying answer cannot be understood unless we understand the point of Plantinga's project. Plantinga's project is not an *offensive* one; it is a *defensive* one. A Christian should not appeal to her own cognitive operation according to design in order to *prove* to the New Atheist that her Christian belief is true and therefore warranted and rational. It is at this point that the expected, familiar Christian strategy against nonbelief, however valid it may be in its own right, can distract us and make it harder to understand what's going on, by predisposing us to hear what we expect to hear. The familiar Christian strategy is to argue that Christianity is *true*; but that's *not* what's going on here.[5] If we *can* show that Christianity is true, showing that isn't part of this project. For all that we need to say here, it's

---

5. Plantinga ends his massive volume (*Warranted Christian Belief*, 499) by asking whether the model of God's operating in the world according to the Christian tradition, which model he's been assuming hypothetically to hold all along in order to argue for a correlative warrant, is true. But he can't settle whether the model is true, to the satisfaction of his opponents. His aim, he reminds the reader, has been:

the Holy Spirit's job to get us to see that Christianity is true, period. It's not that you have to believe that final statement, and so end your account of Christian apologetics as a whole here, with that period; instead, you'll probably insist that *humans* have an important role to play, in helping to move hearts and minds to assent to the Gospel. Granted. But that isn't relevant to what's going on here, in this paper (or this section of it). Perhaps Christians are to carry out an "offensive," so to speak, by testimony, or perhaps through stories, or perhaps through suggestive arguments, or perhaps even through conclusive arguments starting from neutral premises to the effect that Christianity is true. But set all that aside. It only shows there's more to a full account of Christian apologetics than the defensive strategy at issue here. What more there is, however thin or rich, doesn't matter for our purposes. With or without the rest, and however the rest is to be understood, the project here remains: it is the *purely defensive* project of showing that believers have been given *no convincing reason to buckle* to the atheist's objections—whether or not Christianity is true.

The *New Atheist*—not the Christian epistemologist—is the one on the offensive, so far as issues relevant here are concerned. The New Atheist is on the attack, trying to convince Christians that their belief is kooky, irrational, unwarranted, wildly speculative, or arbitrary (like Aunt Dee Dee's). Further, the *New Atheist* is the one *begging the question*—not the Christian epistemologist sharing Plantinga's idea. The New Atheist thinks she has the Christian in a bind: her accusation is,

> you can't show how your belief is more rational than some kook's belief in a flying spaghetti monster. For all you can tell, it isn't any different. For all you can tell, all supposedly divine testimony is a delusion or confusion of some sort. So *your* belief is kooky because it's unestablished. It's out on a limb. It's without any solid basis or credentials. It's like Aunt Dee Dee's belief.

The defensive parry to the charge ("not convincing") is that in order to have any claim on the Christian, you have to establish first that her Christian belief is *false*. Only if the Christian story is false can you go on to establish that therefore the belief is without solid epistemic credentials. If in fact the belief is true, then it's got *excellent* epistemic credentials, because

---

> To clear away certain objections, impedances, and obstacles to Christian belief. Speaking for myself and of course not in the name of philosophy, I can say only that it does, indeed, seem to me to be true, and to be the maximally important truth.

it's produced, like your typical visual belief that your friend is before you at the café, by proper function.[6] That's just the sort of belief the café patron or the Christian is *supposed* to form, respectively, if she's working properly, in the circumstances.

The atheist is entitled to her *own* Naturalist Hypothesis (or other anti-Christian hypothesis), according to which Naturalism is true. She can argue that *if her* hypothesis is true then Christian belief is *not* inspired by any alleged Holy Spirit and accordingly not produced by way of God's design. But to *show* not (hence, gullibility), you can't just *assume* not. The Christian won't be talked out of her story, which the New Atheist has entertained by hypothesis, merely by a counter-story that the atheist can ask the Christian in turn to assume by hypothesis.

Seldom does the New Atheist try to take the bull by the horns and show from the start that Christian belief is false and that we aren't operating properly in forming Christian belief, probably because that is a very hard thing to establish. In my own experience, the most tempting efforts at proceeding tend to drift back into question-begging ways of assuming that the Christian's take on this or that feature of the world is kooky and not formed by design.

I've given a whirlwind tour of Plantinga's reply to the New Atheism. I have left alone, for the sake of space, any discussion of what science establishes, or whether it harmonizes with Christian belief or jars against it. For details and extensions like these, I refer the reader to Plantinga's terrific work. I recommend *Warranted Christian Belief* and *Where the Conflict Really Lies*. Plantinga has other *Warrant* books, but they're better suited for other epistemologists than for the intelligent laity.

What's left for this section is to situate Plantinga's line with respect to salient Christian traditions—however cursorily. Plantinga began calling his work "*Reformed* Epistemology" and it's still often discussed as such. But the parts I've discussed, at least, are certainly compatible with, say, Catholic tradition. There are a couple of salient sticking points.

6. Similar words apply if we replace talk about *truth* with talk about *probability*. The New Atheist might say that she only has to show that Christian belief is improbable, not that it's false. Reply: improbable in some sort of objective respect (e.g., "three out of four balls in this urn are red")? If Christian belief is true, then the relevant probability is very high (100%, because it's just true, not mostly true or true most of the time or in most cases). So you have to establish falsity before you can establish that. If the relevant probability is epistemic, as seems more likely, then the charge is that Christian belief is in some way unreasonable, implausible, something not to be bet on, etc.; but that's just another variant of the charge that it's irrational, with which we've been dealing all along.

First, many of the specifics about just *how* God in his providence has designed us to form Christian or theistic belief will have to be adapted to different faith traditions (is it by way of the natural intellect[?]; the infused gift of faith[?]). But the project of filling out these specifics appears to me to be hopeful.[7] And the basic idea of *warrant by way of proper function* seems harmonious with many Christian traditions (it's implicit in, say, Aquinas, as Jenkins argues).

Second and relatedly, it might seem that faith is precisely *not* knowledge, because there is a sort of leap-in-the-dark aspect to it, or inconclusiveness about it. But much of the tension here, it seems to me, is linguistic and not substantial. Christians talk past each other. For example, Augustine "avoided the term *knowledge*" even for *historical* belief, in well-known writings on faith, in order to say that "belief, that is, faith, is a constituent part" of what a good head will accept.[8] Whether it's that Jesus is Lord or that Caesar crossed the Rubicon, "it is not proper, says Augustine, to say, 'I *know* it';" I can only say I *believe* it.[9] So there's a surface-level conflict between what Augustine says and what Plantinga says, because Plantinga says we *know* that Jesus is Lord, and we know that Caesar crossed the Rubicon; we don't merely *believe* these things. Happily, the conflict here is superficial. Consider that Augustine himself later "changed his mind . . . about the appropriateness of the word *know*," in order to respect "common usage."[10] It's precisely common usage that epistemologists like Plantinga try to capture today, in analyzing what it is to "know" something as opposed to merely believing it without sufficient warrant. So the conflict between Plantinga and Augustine is superficial. So is what seems at first to be a tension between Plantinga and other eminent theologians (Kierkegaard, if anyone, would seem opposed).[11]

---

7. See Jenkins, *Thomas Aquinas*; Mulder, *Kierkegaard*, 28–31.
8. Wilken, *Spirit*, 169.
9. Ibid.
10. Ibid.
11. See Evans, "Kierkegaard"; on interpreting Aquinas harmoniously, see Plantinga, *Warranted Christian Belief*, 91n.

2. ON EXPERIENTIAL KNOWLEDGE AS OPPOSED TO PROPOSITIONAL KNOWLEDGE

My 14-year-old son Philip mused on a puzzle yesterday at dinner, which highlights the important difference between two types of knowledge. Isn't it strange, he remarked, that you might be struck, even surprised, how massive a whale is, when you see it, even if you didn't really *learn* anything new because you already *knew* the whale's massive dimensions before you *saw* it. You're awestruck as if you'd just learned something about how massive the whale is; but you didn't just learn it. This puzzling situation highlights the difference between two ways of knowing something: knowing it "experientially" and knowing it "propositionally" as it is sometimes put.

Experiential knowledge or understanding is important to have for reasons suggested by theologians from Augustine to Jonathan Edwards, John Henry Newman, and beyond.[12] Suppose, to take an extreme case, that I had *no* experiential knowledge about joy or happiness, having suffered through a uniformly drab life. Even so, "though I had never experienced a moment of happiness, I could nevertheless understand perfectly well what happiness is, even what a paradisal life of complete happiness would be," purely propositionally: or anyway, it seems plausible to say so, following Matthews.[13] The reason that it seems plausible to say that I might understand, propositionally, what happiness is, is because I might be able to *define* "happiness" and *use* the term sensibly, explaining people's behavior by reference to their pursuing "happiness," and so on. My *experiential* impoverishment—I have not gone through it—seems to issue in a corresponding but distinct *conceptual* impoverishment. We can easily imagine someone telling me, "You don't understand what I'm going through," in their times of joy. They might say that I don't know what it's like to be happy even though I know what happiness is.

My conceptual impoverishment would have deleterious effects. Perhaps the most substantial or salient effect of the conceptual impoverishment is that I would probably not have the understanding it takes to be *motivated*

---

12. For secondary literature about Augustine's thoughts on experiential knowledge, see Matthews, *Augustine*, 134–45 (chapter 15, "Happiness"); Edwards's thoughts on the matter are discussed by Plantinga, *Warranted Christian Belief*, 294–95 (§2, "Jonathan Edwards"); Newman's thoughts on experiential understanding are discussed in several of John Crosby's 2011 lectures (see especially Lecture 1: "The Personalist Spirit of Newman's Thought," and Lecture 2: "Newman on the Human Person as a World of His Own.").

13. Matthews, *Augustine*, 143.

to do what I know, propositionally, that I ought to do to be happy: from a Christian perspective, that would be to commit my life to Christ. Newman accordingly warns that "there cannot be a more fatal mistake than to suppose we see what the doctrine" of eternal joy in Christ "means as soon as we can use the words which signify it." On the contrary, he insists, *experiential* understanding of doctrinal matters like this "is all one with being serious" about orienting our lives.[14]

So it seems fitting that Aquinas closely associates the highest *wisdom*, whereby we "judge and order" our lives and actions, with an "intimate"—I suggest *experiential*—comprehension of what the Divine ways are all about.[15] Aquinas juxtaposes the highest wisdom with merely propositional knowledge that any student of ethics might have "if he has learnt the science of morals." That inferior sort of wisdom "which is acquired by the study and research of reason" does not hold us back from sin. But the highest wisdom does. The highest wisdom is backed by a comprehension from the insider's perspective of an experiential union with God in the act of love, by means of which the agent "contemplates Divine things in themselves."

From the outsider's merely speculative perspective, whereby we lack real appreciation of what they're really all about in spirit, "Divine rules" can appear to be cold and commanding fiats, instead of the benevolent directives of a solicitous nurse and lover. Merely being well catechized or propositionally sophisticated is not enough to lift us from this misunderstanding and thereby to give us "sympathy" for God's directives. Someone without the highest wisdom, who is nevertheless well catechized, might say, in a manner of speaking, "I *know* these precepts are good for me, but I just can't get myself to *believe* it!" The connection between an experiential/propositional distinction, on the one hand, and wisdom in living, on the other hand, sheds light on puzzling biblical pronouncements, such as "my yoke is easy, and my burden is light" (Matt 11:30). Jesus's teachings are hard. However, because the wise understand deeply the benevolent spirit behind divine commandments, it can be "sweet" for them to do what would otherwise be hard, as Aquinas says. Just so, if I have had firsthand

---

14. Newman, "Immortality."

15. Aquinas, *Summa*, 2a2ae.45, "The Gift of Wisdom." Aquinas isn't directly addressing the topic of experiential understanding and his discussion does leave interpretive mysteries. I recall some years ago discussing this with Alfred Freddoso, who piqued my interest by his own searching into puzzles about why Aquinas would organize his *Summa*'s coverage of seven key virtues by putting the discussion of the highest wisdom under the topic of love, rather than prudence.

experience of your kindness, it can be easy for me to do what you ask me to do, even if you can't explain your reasons to me. Alternatively, if I've had firsthand experience with a miserable consequence, it can be easy for me to do what it takes to circumvent that outcome in the future, even if it means some effort on my part. After all, I can vividly imagine the troubles I will otherwise bring upon myself. Hence, imagination is closely associated in the literary tradition with what I've been calling "experiential knowledge." As C. S. Lewis says in a related vein, "If the imagination were obedient, the appetites would give us very little trouble."[16]

The connection between an experiential/propositional distinction, on the one hand, and wisdom in living, on the other hand, also lends new dimensions to such readily understood pronouncements—understood at face value anyway—as "thou hast hid these things from the wise and prudent, and hast revealed them unto babes" (Matt 11:25). Sometimes it is *propositional* knowledge that separates the wise from children: hence, John Duns Scotus observes that Aristotle, for all his wisdom, had no information about the happiness "far more perfect than anything possible in this life," because Aristotle didn't know about Yahweh's special revelation through the prophets and Scriptures. Mere intelligence, which Aristotle had in plenty, isn't enough to learn anything about that kind of happiness. "From all this it is apparent how much thanks must be given to our Creator, who through faith has made us most certain of those things which pertain to our end and to eternal life—things about which the most learned and ingenious men

---

16. Lewis, *Prayer*, 17. The connection between epistemology and motivation here is clearly of *practical* importance, but also has important *theoretical* applications. Thus, we sometimes hear that God might allow us to suffer so much in part, at least, because God knows that we would assent to going through with it if we were offered the opportunity. Here's an interesting objection: saying that "Christians who suffer horrendously *would* have consented had they been asked for prospective consent" ignores that we "tend to weight temporally near effects over temporally distant effects and the aversion of harm over the procuring of greater goods" (Vitale, Review of *Wandering in Darkness*, 1196). True, we do. I suggest even so that perhaps we *would* assent if we *understood* better—intuitively, experientially—just what's at stake with the choice (observe that understanding what's at stake is anyway important to our *freely* choosing anything). As we anticipate the future, the vivid, experiential side to our understanding fades away. Newman says tellingly that "a sluggish will and a lukewarm love" might betray a myopic heart, which "cannot see afar off," to the redemption of promises (Newman, "The Power of Will," 353).

Additionally, the connection between the imagination and experiential knowledge is not straightforward. Strictly speaking, one might *imagine* something that one has had no firsthand experience with; on the other hand, one might consider it to be a form of experience for the imagination to bring *that very thing* to mind.

can know almost nothing" (I don't necessarily recommend Scotus to the uninitiated but some connections to experiential knowledge may be found in more accessible secondary literature).[17] Yet it is not always *propositional* knowledge that separates the learned from children. On the contrary, great propositional sophistication leaves room for a deeper, tacit understanding formed from experiential contact.

I close with three further insights that a firm grasp on the epistemological distinction between experiential and propositional knowledge promises to yield. First, the distinction seems crucial for understanding conceptual change and enlightenment. Our dim experiential contact with God now—"For now we see through a glass, darkly" (1 Cor 13:12)—permits just so much experientially grounded vision about God and God's ways to whet our appetites. So our longing for, say, final happiness is puzzling at face value. "For who would want something of which he is unaware, or run after something he does not know?" as Boethius asks,[18] echoing forbears like Augustine, who worried, "How then shall I seek for the happy life?" Augustine never offers a settled response to the puzzle: "Certainly we have the desire for it, but how I do not know," he concedes.[19] But he hints that we understand *enough* experientially to long for the fulfillment of God's promise.[20] Just so, if God's promises hold out, we will someday say, with a character in Lewis's stories, that we've received just what we've "believed in and longed for"—despite our gaps in understanding. Indeed, when you experience God's gift, you might characterize it as what "I have been looking for all of my life, though I never knew it till now."[21]

The contrast here to finding *what we were desiring all along* might be to this: receiving a conceptual *overhaul* so great that none of our experiences now provide enough grasp on what God promises even for us to be able to long for them—at all. That suggests unfortunately, as James Alison might say, something more like a diabolical cult's "displacement of 'self'" and all of its hopes and loves, than Christian redemption.[22] All of the

---

17. Scotus, *Philosophical Writings*, 162. For the uninitiated, see Mackey, "Singular and Universal."

18. Boethius, *Consolation*, 108.

19. Augustine, *Confessions*, 196.

20. The connections here to the ancient tradition of negative theology are rich but I leave the reader with only this prompt.

21. Lewis, *Last Battle*, 30, 196.

22. Alison, *On Being Liked*, 143.

conceptual groundwork that Augustine, Lewis, and Alison take for a *start* in our conceptual understanding of the kingdom of heaven, visible now in, say, a parent's love for a child, would, instead, yield to something absolutely foreign, something that we will find to be unrecognizable (cf. Jesus's indications that the kingdom is already in our midst [Luke 17:20f.], albeit in seed form [Matt 13:31–32; Mark 4:30–32; Luke 13:18–19]).[23]

One can understand the reluctance, on the part of some, to invite God to move them. They're afraid to pray "Thy will be done." To be sure, there is sin on our part, there is selfishness. But there may also be fear rooted in ignorance for which one is *not* culpable, ignorance stemming from experiential impoverishment, or from misleading experiential associations (imagine someone having had a bad experience with an earthly father),[24] etc., concerning what God or God's invitation is like. Such ignorance should not be thought to be inexcusable on account of proper schooling in the faith, say; it is not, or not primarily, an ignorance of catechesis or a lack of other propositional sophistication. We know less about others' experiential blindspots in moral and spiritual matters than we do about their propositional deficiencies, which are easier to discern in discussion: so we should take care not to assign personal blame lightly. Compare Jesus's warnings against judging others (Matt 7:1; Luke 6:37) and his statement of

---

23. To be sure, there are opposing strains in the great theological traditions. I don't mean to present the uncontroversial here; I only hope to present a possible takehome message, which I hope moves the reader. So I intend to present Aquinas under a favorable interpretation, as Aquinas himself presents his own forbears. I've filled in ellipses. Certain strains in Aquinas suggest, by contrast to my interpretation here, "that God's goodness is different in kind from our own" (Harrison, "Animal Souls," 533), so utterly different that we lack even an experiential *start* in understanding or intuiting the spirit behind divine law: in that case, we "should expect no more than oblivion, or considerably worse," say, for a child who dies before baptism, even if that seems unjust to us. No *greater understanding of the circumstances*, say, would in that case help us; *only erasing and replacing our values*. Compare, by contrast, more recent Catholic tradition in the works of John Paul II (winsomely introduced by Robert Barron, "Hell is Crowded"). There is similar tension between some of Calvin's proclamations and more moderating strains found in the Calvinist tradition (Harrison, "Animal Souls," and Kolakowski, *Is God Happy?*, discuss parallels between Calvinism and Catholicism here).

24. See Plantinga, *Warranted Christian Belief*, 216n. Related mishaps are many and varied: another example would be to think propositionally that certain experientially understood features of fun—like its risk, as in skiing—would *have* to attend fun. This mistake might come from limits to our range of fun experiences. We might thereby conclude that heaven would be boring: for a quick, intuitive, sympathetic account of that way of thinking about the afterlife, see Baggini, *The Pig That Wants*.

forgiveness on the cross: "Father, forgive them; for they know not what they do" (Luke 23:34; see also Acts 3:17).

There are many further applications of the experiential/propositional distinction at hand, many of which have practical interest. Teaching and preaching come especially to mind. The epistemological distinction at hand suggests the urgency of making truths manifest by way of a battery of conduits, in order to help the listener to unpack experientially the rich content of verbal articulation, the whole relevance of which can be otherwise missed. Consider the importance of personal *relationships* in mentoring, by which we may express our thought with gestures and nonverbal cues. Consider the value of *beauty* in liturgy or art to convey sublimity. These are nonverbal conduits. *Verbal* communication, too, can be more or less experiential: the personal touch in storytelling and concrete narrative can effectively illustrate philosophical and theological truths (here see Stump's arguments concerning the problem of evil).[25] A proper understanding of the experiential/propositional distinction upgrades these distinct avenues of communication as concomitants to the teaching of doctrine, which is of course propositionally conveyed as well.

BIBLIOGRAPHY

Alison, James. *On Being Liked*. New York: Crossroad, 2003.
Aquinas, St. Thomas. *Summa Theologica*. Rev. ed. Translated by Fathers of the English Dominican Province. 2008. http://www.newadvent.org/summa/.
Augustine. *Confessions*. Translated by Henry Chadwick. Oxford: Oxford University Press, 1991.
Baggini, Julian. *The Pig that Wants to be Eaten: 100 Experiments for the Armchair Philosopher*. New York: Penguin, 2006.
Barron, Bishop Robert. "Bishop Barron on Whether Hell is Crowded or Empty." YouTube. Mar 28, 2011. https://www.youtube.com/watch?v=dmsa0sg4Od4.
Boethius. *The Consolation of Philosophy*. Translated by Richard H. Green. New York: Macmillan, 1962.
Crosby, John. "The Christian Personalism of Blessed John Henry Newman." http://www.thepersonalistproject.org/comments/audio_of_the_christian_personalism_of_j.h._newman.
Evans, C. Steven. "Kierkegaard and Plantinga on Belief in God." *Faith and Philosophy* 5 (1988) 25–39.
Harrison, Peter. "Animal Souls, Metempsychosis, and Theodicy in Seventeenth-Century English Thought." *Journal of the History of Philosophy* 31 (1993) 519–44.
Jenkins, John. *Knowledge and Faith in Thomas Aquinas*. Cambridge: Cambridge University Press, 1997.

25. Stump, *Wandering*.

Kolakowski, Leszek. *Is God Happy?: Selected Essays.* New York: Penguin Limited, 2012.
Lewis, C. S. *The Last Battle.* New York: HarperCollins, 1956.
———. *Prayer: Letters to Malcolm.* London: Fount, 1964.
Mackey, Louis. "Singular and Universal: A Franciscan Perspective," *Franciscan Studies* 39 (1979) 130–64.
Matthews, Gareth B. *Augustine.* Malden, MA: Blackwell, 2005.
Mulder, Jack. *Kierkegaard and the Catholic Tradition.* Bloomington: Indiana University Press, 2010.
Newman, John Henry. "Immortality of the Soul." In *Parochial and Plain Sermons*, Vol. 1. London: Longmans, 1907. http://www.newmanreader.org/Works/parochial/volume1/index.html.
———. "The Power of Will." In *Parochial and Plain Sermons*, Vol. 5. London: Longmans, 1907. http://www.newmanreader.org/Works/parochial/volume5/index.html.
Plantinga, Alvin. *Warranted Christian Belief.* Oxford: Oxford University Press, 2000.
Scotus, Duns. *Philosophical Writings.* Translated by Allan Wolter, OFM. Indianapolis, IN: Hackett, 1987.
Stump, Eleonore. *Wandering in Darkness: Narrative and the Problem of Suffering.* Oxford: Oxford University Press, 2010.
Vitale, Vince. Review of *Wandering in Darkness: Narrative and the Problem of Suffering* by Stump. *Mind* 122 (2013) 1193–1201.
Wilken, Robert Louis. *The Spirit of Early Christian Thought.* New Haven. Yale University Press, 2003.

4

GOD AS THE INDISPENSABLE FOUNDATION FOR ETHICS

Jesse K. Mileo

If things on earth may be to heaven resembled,
It must be love, pure, constant, undissembled.

– Aphra Behn, "And Forgive Us Our Trespasses"[1]

Ethics, or moral philosophy, is the discipline that addresses questions about what constitutes a morally good life. If I were asked what kind of moral life I wanted to live, if the word "God" or "Christ" isn't one of the next words that comes out of my mouth, I should say I am hardly worth my salt as a Christian. This is because, as I will argue, the Christian view of morality involves an intimate connection between God and morality. In this chapter, I will first address a major objection to this intimate connection, called the "Euthyphro Dilemma." After critiquing this dilemma, I will present a theory of God as the source of all moral value and obligation. We can call this theory a version of "Divine Command Theory" (hereafter, DCT), which, roughly speaking, refers to a family of moral theories where right and wrong are related to God's commands. Two additional objections

---

1. Behn, "And Forgive Us Our Trespasses," 33.

will be addressed, and then I will build a bridge to theology by arguing that two crucial areas of Christianity are at stake in this debate: the gospel of Jesus Christ and the glory of God.

THE NEED FOR THIS STUDY

The Scriptures have much to say about living a morally good life.[2] Even a cursory reading of the Bible reveals that God cares very much how we live. Let us name just a few passages that show this: love for God is the greatest commandment (Matt 22:37–38); love for neighbor is second (Matt 22:39); honoring one's parents is commanded (Exod 20:12); courage is commanded (Deut 31:6); God desires that we be truthful (Ps 51:6); gratitude is commanded (Col 3:15); generosity to the poor is commanded (Deut 15:7–11); we are to treat others in a way we wish to be treated (Luke 6:31); we are to put away all hypocrisy (1 Pet 2:1); we are commanded to be tenderhearted (Eph 4:32); Jesus praises integrity (John 1:47); and pure motives are extolled (Matt 6:1–6). It's safe to say that, for the Bible, God and morality are inextricably linked.

Not so fast, says the philosopher. Don't you know that any such view connecting God with morality was refuted over two thousand, four hundred years ago by Socrates?[3] That is the attitude of most philosophers I have encountered who address the subject. If God comes up in an ethical discussion, he is often quickly whisked away from the moral scene, likely without even mentioning the best defenders of DCT.[4] One philosopher even says

---

2. One crucial distinction any full-orbed theory of Christian ethics should maintain is between the way a regenerate believer may possess moral properties (through the means of what can be called *special grace*) and the way an unregenerate unbeliever may possess them (through the means of what can be called *common grace*; see Luke 6:32, 33 and Rom 2:14 [for a discussion on the distinction between special and common grace, see Louis Berkhof, *Systematic Theology*, 432–46; see also Jonathan Edwards, *A Dissertation*]). Since this chapter is not intended as a full-orbed theory of Christian ethics and largely focuses on the foundations of such a theory as a response to a secular criticism, I won't delve much into that important distinction.

3. A. I. Melden, for example, dismisses DCT rather quickly in the introductory essay to his historical reader: *Ethical Theories*, 5.

4. For example, all of the following textbooks contain sections dedicated to a critique of DCT, but they offer no responses to those criticisms whatsoever: Steven M. Cahn, *Exploring Ethics: An Introductory Anthology*, 2nd ed. (New York: Oxford, 2011); Lewis Vaughn, *Great Philosophical Arguments: An Introduction to Philosophy* (New York: Oxford, 2012); and Louis P. Pojman and Lewis Vaughn, *Philosophy: The Quest for Truth*,

that it is "practically a philosopher's platitude that even if God did exist, that would not, to a clear-headed and moral thinker, make any difference to the situation of morality."[5] The late Derek Parfit, an influential moral philosopher of our time, also reflected this dismissive attitude when he wrote, in a passing comment, that moral truths "do not have to be grounded in claims about Nature or God. Nor could all such truths be so grounded."[6] Saying that moral truths *could not* be grounded in God is the strongest kind of claim, since that means it is not even possible for morality to be grounded in God and all such views are necessarily false. Christians must be prepared to offer a plausible account of the way God relates to morality that avoids the problems so often thought devastating to DCT. We now turn to the main objection.

THE MAIN OBJECTION TO THEISTIC ETHICS: THE EUTHYPHRO DILEMMA

In Plato's dialogue, entitled the *Euthyphro*, Socrates famously asks the supposed religious expert Euthyphro the following question: "Is what is pious loved by the gods because it is pious, or is it pious because it is loved?"[7] Philosophers have ingeniously adapted this question and posed it to advocates of DCT. While there are various ways we can put this, let's pose the question fueling the Euthyphro Dilemma like this:

(a) *Are actions right because God commands them, or* (b) *does God command us to do actions because they are right?*

Suppose we take option (a). What is wrong with this? If actions are right just because God commands them, then this threatens to make morality arbitrary, so the argument goes. James Rachels argues, "It means that God could have given different commands just as easily. He could have commanded us to be liars, and then lying, and not truthfulness, would be right."[8] Suppose we reply that God would never do that. "Why not?" asks the objector. If we say God would not do that because it would be wrong, we've effectively given up DCT, because wrongness then is not dependent

---

9th ed. (New York: Oxford, 2014).

5. Williams, "God, Morality, and Prudence," 136.
6. Parfit, *On What Matters*, 444.
7. Plato, "Euthyphro," 31.
8. Rachels, "The Divine Command Theory," 568.

upon God's commands. In fact, we cannot offer any reasons for why God commands as he does, because then, says Russ Shafer-Landau, "*these reasons, and not God's commands, are what makes* [sic] *actions right or wrong.*"[9] This too departs from DCT. But if God can have no more reason for commanding one action than its opposite, his command is arbitrary. God might as well create morality with a coin toss![10]

Not only does (a) potentially make morality arbitrary, but it might call into question our ability to make any sense of God's goodness. Rachels explains, "If 'X is good' means 'X is commanded by God,' then 'God's commands are good' would mean only 'God's commands are commanded by God,' an empty truism."[11] We normally think we are saying something substantial when we say, "God's commands are good," but if Rachels is right, then what we say is trivially true. And it raises the question why we should praise God for commanding some action if he would be equally praiseworthy if he commanded its contrary.[12] So (a) does not look promising as it stands here. We can call this the *arbitrary horn of the dilemma*. We now turn to (b).

Suppose we answer the Euthyphro Dilemma by saying that God commands us to do actions because they are right. On this view, God's commands don't make rightness or wrongness. Rather, he recognizes, say, that dishonesty is not right, so he forbids that. If that is the case, then there is a moral standard independent of God. Is that so bad? Yes, if you think it's bad that the Almighty should be subject to a moral law. Shafer-Landau writes that, on this view, God "is one who fully understands, embraces, and *adheres to a moral law not of His own making.*"[13] Since moral truths prescribe behavior, this involves an authority above God where he is beholden to various obligations. So this view calls into question God's sovereignty and, hence, his omnipotence. William Alston rightly says that if it is true independently of God "that loving communion is a supreme good, and that forgiveness is better than resentment, then God is subject to these truths. He must conform himself to them and so is not absolutely sovereign."[14]

---

9. Shafer-Landau, "The Divine Command Theory," 487 (emphasis original).
10. Ibid.
11. Rachels, "The Divine Command Theory," 568.
12. Rachels quotes from Leibniz's *Discourse on Metaphysics* in this regard (ibid.).
13. Shafer-Landau, "The Divine Command Theory," 488 (emphasis added).
14. "What Euthyphro Should Have Said," 291; see also Bagget and Walls, *Good God*, 85.

This seems also to contradict the Bible, where God (through Christ) is shown creating all things, including all authorities: "For by him all things were created, in heaven and on earth, visible and invisible, whether thrones or dominions or rulers or authorities—all things were created through him and for him" (Col 1:16; see also Eph 1:20–21). Furthermore, if we take God to be the greatest conceivable being, it seems we can conceive of a being that is greater than the one who is subject to an authority: a being that is wholly good *and* completely sovereign (as I will argue below). Plus, this would potentially make God superfluous to morality. Many philosophers think we can discover moral truths through reason. If that is true, then what purpose does God serve in the matter? A mere informer. So if a person were informed by God of a certain moral obligation they have, they could snarkily reply, "You, O Lord, are subject to the same obligation!" Such a view should be offensive to theists.[15] We can call this the *independent horn of the dilemma*.

SOME DISTINCTIONS AMONG ETHICAL CONCEPTS

If we are going to navigate past this difficult dilemma and craft a sensible theory, then getting a grasp on a variety of moral concepts is essential. We will look at the terms "good," "bad," "right," and "wrong" and make some crisp distinctions. While our typical moral conversations don't require these fine distinctions and often blur them, they will be necessary since we are attempting to set forth a formal moral theory. The terms "right" and "wrong," as Barbara Mackinnon writes, "prescribe things for us to do or not to do."[16] So to say "stealing is wrong for us" is to say that we have a moral obligation not to steal. To say "truth-telling is right" is to say that we have a moral obligation to tell the truth. But "right" can mean something weaker than "morally obligatory." It can also mean "morally permissible." Consider an example from the abortion debate. Pro-choice advocates do

---

15. Not all theists agree with me here. See Keith Yandell's defense of the position that there can be moral principles independent of God in "Moral Essentialism," 110–16. Richard Swinburne argues that God's commands can increase the strength of an already existing obligation, thus taking the position that moral obligations do exist independent of God ("Duty and the Will of God," 130–33). Peter Geach shares that on one occasion when he attacked the Euthyphro argument, his chief opponents were professing Christians, and he mentions the Cambridge Platonist Christians as ones who believed that moral obligations were independent of God ("The Moral Law and the Law of God," 165).

16. Mackinnon, *Ethics*, 6.

not argue that abortion should be morally *obligatory* for women, but morally *permissible* (usually before a certain point in the pregnancy). That is, they want to say that a woman *may* have an abortion, not that she *has* to. So if a person says "Abortion is morally right," presumably, they believe it is morally permissible; that is, it is not wrong if she has an abortion. So "right" and "wrong" prescribe, permit, or prohibit actions. "Good" and "bad" do not necessarily serve the same purpose.

Mackinnon rightly notes, "[W]hen we say that something is morally good, we are not explicitly recommending doing it. However, we do recommend that it be positively regarded."[17] To say "love is good" isn't necessarily the same as saying "we are obligated to be loving." "Love is good" is to say something like, "love is morally valuable," "love has moral worth," or "love is worthy of admiration." Conversely, "morally bad" would refer to things that are to be negatively regarded, like cruelty, stealing, and rape. One difficulty with understanding these terms is that they often overlap. Molesting children is *bad*, but it is also *wrong*. Yet, just because they overlap doesn't mean there is no distinction between these terms. Consider this statement:

(1) It is morally good for me to do volunteer work for Habitat for Humanity three Saturdays a month.

Habitat for Humanity is an organization that helps people have adequate and affordable housing. Suppose that out of compassion for others, I decide to volunteer with them three Saturdays a month. We can say this is morally good of me, but this does not logically entail the following:

(2) It is morally obligatory for me to do volunteer work for Habitat for Humanity three Saturdays a month.

If (1) is true, then perhaps I am morally *permitted* to volunteer three Saturdays a month, but we would not say I am obligated to do so. This additional example should show that the concepts "good/bad" and "right/wrong" are not identical. The "good/bad" pair primarily speaks of values, and the "right/wrong" pair about duties.

We need to understand another aspect of the way we use "good": *intrinsically good* versus *instrumentally good*. To say that something is intrinsically good is to say that it is good in itself, or "that which is good apart from any of the results it produces."[18] Candidates for intrinsic goodness would

---

17. Ibid.
18. Ross, *The Right and the Good*, 68.

be God, truth, friendship, and knowledge. It seems those things are inherently good. This kind of goodness is to be distinguished from instrumental goodness. Money is a great example of something that is not intrinsically good (or evil), but instrumentally good. It is *good for* buying things that you want or need. Going to the gym, for me, is not really good in and of itself; rather, it is *good for* my health. We could also say that going to the gym is a *non-moral* good, since it has nothing necessarily to do with morality. We can refer to specific things as non-morally good as well such as a "good knife" or a "good hammer," since those may be good or successful in what they are intended for. Strangely enough, then, we can even refer to someone as "that bad man over there who is a good terrorist" without contradiction! This uses "bad" in a moral sense and "good" in a successful or effective sense. These distinctions will help us deal with the Euthyphro Dilemma.

THE PROBLEM WITH THE EUTHYPHRO DILEMMA

Recall James Rachels's claim that if DCT were true, then God could give other commands just as easily; God could command us to be liars. But why believe that? What kind of shabby view of God do philosophers who make such claims have in mind? Surely it must not be the one who is wholly good and morally perfect. God is necessarily good. That is, he is good in all possible worlds. One philosopher aptly comments on this point,

> God is what He is by necessity. To suppose that God "might" have been different, or that there are possible worlds or possible futures where He has an entirely different character, is simply to demonstrate a total misunderstanding of what God is. Theists do not worship an occult Abominable Snowman, nor a peculiarly inaccessible Galactic Emperor.[19]

As I will argue, one of the essential good-making properties God has is truthfulness, so it is not reasonable to believe that God would command his creatures to be liars.[20] This fits nicely with the Scriptures that say "it is impossible for God to lie" (Heb 6:18). Lovingness is also a good-making property that God has essentially. So if one were to say that if DCT were true, then God could command cruelty for its own sake, they would have

---

19. Clark, "God's Law and Chandler," 204.

20. There may be possible situations where God permits lying (Exod 1:16–21; Josh 2), but commanding us to *be liars* is an entirely different matter.

to describe a possible world where the God who loves his creatures would command one of them to torture another one of them just for the sake of being cruel. This is not sensible. Such a world contradicts God's character and is impossible.[21] As Alvin Plantinga says, "God's very nature constrains what he commands."[22] So on this view, God can't command just anything since he is necessarily good. Hence, morality is not arbitrary.

Rachels also claimed that equating "X is good" with "X is commanded by God" leads to an empty truism. This seems right, but we don't have to allow that "X is good" means the same as "X is commanded by God." I have already argued that "good" has to do with value, so we can say that "X is good" means something like "X is morally valuable" or "X is worthy of admiration."[23] Having addressed the arbitrary horn of the dilemma, let us move on to the second horn, the independent horn.

Saying God cannot command certain actions only gets us out of half the problem. If we claim that God has reasons why he commands as he does, are we not left open to Shafer-Landau's charge that those reasons, and not God's commands, are what make actions right or wrong? It doesn't seem we have to go that route. We can just deny that those reasons have to make actions right or wrong by providing examples of reasons God *could* have that do not appeal to some standard independent of God. William Alston offers some help here: "God can have an adequate reason for issuing the commands he issues, namely, that it is *best* for us to behave as he commands us to behave."[24] "Best" is a cognate of "good," so are we just sneaking in a moral standard of goodness independent of God? Not at all. Alston is simply referring to what is best for us in the sense of what is *instrumentally good* for us, and this is a *non-moral* good having to do with our well-being.

---

21. This doesn't have to contradict God's omnipotence, Robert Adams rightly argues, because it doesn't limit God's power in the relevant sense: "Things can have powers that they are prevented from exercising. You can have the physical power to accomplish a certain result even if for some reason it is impossible that you should choose to do so, perhaps because you are too nice to do it. A fully armed soldier may have the power to kill an enemy solider, but be 'unable to bring himself' to do it . . . Something similar can be true of God" (*Finite and Infinite Goods*, 47). A helpful definition of "omnipotence" that follows this line of thinking is the following: "God's ability to bring about any state of affairs that is logically possible in itself as well as logically consistent with his other essential attributes" (Trakakis, "The Evidential Problem of Evil," para. 4.).

22. Plantinga, "Naturalism, Theism, Obligation and Supervenience," 269.

23. I will discuss additional issues about how my theory relates to the meanings of moral terms more fully in a subsequent section.

24. Alston, "What Euthyphro Should Have Said," 290 (emphasis added).

CONVERGENCE

Well-being doesn't have to be the only reason God can have, but it's one that Bible believers should get behind since, at least sometimes, this seems to be involved in his reasons for commanding: "Honor your father and your mother, as the LORD your God commanded you, *that your days may be long, and that it may go well with you* in the land that the LORD your God is giving you" (Deut 5:16, emphasis added).

Some philosophers see phrases like "having a reason" as implying a distinct realm of obligations.[25] Obviously, I am not using "reason" here in that sense, or else we are subject to Shafer-Landau's criticism. I am using "reason" in the sense of God performing some action simply because he desires something. Simon Blackburn calls this the "ordinary, everyday reason for acting" distinguished from *Reason* with the capital letter, which sometimes denotes a kind of obligation.[26] Before we look at some additional examples of reasons God could have for commanding that do not appeal to a standard independent of himself, let me point out that it's entirely plausible God would have reasons we are not aware of. It should not be shocking to us that the all-wise and infinite God should have reasons and purposes of which we know nothing.

Turning to some reasons we might know, however, we will assume as the Christian faith has it, that God has commanded husbands to love their wives. We might suppose that God has issued that command *because*:

(3) Men have the tendency to be selfish, unkind, and lazy, and God doesn't want them to behave that way.

(4) God values wives and wants them to be treated lovingly, and this will spill over into how women are treated in general.

(5) Marriages where the husband loves his wife tend to be happy marriages, and God desires us to have happy marriages.

(6) Happy marriages are (non-morally) good for society, and God desires the well-being of society.

(7) Marriages where the husband loves his wife provide a healthy environment for their children to be reared, and God wants children to have a healthy childhood.

---

25. See Parfit, *On What Matters*, 268; and Shafer-Landau, *Moral Realism*, 112.
26. Blackburn, *Ethics*, 93–4.

(8) A husband loving his wife is a picture that God intends to represent Jesus Christ's relationship to his church, and God desires a variety of ways of telling the world about that relationship.

I think all these reasons are actually true (at the same time), but all we need to refute Shafer-Landau's point is one reason that could *possibly* be true, and these seem like great candidates. None of them appeals to a moral standard independent of God. Thus, it is not necessarily true that if God has a reason for commanding as he does, then that reason, and not God's command, is what must make the action right or wrong.

So, we have seen that the following two propositions are not necessarily true[27]:

(9) If actions are right (or wrong) just because God commands (or forbids) them, then morality is arbitrary.

(10) If God has reasons for commanding as he does, then those reasons, and not God's commands, are what make the action right (or wrong).

Therefore, since (9) and (10) comprise both options given to us in the Euthyphro Dilemma, the dilemma is built upon faulty assumptions. The arguers have given us only these two options. Since, as I will now argue, we have another option, they commit the fallacy of *false dilemma* or *false dichotomy*. That is, the Euthyphro Dilemma is a false dilemma. This is a fallacy of presumption where the arguer assumes there are only two options for something, when in fact, there may be one or many more options. It's like someone saying they can't get to work because their car broke down and they don't have money for a taxi, when actually there are plenty of other options—they can get a ride with a coworker, take a bus, wake up early and ride a bike, or even walk! Now that we have shown that the Euthyphro Dilemma does not have to pose a problem for DCT, we need to understand how God is the source of all moral value.

GOD AS THE INFINITE GOOD

Suppose I say, "Rachel is a good person." Among other things, I might have in mind that she generally does the things she's morally obligated to do and refrains from doing what she ought not to do. She tells the truth, keeps her

---

27. And if the theory I am presenting in this chapter is true, then these two propositions are necessarily false.

promises, and treats people with dignity. She does not steal from others, engage in racial discrimination, or mistreat other persons or animals. In short, Rachel acts in keeping with her obligations. We should not say that God is good in this sense since he does not have any obligations.[28] So how are we to understand God's goodness? We can understand his goodness by considering various properties that describe his character. God is good by virtue of being loving, kind, faithful, compassionate, generous, gracious, just,[29] merciful, tenderhearted, truthful, and forgiving.[30] Just as we should be open to God's having reasons for commanding that we know nothing about, so also we should say that God may be good in other ways we don't fully understand. As the apostle Paul says, "For now we see in a mirror dimly" (1 Cor 13:12). But this list of properties fits nicely with our common moral intuitions, and more importantly, with the Scriptures.[31]

This list of virtues does not have to hearken back to some independent standard by which we can say they are good. Rather, God's nature *determines* the good, on this view. This is why Robert Audi says that moral principles are not "*above* God," but are "instead *within* God."[32] Robert Adams, in his masterful book *Finite and Infinite Goods*, writes that "the infinite or transcendent Good *is* God."[33] Augustine and Calvin would concur.

---

28. I have claimed that there is no authority above God that would be the source of moral obligations, and I have rejected views involving a realm of moral facts that are independent of God. As Alston says, "[T]he closest we can get to a moral law requiring God to love others is the modal factual statement that God necessarily loves whatever others there are" ("What Euthyphro Should Have Said," 288–89). So if we were to apply the language of obligation to God, we would have to be speaking loosely, in a non-regulative or deflationary sense.

29. Robert Adams writes, in regard to the idea of God's being just, "Here, if my theory of obligation is not to be circular, I must be using a 'thin theory' of justice, so to speak, which does not presuppose moral obligation as such. Without going beyond such a thin theory I can say, for example, that God judges in accordance with the facts, and cares about each person's interests in a way that is good." (*Finite and Infinite Goods*, 254). In a footnote to this quote, he says he is borrowing the term "thin theory" from John Rawls, even though he is making a "most un-Rawlsian use of it" (ibid.).

30. Alston, "What Euthyphro Should Have Said," 289.

31. God is loving (1 John 4:8), kind (Luke 6:35), faithful (2 Cor 1:18), compassionate (Isa 63:7), generous (Jas 1:5), gracious (Exod 34:6), just (Gen 18:25), merciful (Ps 86:15), tenderhearted (Hos 11:8), truthful (Rom 3:4), and forgiving (Neh 9:17).

32. Audi, "Divine Command Morality and the Autonomy of Ethics," 126 (emphasis original).

33. Adams, *Finite and Infinite Goods*, 3 (emphasis added).

God as the Indispensable Foundation for Ethics

Augustine saw God as the "Supreme Good,"[34] and John Calvin eloquently calls God the "fountain of all goodness."[35] C. S. Lewis falls in line with this great tradition, calling God "Love Himself" and "Good Himself."[36] Moral virtues in us such as love and mercy, then, are finite goods insofar as they *resemble* God the Infinite Good. So it would be an objective fact to say that compassion in some person is morally good, since such a person images the Infinite Good, who is compassionate. Understanding goodness in this way, we can add one other reason to (3)–(8) from the previous section as to why God might command husbands to love their wives. He can command them to love their wives because:

(11) Loving one's wife is morally good, and God desires husbands to be good as he is.

This reason also does not require a standard independent of God since lovingness is a feature of God, and a husband's love for his wife simply mirrors what God is like.

A few analogies may be in order. I once heard David Stern, former commissioner of the National Basketball Association, say that Michael Jordan was the standard by which basketball excellence is measured.[37] Similarly, God is the standard by which moral excellence is measured. This is a helpful analogy, with one major qualification. We have to understand Michael Jordan's being the standard of basketball excellence loosely, for we can conceive of a greater player than Jordan, and he might not have even been a professional basketball player. When we refer to God as the standard by which moral excellence is measured, we mean it *literally*. We cannot conceive of a morally greater being than God, by definition,[38] and it's not the case that he might not have been good. William Lane Craig provides another helpful analogy with the concept of "high fidelity":

> By analogy think of some audio recording's being "high fidelity." Whether or not a symphony recording is high fidelity is determined by its approximation to the sound of a live orchestra. The sound of the live orchestra does not exhibit fidelity to anything

---

34. Augustine, *The Nature of the Good*, 326.
35. Calvin, *Institutes*, 1.2.2.
36. Lewis, *The Problem of Pain*, 159.
37. Stern, David. *Hardwood Classics Series,* 1999.
38. I'm assuming that God should be understood as the greatest conceivable being, and this entails moral perfection.

else; it just is the standard that determines whether some recording is high fidelity or not. Similarly with God's nature.[39]

God's nature or character just *is* the standard of goodness. The standard, on this view, is a particular personal being and not some general idea, which is why it is sometimes called *particularism*.[40]

If virtues are grounded in God as the infinite Good, what then of vices or morally bad qualities? Shall we ground these in something like an Infinite Bad? God's evil twin perhaps? Any attempt to do so would lead to an incoherent position, since there can only be one infinite being.[41] Moral badness also can be understood in relation to God, in what Adams calls "negative relations to the good."[42] He notes two main types of badness: one is "mere lack of goodness; the other attacks or opposes something good."[43] A person who is untrustworthy, unkind, and unjust is very ungodlike; this individual is far from the character of God. Or take a cruel and hateful person. Not only is this one far from the character of God, but their badness may very well be expressed in an outright antagonism to good. Douglas Groothuis rightly points out that evil "frustrates human goods"[44] and is a "corruption or twisting of the good."[45] The best villains, we all know, are those who not only lack good qualities, but who viciously oppose various

---

39. Craig, "The Euthyphro Dilemma Once More," para. 5.

40. William Alston calls it "valuational particularism" and shows how it is different from Platonism: "We can think of God himself, the individual being, as the supreme standard of goodness. God plays the role in evaluation that is more usually assigned, by objectivists about value, to Platonic Ideas or principles. Lovingness is good (a good-making feature, on which goodness is supervenient) not because of the Platonic existence of a general principle or fact to the effect that lovingness is good, but because God, the supreme standard of goodness, is loving. Goodness supervenes on every feature of God, not because some general principles are true but just because they are features of God" (Alston, "What Euthyphro Should Have Said," 291–92).

41. An infinite being would be one of infinite power or omnipotence. An omnipotent being would necessarily have power over every other being that might exist, so it cannot be that there would be two omnipotent beings, since that would entail they each have power over the other, but that is contradictory. This does not contradict the Christian doctrine of the trinity, however, since that entails there is one being shared by three persons (for a detailed discussion of the trinity, see Frame, "Part Six: The Triune God," 617–735).

42. Adams, *Finite and Infinite Goods*, 103; see also 102–04.

43. Ibid., 103.

44. Groothuis, *Christian Apologetics*, 615.

45. Ibid., 617.

goods like justice and peace, even increasing their wickedness as they diabolically delight in evil. In the Scriptures, it's no wonder that Satan is depicted as God's adversary who attempts to thwart God's good purposes (Gen 3:1–4; Luke 22:31; Eph 6:11–13).

In this section, we have looked at various good and bad character traits as they relate to God. Previously, I argued that proposition (1) did not entail a moral obligation, since all it said was that volunteering for Habitat for Humanity was morally *good*, not morally *obligatory*. I would say the same for the virtues I've been speaking about.

(12) Possessing the attribute of truthfulness is morally good.

Proposition (12) means that truthfulness has moral worth or is worthy of admiration. It doesn't necessarily entail, by itself, that I *should* be a truthful person. For all I have said in this section, this may only be a theory of virtues and value, but a moral theory should also account for obligations. That's where God's commands come in.

THE INFINITE GOOD AND MORAL OBLIGATIONS

Robert Audi distinguishes between *semantic* versions and *ontic* versions of DCT.[46] Semantic versions argue that moral claims have theological meaning in that "obligatory" might be synonymous with "commanded by God," and "wrong" might be synonymous with "forbidden by God." Ontic versions deny semantic equivalence but affirm that moral obligations are identical with divine commands.[47] This distinction is essential and needs some teasing out. Consider (13):

(13) It is wrong to torture children just for fun.

Most atheists I know of believe that (13) is true, and every Christian I know also believes this. If the theory being presented in this chapter were a semantic version, then my atheist friends who think (13) is true do not

---

46. Audi, "Divine Command Morality and the Autonomy of Ethics," 121–22. I should point out, however, that in a 2011 article, Glenn Peoples said there were actually no semantic versions of DCT in the literature (Peoples, "The Epistemological Objection to Divine Command Ethics," 389). For a discussion of three different interpretations of ontic DCT, see Murphy, "Divine Command, Divine Will, and Moral Obligation."

47. Specifically, Audi says that "the *property* of being obligatory is identical either with that of being commanded by God or with some property closely related to this" ("Divine Command Morality and the Autonomy of Ethics," 122) (emphasis original).

correctly understand moral language. This seems implausible, and from a Christian perspective in particular, it seems wrong as well. We believe the moral law is written on the heart of everyone (Rom 2:15), so we should expect that the typical person (believer or not) will have moral beliefs and be able to express them correctly. This is why Jonathan Edwards, in his work *On the Nature of True Virtue,* argued that the moral sense common to all mankind is what "chiefly *governs* the use of language, and is the mind's *rule* of language in these matters."[48] So we think atheists' moral foundations (whatever those may be) are wrong, but we don't have to argue that they never use moral language correctly. Thus, the theory I am presenting is an *ontic* version of DCT, not a *semantic* version.

To understand this further, consider some more propositions:

(14) "X is morally wrong" is synonymous with "X is not morally permitted."

(15) An action's being wrong is the same thing as an action's violating God's commands.

Proposition (14) is a claim about moral semantics, and (15) is a claim about moral metaphysics. Moral semantics addresses questions about the *meaning* of moral claims, and moral metaphysics involves questions about the *existence* of moral properties. A moral *nihilist*, to illustrate this distinction, does not believe there are any moral facts, so (appallingly) she rejects (13). However, she can be perfectly consistent with her nihilism and believe that (14) is true. This nihilist would have no problem affirming that moral judgments have a certain meaning, but she would just say that no actions actually have the property of being wrong, since nihilists do not believe any moral properties exist. This should help us see further that the distinction between the meaning of terms and the nature of things is a sensible one. So then, what does our theory say about moral obligations?

Moral obligations are identical with divine commands. A command, as I see it, is simply God telling us to do (or not to do) something. Adams puts it like this:

(16) [E]thical wrongness *is* (i.e., is identical with) the property of being contrary to the commands of a loving God.[49]

---

48. Edwards, *A Dissertation on the Nature of True Virtue,* 142 (emphasis original).
49. Adams, "Divine Command Metaethics Modified Again," 139 (emphasis original).

Proposition (16) says wrongness is identical with God's commands (his forbidding certain actions), but this is not saying that the word "wrong" means "forbidden by God," which I've just argued is an implausible meaning. Before I offer more reasons why this is important, let us turn to an analogy in science that will help us see this point more clearly. It is an example that comes up frequently in philosophical literature and is applied to a variety of issues.[50]

Take the following proposition:

(17) Water is H2O.

While "water" and "H2O" refer to the same stuff, those terms do not have identical meanings. William Shakespeare, for instance, clearly understood the meaning of the word "water," but he did not know that (17) was true. We had to engage in a lot of scientific experimentation in order to find out that (17) was true. Given that someone could competently use the term "water" before we had the science to know water's chemical compounds, this shows that the meaning of "water" and "H2O" are different. If they had identical meanings, then we could have known that (17) was true *a priori*, or prior to experiencing the world with our senses. That is, we could have known that (17) was true in the same way we know (18) is true:

(18) All bachelors are unmarried males.

We know (18) not through empirical means, but merely because we understand that the word "bachelor" is synonymous with "unmarried male." But surely we did not come to learn (17) that way. As we said, we came to learn this *a posteriori*, or through our five senses that we employed in investigating the nature of water. An example with names further illustrates this point. We know that (19) is true *a priori*:

(19) Mark Twain is Mark Twain.

But we do not know (20) in the same way:

(20) Mark Twain is Samuel Clemens.

We have to be informed somehow that (20) is true, that those names are referring to the same individual. This is somewhat similar to the example with water and H2O. The parallel we are making in this analogy is the following: just as "water" and "H2O" do not have the same meaning but refer

---

50. See Kripke's *Naming and Necessity*.

to the same stuff, so also "right" and "commanded by God" do not have the same meaning but can refer to the same thing. Why is this important?

This allows us to have an intimate connection—indeed, a necessary connection[51]—between God and morality, without being forced to embrace radical semantic positions entailing that everyone who does not believe in God does not understand moral language correctly. As Adams says, we are speaking of the morality "that *everybody* (or almost everybody) is talking about."[52] And this protects us from other objections as well. Recall one of James Rachels's objections to DCT. If we give "good" a religious meaning, then we risk making certain statements about God's goodness empty truisms. The same could be said for statements about wrongness. Suppose my daughter asks me why it is wrong to steal, and I reply, "Stealing is wrong because it is forbidden by God." If "wrong" means "forbidden by God," then all I have really said is (21):

(21) Stealing is forbidden by God because it is forbidden by God.

This is trivially true and I wouldn't really have answered her question. But when I say that stealing is wrong *because* it is forbidden by God, I am saying something substantial, like (22):

(22) God's commands *make it true* that stealing is wrong.

This theory, then, protects against certain objections and accords nicely with the way we use moral language.

TWO ADDITIONAL OBJECTIONS ADDRESSED

There are many objections we will have to face in postulating this theory. Space permits only dealing with two. First, what about the obligation to obey God? Are we morally obligated to obey God's commands? If we say yes, then the objector is sure to pose a following question: Why are you morally obligated to obey God, or what grounds the obligation to obey God? Suppose we say that we are obligated to obey God because God commands us to obey him. After all, the Scriptures contain such commands to obey God. Leviticus 22:31 reads, "So you shall keep my commandments and do them: I am the Lord." So if we answered this way, we speak truthfully.

---

51. I take it that "Water is H2O" is a necessary truth since a thing is always identical to itself.

52. Adams, "Divine Command Metaethics Modified Again," 139 (emphasis original).

God as the Indispensable Foundation for Ethics

Surely it's not incoherent for God to tell us to obey him, just as it is sensible that a commanding officer might tell his troops that they must obey him. But this objector has something much more subtle in mind. Suppose we call God's command to obey his commandments a *second-order command*. This objector will then simply ask why we are morally obligated to obey second-order commands. Shall we then postulate a *third-order command*? Certainly not, for this will lead to an infinite regress.

Suppose we reply by saying we don't have to ground obedience to God in God's commands. It's just a simple fact that we are obligated to obey our superiors. We might as well shoot ourselves in the foot if we give this answer! This would impale us on the independent horn of the Euthyphro Dilemma, for there would then be moral obligations independent of God and we would have given up DCT. Every single command given to us by God would presuppose this independent moral framework that obligates us to obey our superiors. So this is not a good option.

So how shall we respond to the question about why we are morally obligated to obey God? Sometimes the best way to answer a question is to point out it is actually a poor question. The one asking this question hasn't really understood our theory. It's like asking, "Why is water H2O?" We might respond, "That's just what water *is*." In a similar way, the answer to the question why we are morally obligated to obey God, is to say that fulfilling a moral obligation *just is* heeding God's commands. The objector seems to be assuming that facts about our obligations and facts about God's commands are separate facts, but we have argued that obligations and God's commands are identical.[53] If the questioner is implying they are different, then they are just begging the question, because that simply assumes our theory is false. And that is hardly an objection at all. So the one bringing this objection either doesn't understand our theory or begs the question.

The second objection deals with the virtue of courage. Dean Kowalski argues,

> Courage is, or at least can be, a moral virtue for human persons. However, because being courageous requires (roughly) focused effort in the face of adversity when the resulting outcome is uncertain, it is very difficult to see how the omnipotent, omniscient, and existentially secure Creator could be courageous. God's

---

53. I am referring to *ontic* identity, not *semantic* identity, as I have argued in the previous section.

> omnipotence entails that all activity is effortless, and God's omniscience entails that no outcome is uncertain to Him.[54]

Kowalski seems right when he says that courage requires effort in the face of adversity and a risk in the face of uncertainty. Consider Wesley Autrey, who in 2007 risked his life to save a man who had had a seizure and fell onto the subway tracks. As he saw the subway train coming, Autrey jumped down onto the tracks to hold the man down so the train could pass over them. With just inches to spare, both men survived and Autrey was rightly heralded a hero.[55] Imagine if Autrey had the power to stop time when the man fell, so he could just go down with no risk and carry the man to safety, and then he would start time back up to let the train pass. Would we praise him to the same degree as a courageous hero in that instance? I don't think so. What he actually did was an amazing and morally *good* act of courage.

How can our theory account for courage as morally good if God cannot be courageous? We have said that goodness in us is that which resembles God, but since God cannot be courageous, then we may not be able to say that courageous acts are good. But, intuitively, they are good.

One way to tackle this problem is to try and gain clarity on the nature of courage. Yes, courageous acts are good, we can admit, *sometimes*. But is courage necessarily good? Kowalski is operating under the idea that courage requires "focused effort in the face of adversity when the resulting outcome is uncertain." Going with that idea, it's not difficult to see that courage may be *morally bad* in some cases. The terrorists on 9/11 can be said to have exhibited intense effort in the face of adversity when the outcome was uncertain. It takes a lot of fortitude to hijack a plane and go forward with the plan at the risk of failure and being caught and prosecuted on display for the whole world. Though we would never praise their actions since they were abominable, we can admit that they were courageous in a sense, since courage is not necessarily good.[56] Kowalski would probably agree with this since he says courage "*can* be" morally virtuous in persons, but highlighting how courage is only contingently good will show how we can deal with this objection.

If courage is only good sometimes, we can ask what would *make* an instance of courage good. The example with Wesley Autrey can help here.

---

54. Kowalski, "Remembering Alston's 'evaluative particularism,'" 280.
55. Mackinnon, *Ethics*, 33.
56. I first heard Bruce Russell speak of courage in this way.

His action was a good instance of courage because it was a loving[57] and sacrificial action, which the Christian is happy to say does resemble what God did in sacrificing his own Son (Rom 8:32). So courage doesn't have to be seen as a virtue that is always good in and of itself, but it can derive its goodness from something else. And we can see this "something else" as ultimately being grounded in God's goodness.

Attaching to some virtue like love is not the only way we can see how courage can be good. Courage can be good in certain instances *because God commands it*. Courage is commanded to Joshua when he was commissioned to lead Israel after Moses was going to die (Deut 31:6–8). We can understand courage to be good in this instance, not necessarily because it attaches to some virtue that is grounded in God,[58] but because it relates to God through his commands. The resemblance-to-God relation is only one of the ways actions and character traits can be good. This occurrence of courage would be morally good for Joshua to exhibit because the Infinite Good is telling him to do it. This case of courage, then, derives its value from God who is infinitely valuable and has good purposes in directing Joshua to have courage.

This is just how value works for non-consequentialist moral theories—theories in which right and wrong are *not* fundamentally based on the results or consequences of the action. Previously, I argued that "good" and "right" were not identical moral concepts, but that there is an overlap between them. Here we see some of that overlap. I pointed out that just because some action was good, it doesn't necessarily follow that we are obligated to do it. Yet the opposite of this does seem necessarily true: If some action is morally obligatory, then performing it is morally good. If I have an obligation to refrain from harming animals for fun, then it is morally good that I refrain from harming animals for fun. If I have an obligation to keep my promises, then it is morally good that I keep my promises. This is important for our theory because we can not only see various character

---

57. I'm assuming it was loving and I don't think there's any reason to doubt this, but we should point out it is possible for someone to give their life and it actually not be loving (1 Cor 13:3).

58. We should note, however, that courage in this case with Joshua does really resemble God in that it is *for the good* and *opposed to the bad*. Take, for another example, when someone has courage in telling the truth; they demonstrate a firm commitment to goodness, which does image God. Courage may also be good in that, when connected to God's purposes, it magnifies God's worth by showing he is infinitely worthy to be obeyed; that is, it simply "speaks" the truth about God.

traits and actions as having value in faithfully imaging God, but also actions as having a value that flows from the source of the obligation, namely, God. In both cases, God is the ultimate source of the value.[59] Good instances of courage, then, are no objection to our theory.

SUMMARY OF THE PHILOSOPHICAL ARGUMENT

Before I build a bridge to theology, I shall recap the philosophical argument of this chapter up to this point. We saw that the Bible assumes there is an inextricable link between God and morality. Most philosophers don't think such an account makes sense, because—following the Euthyphro Dilemma—either morality is arbitrary or there is a moral standard independent of God. This dilemma is built on faulty assumptions and its arguers commit the fallacy of false dichotomy, since only two options are given. One way out of the dilemma, I argued, was to understand God as the Infinite Good who creates moral obligations for us. That is, moral obligations are identical with God's commands even though moral language itself does not necessarily involve theological semantics. We then dealt with two additional objections, one from the supposed obligation to obey God, the other from the nature of courage.

DIVINE COMMAND THEORY AND THEOLOGY

While I have touched on several theological issues in this chapter, this section explicitly builds the bridge to theology by providing two additional reasons why Christians should embrace DCT. The first reason relates to the gospel of Jesus Christ, and the second reason relates to the glory of God.

For this first reason, perhaps ironically, we will get some help from the skeptic David Hume. In crafting his theory of morality as based upon human sentiments, Hume required an important distinction. He distinguished between private affairs whereby one man offends another personally and that of "the common point of view" where humanity together can

---

59. A parallel from Kant's ethical theory may help here. A non-consequentialist, Kant thought that the moral worth of an action stemmed from the principle of duty, what he called the *categorical imperative*. So, for Kant, an action has moral value *because* it is an instance of one's duty in following the categorical imperative. Similarly, for the theory we are considering, one way an action has value is *because* it is an instance of one's duty in heeding the commands of God.

employ language of praise and blame. Here's this distinction in his own words:

> When a man denominates another his *enemy*, his *rival*, his *antagonist*, his *adversary*, he is understood to speak the language of self-love, and to express sentiments peculiar to himself, and arising from his particular circumstances and situation. But when he bestows on any man the epithets of *vicious* or *odious* or *depraved*, he then speaks another language, and expresses sentiments in which, he expects, all his audience are to concur with him.[60]

This distinction is important for our theory as well. First, let me point out how our theory beautifully captures this common point of view. Moral truths may be rightly discovered by both believers and unbelievers, and they can even agree on the language with which to express these truths. But where Hume is moving from the private realm to the public realm, I'd like to move in the opposite direction, from the public realm where all may discover moral truths to the private realm where one encounters God himself, the source of the moral truths. Our view entails that moral obligations are identical with God's commands. If this is true, then *necessarily*, every real moral violation is also a *sin that is personally against God*, since sin, by definition, is a violation of God's commands.[61]

Isaiah says, "The LORD was pleased, for his righteousness' sake, to magnify his law and make it glorious" (Isa 42:21). This shows that God's law is a glorious manifestation of the greatness of his character. This is why to obey his law is to render him the proper reverence (Deut 28:58), and to fail to do this dishonors him. When the wife of Joseph's master requested to sleep with him, Joseph replied, "How then can I do this great wickedness and sin *against God*?" (Gen 39:9, emphasis added). David reflects the same understanding. After committing adultery with Bathsheba, constantly lying to cover up his sin, and finally murdering her husband Uriah, he repents and says to God, "*Against you, you only*, have I sinned and done what is evil in your sight . . ." (Ps 51:4, emphasis added). God interprets David's sin in a similar way: "[Y]ou have despised *me* and have taken the wife of Uriah the Hittite to be your wife" (2 Sam 12:10, emphasis added). Paul falls in

---

60. Hume, *An Enquiry Concerning the Principles of Morals*, IX, 272–73, as cited in Blackburn, *Ethics*, 111 (emphasis added).

61. One helpful definition of "sin" is the following: "Any act, attitude, or disposition that fails to completely fulfill or measure up to the standards of God's righteousness. It may involve an actual transgression of God's law or failure to live up to his norms" (Erickson, *The Concise Dictionary of Christian Theology*, 182).

line when he speaks of unbelievers who "did not honor him as God or give thanks to him" (Rom 1:21). Thomas Schreiner rightly notes, "At its root, sin does not acknowledge the *Godness* of God, refusing to give him the glory and honor and praise he deserves."[62] Sin is personal to God, and this is why the Bible even describes offenders as God's *enemies*.

We see this in a variety of places in the Bible,[63] but let us look at one: "Our God is a God of salvation, and to God, the Lord, belong deliverances from death. But God will strike the heads of *his enemies*, the hairy crown of him who walks in his guilty ways" (Ps 68:20, 21, emphasis added). This is not only an Old Testament teaching, but it reflects Jesus's view as well (Mark 12:35–37). And God, being a just God (Gen 18:19; Rom 3:26), requires that everyone be held accountable for their transgressions: "Now we know that whatever the law says it speaks to those who are under the law, so that every mouth may be stopped, and the whole world may be held accountable to God" (Rom 3:19). So DCT preserves this idea that human beings have broken God's moral law and are under his judgment. Why is it important to preserve this?

If people haven't really offended God and incurred a debt to him, then why should they be in such desperate need of *his* forgiveness? What great need is there for salvation for those who have merely "sinned" against some abstract idea that has nothing to do with God?[64] The greatest need of humanity is forgiveness and reconciliation with God. Thankfully, in magnificent love and mercy, God has made a way that even his enemies may be reconciled to him through what Jesus Christ accomplished on the cross, which is to be received, not by works, but by faith (Rom 3:20–4:25). Paul explains:

> God shows his love for us in that while we were still sinners, Christ died for us. Since, therefore, we have now been justified by his blood, much more shall we be saved by him from the wrath of God. For if *while we were enemies* we were reconciled to God by the death of his Son, much more, now that we are reconciled, shall we be saved by his life. (Rom 5:8–10, emphasis added)

---

62. "A Biblical Theology of the Glory of God," 219 (emphasis added).

63. See, for example, 1 Sam 30:26; Ps 37:20; Luke 19:27; and 1 Cor 15:25.

64. If the moral law is independent of God, then one candidate for what it consists in is a realm of abstract ideas or necessary, brute moral facts (see Shafer-Landau, *Moral Realism*). A brute fact is a fact for which there can be no explanation; it is ungrounded, and hence, nothing makes it true.

Far from the idea of God having enemies as contradicting the love of God, notice it is the love of God that is demonstrated in Christ's death for those who were his enemies. How amazing a love it is that the offended God loves even his enemies and invites them to be reconciled to him! In fact, it is God's merciful love of his enemies that grounds Jesus's command to love *our* enemies and to be merciful: "But love your enemies, and do good . . . and your reward will be great, and you will be sons of the Most High, for he is kind to the ungrateful and the evil. Be merciful, even as your Father is merciful" (Luke 6:35). So then, we have seen that DCT preserves the notion that people have broken God's law, and this highlights their need for the salvation he has provided in Jesus Christ. Now let us look at a second theological reason Christians should hold to DCT.

If moral goodness itself is independent of God, then he might conform to this standard and be good, but we could not say that goodness is somehow owing to him. That is, he would not get the credit for goodness; he would not receive the *moral glory* he is due. The goodness of our works would not necessarily result in praise of God, since their goodness primarily would be derived from this independent standard, and not God. Jesus said to "let your light shine before others, so that they may *see your good works and give glory to your Father* who is in heaven" (Matt 5:16, emphasis added). Our good works can bring praise to God in that they resemble what he is like. Thus, they "speak" the truth about God.

Recall that one of the acceptable meanings of the moral sense of "good" is "worthy of admiration." So to say some action or character trait is morally good is to say that it is worthy of being admired. It is fitting to express this admiration in terms of praise. We rightly applaud people like Wesley Autrey who lovingly risk their lives to save others. We appropriately praise someone for forgiving a great evil they have endured or for enduring persecution in standing up for truth or justice.

Now consider a story that offers an analogy to show how appropriate praise of other people relates to God. Some friends are backpacking in the mountains, and they have run out of water. Having hiked for several hours in the scorching sun, legs caked with dust and shoulders sore from fifty-pound packs, they long for the trail to descend into the valley where they will find streams of water. As the trail moves downward, the foliage becomes more green and lush; soon they can hear rushing water. They have been told the water is not completely pure, but it is clean enough to drink straight from the river. Finally arriving at the banks of the river, with throats and mouths parched from the heat, they drink deeply. Unable to contain themselves, they exclaim, "How wonderful is this pristine and refreshing water!" If these men praise this relatively clean water, much more—if they are sane—would they marvel at water that is absolutely pure. So it is with God and goodness. If we praise goodness in people, much more should we praise the fountain of goodness himself.

If God is the Infinite Good, then every moral action and character trait worthy of admiration *necessarily* is an opportunity to heap praise upon God. When I delight in loving and playing with my young daughter and spending time with her, I magnify my heavenly Father who rejoices and sings over his children (Zeph 3:17). Or when a single mother works three jobs so she can provide for her children, this love is a beautiful display of the character of God. Even moral badness unwittingly praises him. We can rightly say of some morally awful person, "How far from God is this poor wretch!" But if morality ultimately has nothing to do with God, then God is robbed of his due worship and honor. The whole world rings with praise to God, if we have eyes to see it. Only if moral goodness is grounded in God can we truly say with the apostle Paul, "For from him and through him and to him are *all things*. To him be glory forever. Amen" (Rom 11:36, emphasis added). Let us never move from that.[65]

BIBLIOGRAPHY

Adams, Robert M. "Divine Command Metaethics Modified Again." In *The Virtue of Faith and Other Essays in Philosophical Theology*, edited by Robert M. Adams, 128–43. New York: Oxford, 1987.

———. *Finite and Infinite Goods*. New York: Oxford, 1999.

Alston, William. "What Euthyphro Should Have Said." In *Philosophy of Religion: A Reader and Guide*, edited by William Lane Craig, 283–98. New Brunswick, NJ: Rutgers University Press, 2002.

Audi, Robert. "Divine Command Morality and the Autonomy of Ethics." *Faith and Philosophy* 24, no. 2 (April 2007) 121–43.

Augustine. *The Nature of the Good*. In *Augustine: Earlier Writings*, 324–48. Translated by John H. S. Burleigh. The Library of Christian Classics: Ichthus Edition. Philadelphia: Westminster, 1953.

Baggett, Dave, and Jerry L. Walls. *Good God: The Theistic Foundations of Morality*. New York: Oxford, 2011.

---

65. I would like to thank the following friends and colleagues for their valuable insights into this essay: Robert Jooharigian, Elliott Crozat, Richard Ostella, Gary Papp, and Stephen Kovacs. My lovely and supportive wife, Rachel, also provided excellent feedback.

Behn, Aphra. "And Forgive Us Our Trespasses." *One Hundred and One Classic Love Poems*, compiled by Sara L. Whittier, 33. Chicago: Contemporary, 1988.

Berkhof, Louis. *Systematic Theology*. Grand Rapids, MI: Eerdmans, 1996.

Blackburn, Simon. *Ethics: A Very Short Introduction*. New York: Oxford, 2001.

Cahn, Steven M. *Exploring Ethics: An Introductory Anthology*. 2nd ed. New York: Oxford, 2011.

Calvin, John. *Institutes of the Christian Religion*. Translated by Henry Beveridge. Peabody, MA: Hendrickson, 2008.

Clark, Stephen R. L. "God's Law and Chandler." *The Philosophical Quarterly* 37, no. 147 (1987) 203–8.

Craig, William Lane. "The Euthyphro Dilemma Once More." http://www.reasonablefaith.org/the-euthyphro-dilemma-once-more.

Edwards, Jonathan. *A Dissertation on the Nature of True Virtue*. In *The Works of Jonathan Edwards: 2 Volume Set*. Vol. 1. Peabody, MA: Hendrickson, 2007.

Erickson, Millard J. *The Concise Dictionary of Christian Theology*. Rev. ed. Wheaton, IL: Crossway, 2001.

Frame, John M. "Part Six: The Triune God." In *The Doctrine of God*, 617–735. Phillipsburg, NJ: P&R, 2002.

Geach, Peter. "The Moral Law and the Law of God." In *Divine Commands and Morality*, edited by Paul Helm, 165–74. New York: Oxford, 1981.

Groothuis, Douglas. *Christian Apologetics: A Comprehensive Case for Biblical Faith*. Downers Grove, IL: InterVarsity, 2011.

Kowalski, Dean A. "Remembering Alston's 'evaluative particularism.'" *Religious Studies* 47, no. 3 (September 2011) 265–84.

Kripke, Saul A. *Naming and Necessity*. Malden, MA: Blackwell, 1981.

Lewis, C. S. *The Problem of Pain*. New York: HarperCollins, 2001.

MacKinnon, Barbara. *Ethics: Theory and Contemporary Issues*. 7th ed. Belmont, CA: Wadsworth, 1995.

Melden, A. I. *Ethical Theories: A Book of Readings*. New York: Prentice-Hall, 1950.

Murphy, Mark C. "Divine Command, Divine Will, and Moral Obligation." *Faith and Philosophy* 15, no. 1 (January 1998) 3–27.

Parfit, Derek. *On What Matters*. Vol. 2. New York: Oxford, 2012.

Peoples, Glenn. "The Epistemological Objection to Divine Command Ethics: Morriston on Reasonable Unbelievers and Moral Obligations." *Philosophia Christi* 13, no. 2 (2011) 389–401.

Plantinga, Alvin. "Naturalism, Theism, Obligation and Supervenience." *Faith and Philosophy* 27, no. 3 (July 2010) 247–72. http://www.ccel.org/ccel/plantinga/warrant3.vi.iv.ii.html.

Plato. "Euthyphro." In *The Last Days of Socrates*, 19–41. Translated by Hugh Tredennick, New York: Penguin Books, 1980.

Pojman, Louis P. *Philosophy: The Pursuit of Wisdom*. 5th ed. Belmont, CA: Wadsworth, 2006.

Pojman, Louis P., and Lewis Vaughn. *Philosophy: The Quest for Truth*. 9th ed. New York: Oxford, 2014.

Rachels, James. "The Divine Command Theory." In *Philosophy: The Quest for Truth*. 9th ed. New York: Oxford, 2014.

Ross, W. D. *The Right and the Good*. Edited by Philip Stratton-Lake. British Moral Philosophers. Oxford: Clarendon, 2002.

Schreiner, Thomas R. "A Biblical Theology of the Glory of God." In *For the Fame of God's Name: Essays in Honor of John Piper*, edited by Sam Storms and Justin Taylor, 215–34. Wheaton, IL: Crossway, 2010.

Shafer-Landau, Russ. "The Divine Command Theory." In *Great Philosophical Arguments: An Introduction to Philosophy*, edited by Lewis Vaughn, 486–88. New York: Oxford, 2012.

———. *Moral Realism: A Defence*. Oxford: Clarendon, 2003.

Stern, David. *Hardwood Classics Series: Michael Jordan: His Airness*. DVD. Burbank, CA: Warner Home Video, 1999.

Swinburne, R. G. "Duty and the Will of God." In *Divine Commands and Morality*, edited by Paul Helm, 120–34. New York: Oxford, 1981.

Trakakis, Nick. "The Evidential Problem of Evil." http://www.iep.utm.edu/evil-evi/.

Vaughn, Lewis. *Great Philosophical Arguments: An Introduction to Philosophy*. New York: Oxford, 2012.

Williams, Bernard. "God, Morality, and Prudence." In *Divine Commands and Morality*, edited by Paul Helm, 135–40. New York: Oxford, 1981.

Yandell, Keith E. "Moral Essentialism." In *God and Morality: Four Views*, edited by R. Keith Loftin, 97–116. Downers Grove, IL: InterVarsity, 2012.

5

THE OLD TESTAMENT AND METAPHYSICS: A NEW GROUND FOR THEOLOGY?

Jason Stanghelle

It is one of the tragedies—one could almost say crimes—of Christian theological history that the Old Testament was effectively displaced by Greek philosophy as the theological basis of the doctrine of God, certainly so far as the doctrine of the divine attributes is concerned.
—Colin Gunton, Act & Being: Towards a Theology of the Divine Attributes[1]

INTRODUCTION

The task of this paper is to triangulate the discipline of Old Testament studies with philosophy and theology. The conceptual tool this paper will employ is the concept of space to examine how the three disciplines share conceptual territory which could provide common ground for dialogue. A

---

1. Gunton, *Act & Being*, 3.

main goal of this paper is to connect spatial issues to the issue of history. The place of history is one of the largest rifts between theology, biblical studies, and philosophy. Biblical scholars tend to place more importance upon history than the other disciplines. Since the rise of historical consciousness in early modernity, the relationship between theology and history has been contentious. One issue this essay will develop is that the fateful *Histoire–Geschichte* split, which is a root of the problem, is grounded in deeper topological issues. By exploring these topological issues, the hope is to create new categories in which a more congenial dialogue might be formed between the disciplines. This essay will focus upon the early modern period by tracing two seemingly unrelated stories. From the historical side, it will look at how a container view of space was the operative category for biblical studies and caused problems in interpretation during the rise of historical consciousness. From the philosophical side it will look at the crisis in metaphysics between Kant and Hume. What it will argue is that Kant's response was, at its core, a response to a spatial crisis in which metaphysics was threatened by the loss of the cosmos. Kant attempted to make the human mind do what the hierarchical cosmos once did. In the concluding section, this paper will argue—following the work of both Colin Gunton and T. F. Torrance—that theology and Old Testament studies lack a theology of mediation to overcome these difficulties. The hope is that, by examining the topological aspects of these twin problems, this essay might help spur on new categories and conversations within the disciplines.

Colin Gunton and T. F. Torrance were two of the most influential theologians of the twentieth century to recognize the problem of the classical conception of God, and the attendant flawed categories inherited from the medieval period which became problematic in modernity. Gunton's body of work—from his dissertation, *Being and Becoming*, all the way until the end of his career, in *Act & Being*—can be construed as an attempt to overcome the impasses of classical theological concepts. T. F. Torrance, in a number of volumes,[2] recognized that the Patristics rejected the container notion of space because it was hostile to the Old Testament vision of God. Both scholars argued that theology must go back to the Old Testament to

---

2. See particularly the texts *Space, Time and Incarnation; Space, Time and Resurrection; Divine and Contingent Order;* and *The Ground and Grammar of Theology*. Torrance was one of the first to bring the awareness of the damaging view of the receptacle to the attention of theology (Torrance, *Space, Time and Incarnation*). In *The Fate of Place*, Edward Casey (from a philosophical viewpoint) offers a comprehensive overview of the move from the ancient container to the rise of modern geometric space.

develop its conceptual content and understanding of the God–world relationship. This paper will use both of these thinkers as conversation partners to develop its topological framework.

In the spirit of this volume situating itself at the intersection between the disciplines, the argument is that concepts of space can be a useful way to facilitate constructive dialogue between theology, philosophy, and Old Testament studies. However, flawed spatial conceptions have confused some central theological and metaphysical issues and hindered dialogue. The central problem is that space from the medieval world into the modern period was conceived of as a container and a hierarchical cosmos. The difficulty with construing space in this way held three problems for theology and philosophy. First, the container view was a static system; second, the container view was closed to outside divine influence; and third the hierarchical understanding created a dualist view of the world. This paper will trace out the problem with this view and advance ways to go beyond it by looking at the Old Testament view of God and creation.

FROM PLACE TO SPACE

For various reasons, space and place have been neglected topics in modern philosophical and theological thought. In the last twenty years, place has made a resurgence in a number of different fields of study, especially critical sociology and geography. One of the major works on this subject is Edward Casey's *The Fate of Place* (1997), where he documents the historical reasons for the eclipse of place through two thousand five hundred years of philosophical history.[3] Casey tells a narrative about how the world was originally conceived as having a connected order, where place was a finite, active, and ordering power, until place vanished in the modern period, where absolute and infinite space came to shatter that ancient conception. Although there are many significant conceptual changes along the way, the beginning of the scientific revolution was when the idea of absolute and infinite space began to be broadly accepted. Alexandre Koyré argues that "the destruction of the cosmos and the geometrization of space" were two of the irrevocable changes to impact the human mind.[4] Attendant with this absolutizing of space was the severance of space from time. Galileo's earlier experiments had paved the way, but Newton's physics was the final cut which completed

3. Casey, *The Fate of Place*.
4. See Koyré, *From the Closed World*, vii-viii.

the division of time and space into independent variables. Modern physics has since rejected the possibility of separating space and time. However, the significance of this historical fact for this project is that the metaphysical issues of Hume and Kant, as well as the birth of critical biblical scholarship, came to maturity within the age of Newton. Time and the historical dimension of human experience have gained a special relevance in the modern world and theology due to the Newtonian spatial paradigm.

The idea of space as a container goes all the way back to ancient Greek philosophy.[5] However, what happened during the scientific revolution was that place lost its physicality and became absolute space. The distinction between space and place used in this paper is that space refers to the idea of pure, volumetric extension. When most moderns think of space, they think of it as immaterial, geometric extension. Space denotes this type of abstract extension. Place, in contrast, is a much more physical idea than pure spatial extension. In Aristotle, the spatiality of the cosmos had an *active* part in holding the universe together. Additionally, in the Hebraic account, space carries with it the connotations of *tehom*: that is, a depth and rootedness which connotes a physicality that is more than mere extension. Here, place refers to this active, relational, and dynamic conception of spatiality.

These two great conceptual changes, the idea of space as pure, geometric extension and the splitting of space and time, presaged massive changes for both theology and philosophy. However, this problematically associated meaning almost exclusively with time. The conceptualization between God and the world was conceived as a problem of reconciling time and eternity. Lessing's famous dictum, "Accidental truths of history can never become the proof of necessary truths of reason," is the classic example of this framework.[6] The problem was that history was seen as temporal—therefore, accidental and contingent—and thus incompatible with necessary truth. There are two problems with Lessing's formulation. The first is a sharp dichotomy between contingency and necessity. The second

---

5. There is not sufficient room in this paper to tell the full tale. However, for more information see Casey, *The Fate of Place*. Edward Casey's work is an excellent starting point for anyone interested in that account. Part One, "From Void to Vessel," moves from the ancient void to Aristotle's notion of place as a container. Part Two, "From Place to Space," documents the rise of space in the modern sense of pure extension and the eclipse of place.

6. In German it reads: "*Zufällige Geschichtswahrheiten können der Beweis von notwendigen Vernunftswahrheiten nie warden.*" See "On the Proof of the Spirit and the Power," in *Lessing's Theological Writings*, 53.

problem is that he construed history as a temporal phenomenon with little regard for spatiality.

HISTORY AND THE CONTAINER VIEW OF SPACE IN OLD TESTAMENT STUDIES

These two issues are important, because a dividing line which can often separate philosophy and systematic theology against Old Testament studies is the question of the role of history both epistemologically, as a normative measure of knowledge, and also ontologically in regards to the nature of history. History was not a live category for many of the scholastics. Indeed, one Aquinas scholar argues that perhaps Christianity's chief intellectual weakness in the modern period was a failure to think historically.[7]

Biblical studies is correct to affirm the value of history. However, it must be careful in how it uses history. Iain Provan argues that, because of "narrow specialist training," biblical scholars are often unprepared to deal sophisticatedly with theoretical models applied to the biblical text.[8] Provan's criticism illuminates a harmful tendency within biblical studies to derive its theoretical framework from other disciplines without carefully understanding the philosophical issues at stake. The historical dimension provides an orientation to the study of the Old Testament. However, biblical scholars cannot put aside philosophical issues in regards to their theoretical apparatus and the methodological tools they employ.

An example of this problem would be the biblical theology movement of G. Ernest Wright and Brevard Andersen of the 1970s. The biblical theology movement was defined by searching for the "mighty acts of God" and an attempt to empirically prove these results. This was not a bad impulse. However, Langdon Gilkey's seminal article, "Cosmology, Ontology and the Travail of Biblical Language,"[9] was a devastating critique of this movement, because he succinctly showed that, while these authors spoke of the Bible in a theological sense, the empirical categories they used were modern and at odds with theology. The problem with the biblical theology movement was not their focus upon actual history. The problem, as Gilkey showed, was that their operative concept of history was modernist and not theological. As will become clear throughout the rest of this essay, an empirical history

---

7. Milosz, "The Importance of Simone Weil," 248.
8. Provan, "Knowing and Believing: Faith in the Past," 254.
9. See Gilkey, "Cosmology, Ontology and the Travail of Biblical Language," 143–154.

was placed into a container view of space in which distinct events could only be empirically proved and temporally connected. As Torrance recognized, such a view created the *Histoire-Geschichte* split because there was no way for God to enter into a container.[10] Thus, Gilkey was correct to call out the categories, but that does not impugn the legitimacy of the search to find God within history. The biblical theology movement collapsed in the 1980s because they were so empirically focused that they lost any proper theological (and spatial) frame to undergird it. The problem was a conflation of a modern account of history (and space) with theology.

The same problem befell Wolfhart Pannenberg's project *Theology as History*.[11] Pannenberg was an important figure in the 1960s because he was a reaction to the existential theologies of Bultmann and Tillich, which minimized the importance of history and denied a real resurrection. Pannenberg attempted to create a scientific theology which could affirm an objective view of the resurrection and other biblical events. However, Pannenberg argued that all of the events in history and the meaning of these events were *provisional* because the final coming of Christ had not yet come. Pannenberg argued that only in the full course of history (by which he meant time) was it possible to determine the meaning of any one event.

The problem with both Pannenberg and the biblical theology movement was not their attempt to create a scientific theology, but rather that there was still too much Newton in their project. They each tried to rework the material along a different temporal pole, but both ultimately failed. The trap that both Pannenberg and the biblical theology movement fell into is what Donald Davidson calls the third dogma of empiricism, or the scheme-content distinction: that meaning can be separated from the structure and categories in which it is framed.[12]

Historical Consciousness, Contingency and Place

A second related historical factor which complicates the relationship between philosophy and the Old Testament is that biblical criticism came

---

10. Torrance, *Space, Time and Incarnation*, 42.

11. It was originally published in 1961 in German under the title *Offenbarung als Geschichte*.

12. For more elaboration on this subject see Vanhoozer's chapter, "On the Very Idea of a Theological System," in *Always Reforming*, pp. 125–182.

out of Germany in interaction with the German Historicist movement.[13] One of the distinctive aspects of the Aufklärer, as opposed to the earlier British and French circles—where the waves of the Enlightenment arrived earlier—was a greater affirmation of history. The British gravitated more towards empiricism via the tradition of Hume and Locke. The French were more rationalist in their orientation stemming from the Cartesian tradition.

A key assumption which unites both empiricism and rationalism is that they tend to hold a similar individualist understanding of knowledge. In both cases the individual—armed through either the scientific method (empiricism) or through the power of the Cartesian cogito (rationalism)—can acquire knowledge. The debate is not in the primacy of the individual, but the way the individual acquires knowledge. In both schools of thought, the emphasis is upon the individual, which tends to minimize the importance of tradition as a means of knowledge. Historicism, on the other hand, placed more emphasis upon tradition and the particularity of place.[14] This did not mean that the Aufklärer were disinterested in reason or method in its relationship to developing tools for a scientific history, but it gave the German Enlightenment its own distinctive flavor. The reason this complicates the relationship between philosophy, theology, and biblical studies is because the Anglo-American tradition in the twentieth century has tended to follow rational-empiricist lines rather than the historical school. There are shared issues and a common language between the analytic theology movement and analytic philosophy which facilitates dialogue. Historicism and hermeneutics developed along a different historical trajectory which hinders dialogue between biblical studies and most contemporary theology.

The German Historicist tradition has not been studied as deeply in the English world partly due to the barrier of language. Frederick Beiser's new work *The German Historicist Tradition* is a welcome corrective. Beiser looks to Justus Möser as the father of historicism:

13. Biblical criticism was not limited to Germany. On the French side, Richard Simon, Pierre Bayle, and the later philosophers were heavily involved in biblical criticism. However, it was in Germany where robust Old Testament biblical criticism in de Wette, Graf, and Welhausen, and New Testament criticism in Strauss's *Das Leben de Jesus*, found its most widely recognized form.

14. Historicism is a way of thinking which assigns particular importance to the place and situated-ness of an individual or society within their unique context. Historicism is a hermeneutical way of looking at human knowledge, as opposed to rationalism and empiricism, which attempt to look at human knowledge separately from their engagement with the world. Kant's great contribution to philosophy is the way he combined empiricism and rationalism together into a coherent system.

> What makes Möser the father of historicism is precisely his recognition of the importance of rootedness, attachment and belonging. . . . The reason this principle became so important to him is precisely because it was the seat or locus of rootedness, attachment and belonging. What we are rooted in, attached to, or belong in, is *per necessitatem* unique and individual, this particular time and place.[15]

The point of emphasis is the orientation to the issues of individuality and the relationship of meaning to place. It is in the contingent realm of life, *per necessitatem,* where individuality finds meaning. The terms contingency and necessity are two important technical terms. "Contingency" means something which depends upon another thing or state of affairs for its existence and meaning. "Necessity" refers to something which is true in and of itself, independently of any other state of affairs or being. Aristotle was the first to technically define these categories,[16] but contingency and necessity became theologically and philosophically loaded terms in medieval scholasticism.

In order to facilitate a dialogue between theology, philosophy, and biblical studies, it is imperative to see how the historical question is worked out between contingency and necessity. The idea of contingency in Christian contexts was an outworking of the doctrine of "creation out of nothing." Contingency holds significance for an understanding of the world; namely, that the world is not true or came to existence in itself, but is dependent upon something else for its existence. Because the world was created out of nothing, creation is dependent upon the will of God. One of Aquinas's five ways of arguing for God's existence is the argument from contingency. Aquinas argues that there is nothing in the universe that necessarily has to be, but it still exists. Therefore something necessary must be outside the universe which called it into being. Hence, according to Aquinas, God exists.

Contingency is a useful category, but it holds the potential to be theologically problematic, due to a non-theological understanding of contingency that emerged in modernity. Ivan Illich defines two notions of contingency.[17] The first notion of contingency is defined as the world being

---

15. Beiser, *The German Historicist Tradition*, 66.

16. See Aristotle's *On Interpretation* sections XII-XIII and *Prior Analytics* sections I:3 and I:13.

17. For a more sustained treatment of contingency and the issues at stake, see Illich, "Contingency, Part 1: A World in the Hands of God," 66–67.

dependent upon God for its being and existence. However, in the modern world, contingency connotes the idea of being arbitrary, without reason or chance. Illich argues that "once the universe is taken out of God's hands it can be placed into the hands of people, and this couldn't have happened without nature having been put into God's hands in the first place."[18] What Illich means is that the idea of contingency was a double-edged sword which lies at the heart of many modern metaphysical and theological problems. On the one side, it was not until the medieval period that the full meaning of *ex nihilo*[19] could be understood. It is hard for moderns to grasp this idea when the Big Bang theory and string theory are part of society's collective imagination. For most of humanity, the universe was considered self-evident and inextricably pointed to some deity or eternal order because it was assumed to be a cosmos. The advent of contingency allowed the world to be explored scientifically because once the universe was no longer considered self-evident, it opened up the search for the rational order or will which founded the universe.[20] Newton was significant here because his system finally broke with the self-evident nature of Aristotle's substances so that the order behind the world could be explored. In this sense, Newton was correct and even theological in trying to understand the patterns of the universe.

However, this same contingency which opened up exploration of the world also threatened to make the world arbitrary and therefore meaningless. This is the second notion of contingency. Modernity in general has had a difficult time coming to terms with contingency. Lessing's famous dictum is an example of modernity's trouble with the concept. The problem for theology has been, how can anything contingent have any ultimate meaning or connection to God? Metaphysically, the problem has been how knowledge of anything contingent can provide absolute truth.

The problem is twofold. Contingency is necessary, it would seem, to affirm a proper sense of individuality, human agency, and even meaning; but at the same time, contingency cannot be allowed to slip into the second sense of the idea of arbitrariness or meaninglessness. This issue, which is

18. Ibid., 70.

19. This is the Latin term meaning "out of nothing" which is common shorthand in theology to refer to the doctrine of creation out of nothing.

20. See, for instance, the Catholic philosopher of science Pierre Duhem's *Medieval Cosmologies,* where he traces the rise of science to the bishop of Paris's Condemnations of 1277. He argues that these condemnations opened medieval thought to explore the contingency of the world and were influential in the rise of the scientific revolution.

deeply topological, lies at the heart of the problem between both classical theology and biblical studies, but more broadly theology and philosophy.

The rest of this essay will show that there is a Hebraic affirmation of contingency, place, and individuality which is essential for theology. Then, with Torrance and Gunton, it will argue that with proper spatial categories there can be a proper sense of contingency and divine order which does not slip into radical contingency, but which upholds a Hebraic notion of the world.

The Affirmation of Contingency in the Old Testament & Historicism

Historicism and contingency illuminate central features of the Old Testament which can often be easily taken for granted. Erich Auerbach was one of the foremost literary critics and philologists of the twentieth century and came out of the historicist tradition. In *Mimesis: The Representation of Reality in Western Literature,* Auerbach begins by noting the difference between the Greek and Hebrew texts.[21] He noted that, in the Greek texts, mythology was always abstracted from everyday life. The gods were involved with the wars of Troy or in an epic sphere away from private life. But in the Hebrew Bible, God comes down into the mundane: "The sublime influence of God here reaches so deeply into the everyday that the two realms of the sublime and the everyday are not only actually unseparated but basically inseparable."[22] The sacred was found in the midst of the everyday. The difference between the Greco-Roman and Hebrew texts is not that one is composed of reason and the other of revelation, but rather where the mythological impinges upon the human.

Auerbach was not the only one to notice the uniqueness of the Hebraic view of creation and history. Harvey Cox, in *The Secular City,* saw the Genesis creation accounts as "demythologizing" the Ancient Near East mythologies and argued that the roots of secularity reach back to the days of the prophets and historical narratives.[23] What Cox meant by "demythologizing" in this context is probably closer to Max Weber's idea of secularism as *Entzauberung*.[24] The word is commonly called "disenchant-

---

21. Auerbach, *Mimesis*.
22. Ibid., 22–23.
23. Cox, *The Secular City,* 21–37.
24. Max Weber himself borrowed the term "disenchantment" from Friedrich Shiller. Weber develops the idea of disenchament in his 1905 work *Die protestantische Ethik und*

ment," but comes from the German *Zauber*, which literally means magic. *Entzauberung* etymologically means to remove the magic from the world. Cox argued that the Hebrew texts removed a magical view of the world so that it could be understood as an ordered and understandable cosmos. This view of the world opened the door for science. It was precisely because the universe was founded in the will of God that it was understandable. This is because primordial supernatural forces and magical forces have no discernible order which can be explored, but a contingent creation based on the will of a good God can be understood.

In sum, Provan is correct to admonish biblical scholars for not being careful in their appropriation of history. However, his admonishment also shows the particular relevance the Old Testament has towards these philosophical issues. The affirmation of history, place, and contingency come out of the Hebraic tradition. The intellectual task is to understand how history, place, and a proper view of contingency can fit into larger philosophical and theological discussions, which give due weight to the reality of creation.

SPACE AND METAPHYSICS: THE ATTACK ON CAUSALITY AND THE LOSS OF HIERARCHY

Having examined contingency's place in the Old Testament, this next section will look at how these same issues played out in philosophy. Kant will be the focal point of this study, because he represents a key turning point which is sometimes called the Copernican revolution in philosophy. The

---

der Geist des Kapitalismus. For English translation, see Weber, *The Protestant Ethic*. In chapter 4, Weber covers the rise of Calvinism, which he argues led to the loss of magic and then the rationalization of the world. Regardless of whether Weber's reading of Calvinism was accurate, there are several analogs to the spatial problem and the consequences Weber saw in how a rationalization of the world led to disenchantment. One in particular was that Weber predicted such a rationalization would lead to an intensification of bureaucracy as a universal reason attempted to coordinate the whole world. Yet at the same time Weber predicted the rise of a new pluralism where each human would be the center of their own values. From a topological point of view, the absolute space of Newton opens itself up to both of these possibilities. On the one hand, Newtonian space is absolute and centered upon a universal reason that could lead itself to such a bureaucratic administration of human affairs. However, seen from another perspective, Newtonian space is highly relative, because every perspective is dependent upon the relative point of view of the inertial framework. The center is simultaneously everywhere and nowhere in Newtonian space, which lends itself to the same consequences Weber saw. It can support a universal bureaucracy or an infinite plurality, since there is no center to the cosmos.

perennial importance of Kant in the history of philosophy is not that he solved the issues of metaphysics, but rather how he changed the contours of the debate. As Gadamer noted in *Truth and Method*, "[t]he epoch-making result of the *Critique of Pure Reason* was not only that it destroyed metaphysics as a purely rational science of the world, the soul, and God, but that, at the same time, it revealed an area within which the use of a priori concepts is justified and which makes knowledge possible."[25]

As the story is usually told, Hume's attack on metaphysics awoke Kant from his dogmatic slumbers. Part of Hume's attack was laid squarely at the problem of causation. The problem Hume saw was that however human reason might try inductively to study the world, such endeavors could not reveal the ultimate causes of things, but only correlations between phenomena. From the previous discussion, it should be clear that Hume is already introducing the idea of radical contingency into the world. If there is no god or metaphysical truth, then every correlation is simply contingent.

The lethality of Hume's attack is highlighted in contrast with the medieval synthesis he dismantled, especially in Aquinas. At the beginning of Aquinas's *Summa*, he outlines his five ways of arguing to God.[26] These five ways are various arguments of causality and teleology which reason back to God. One of the key features of Aquinas's system is the hierarchy of being. Aquinas's cosmology is filled with a strong order and hierarchical under-

---

25. Gadamer, *Truth and Method*, 215.

26. See Thomas Aquinas, *Summa Theologica*, Volume I, Question 2, Article 3. In all five ways to argue for the existence of God, there is a clear Aristotelian framework. There is not sufficient space to go into the extensive discussion and bibliography surrounding modern criticism and defenses of Aquinas's argument. However, the modest contribution this paper would like to make is to show some of the neglected spatial components of the argument. Thomas is arguing from an analogy of being contingent or lower degrees of being outwards to God. A problem that this can cause in the tradition is a pejorative view of this world which makes ordinary existence derivative of a transcendental metaphysic. In contrast, in the Hebraic presentation, the contingency of history and locale are the focal points in which knowledge of God is mediated. God is the God of Abraham, Isaac, and Jacob, and not merely the first necessary being. In fairness to Aquinas, he was correct to understand God as outside of and separate from the world. However, one of the hopes of this project is that through new spatial categories, theology and philosophy could rehabilitate the value of contingency and importance of God using contingent events, people, and places as a focal point of revelation. The hope is that, by rejecting a container view of space, and seeing space as dynamic and relational, that God's otherness from the world could be perceived while also giving a renewed value to mundane existence. The goal here is not to be uncharitable to Thomas or to medieval scholastics, but to offer the possibility of rehabilitating their arguments in an age when we have lost a hierarchical view of the world.

The Old Testament and Metaphysics

standing of the universe. His doctrine of God held similarities to Aristotle's unmoved mover. The way God was thought to interact with his creation was through this hierarchy of being and motion in which he governed the causes of the world.

However, the premise which underlays Aquinas is not only the hierarchy, but also a particular view of space as a container. Torrance notes that, as opposed to the patristics, the scholastics introduced the container notion of space into their system.[27] Torrance's analysis of the spatial problem is similar to our own, although developed independently. As Torrance notes, the problem with construing space in this way held two problems for theology and philosophy. First, the container view was a static system, and secondly, the container view was closed to outside influence. The result of the container view was tendency towards dualism in both philosophy and theology.[28]

The way Plato was able to get around the problem of a container was through his differentiation between the world of forms and the immanent world. The world could not contain the forms, but the forms implanted their shape onto the world. As Casey makes clear, one of the key debates between Aristotle and Plato was over the question of whether the forms were in-place or not.[29] For Aristotle, everything was in-place, whereas for Plato the forms were placeless, although contained within the receptacle of the world, and so ensured the connection between the sensibility and intelligibility of the world.

However, this dualism was integrated into Aristotle's substance-accident scheme, which, as Torrance notes, caused serious problems in the Middle Ages for scholastic philosophy.[30] In the medieval synthesis of Aristotle and Christianity, a similar dualism was created through the *analogy entis*, "the analogy of being." The answer to the question of *how* God related to the world was to say that there was an analogy between the human order and the divine order. The key link was the hierarchical cosmos; the difference between Aristotle and the Christian synthesis was that God was conceived as the unmoved mover. As mentioned above, the problem

---

27. Torrance, *Space, Time and Incarnation*, 1–22.

28. Torrance says, "As far as I am aware the Aristotelian definition of space found no place at all in the Nicene theology. Its rejection meant also the rejection of a strict receptacle view of space and the cataphatic conceptualism that went along with it." *Space, Time, and Incarnation*, 10–11.

29. Casey, *The Fate of Place*.

30. Torrance, *Space, Time, and Incarnation*, 27–28.

with this view of space was that the conception of how God related to the universe quickly became conceived of as the divine watchmaker or through the causal properties and ordered cosmos. The assumption was that theological language had to be grounded in an absolute metaphysic rather than through the dynamic inbreaking of God into creation. There had to be some *analogia* between the created world and the divine. However, Hume's attack on causation and radical contingency threatened the idea that there could be any fixed correlation between a contingent earthly world and the heavens.

The analogy of being was severely threatened by the Copernican revolution and the rise of Newtonian physics. The crisis of faith was that if there was no cosmos, then the correlation or analogy between God and the universe was threatened. This was the danger of Hume's attack against metaphysics and theology. Colin Gunton observes this same flaw in Aquinas's system: "The Third Way is here of particular interest. It depends upon a hierarchy of beings, from the purely contingent through the conditionally necessary, to God, the absolutely necessary. Without the hierarchy there is no reason why, as Hume suggested, the universe should not be the necessary being."[31] In other words, once the hierarchy was destroyed, God became an unnecessary and redundant hypothesis.

To paraphrase Illich, the contingent world that was in the hands of God was transferred to the will of man. Once the hierarchy was destroyed, the contingency of the world made the will of God and the will of man redundant. Without the hierarchy, it was possible to suggest that the order in the world was not part of a divine will, but part of a happenstance which the human mind projected onto a meaningless universe. The challenge for Kant was to find a secure basis to replace the collapsing foundation of the Ptolemaic hierarchical world, and he turned to the structures of the human mind for that foundation.

Kant's Response: The Idealization of Space

These two issues—the problem of causality and the loss of hierarchical space—make Kant's solution to the problem of metaphysics both illuminating and problematic. Kant's *Critique of Pure Reason* and his subsequent work *Prolegomena to Any Future Metaphysics* work together. The *Prolegomena* is more important for our purposes because it was in this work that

31. Gunton, *Becoming and Being*, 4.

Kant tried to lay down the scientific foundations for a future metaphysic. Kant recognized that the first critique was synthetic and preparatory for a science of metaphysics, while the *Prolegomena* was his attempt to lay a new foundation for a scientific metaphysic.[32]

Kant's *Prolegomena* is remarkable for the progressive clarity through which he advances his argument. Kant made two important distinctions: the difference between *a priori* and *a posteriori* knowledge and, secondly, the difference between *analytic* and *synthetic* reason. The difference between *a priori* and *a posteriori* knowledge is that *a priori* knowledge is gained apart from sensory experience and based upon reason alone, while *a posteriori* knowledge is based upon experience. In regards to the analytic/synthetic distinction, an analytic statement is a predication which one could understand sufficiently if one understood the meaning of the words in the statement. The classic example is "all bachelors are unmarried men." The only thing necessary to understand this statement is to know what the words mean and to hold to the law of non-contradiction. Analytic statements do not provide any new knowledge beyond the meaning of the words. Synthetic statements, on the other hand, are statements which predicate new knowledge because their predications are not tautological. For instance, the statement "the dog is on a leash" is a synthetic *a posteriori* statement because it provides new knowledge. For Kant, synthetic *a priori* judgments could be the only possible foundation for a new metaphysics. They had to be *a priori* so as to not depend upon experience and they had to be *synthetic* in order to produce new knowledge and not be based on speculation or mere tautology. For Kant's project to work, he had to show that the principle of causality, as well as space, were not derived from experience, but *a priori* structures of the human mind; otherwise they would be susceptible to Hume's critique.

What concerns us here is not so much causality, but the spatial assumptions of Kant. In the first part of the *Prolegomena*, Kant argues that space, time, and geometry are ideal structures of the human mind. "My doctrine of the ideality of space and of time, therefore, far from reducing the whole sensible world to mere illusion, is the only means of securing the application of one of the most important kinds of knowledge (that which

---

32. "The *Prolegomena* must therefore rest upon something already known as trustworthy, from which we can set out with confidence and ascend to sources as yet unknown, the discovery of which will not only explain to us what we knew but exhibit a sphere of many cognitions which all spring from the same sources." Kant, *Prolegomena*, 22.

mathematics propounds *a priori*) to actual objects and of preventing its being regarded as mere illusion."[33] Hume never extended his attack to geometry or math, but Kant was worried that if he could not provide a basis for space and time in the transcendental structure of the human mind then even math and geometry would fall to Hume's critique. One way to state Kant's project is to say that he baptized the categories of Newton into the *a priori* structures of the human mind in order to provide a foundation for metaphysics. This structure replaced the lost cosmos.

It was this "Copernican turn" in philosophy which Kant presumed would open up new foundations of human knowledge. The problem with Kant was not his illuminating the role of the human mind in knowledge, but rather the way he opposed subjectivity and objectivity, and the way he made space ideal.[34] As developed in the section on Hebraic contingency, there was no room for any meaningful contingency and, more importantly, there was no way place could be a medium and dynamic means of knowledge. In contrast, mundane places in the Hebrew Bible, such as a tent or a threshing pit, are the locations of a relational encounter with God. A container view of space and Kant's idealized space both sever the possibility of place functioning in this dynamic way, because there is no room for God to enter into the world.

The end result in Kant was a rather rigid separation between the subject with no real connection to space and time. This is ultimately the same problem which created the *Histoire-Geschichte* problem and Lessing's ditch.

---

33. Ibid., 39–40.

34. Here again, Beiser's work on Kant and German idealism is helpful. Beiser reads Kant as struggling to overcome subjectivism. He argues that Kant was trying to avoid a radical idealism, as in Berkeley's idealism, which argued that any sensation the world made on the human mind was not real, but a structure of the mind. A more modern form of this would be called psychologism, which argues that math, logic, and geometry are not part of the world, but are just psychological states. Kant has been read both ways on this issue, because his turn to the subject could be construed as falling into idealism. However, read in another way, Kant can be construed as trying to limit the powers of human subjectivity to find a place for reality. This debate exceeds the scope of this paper, but to emphasize the spatial issues even more, Beiser notes that one of the biggest changes in Kant between the first and second edition of the critique is his turn to space in the four-page addendum to the second edition of the *Critique,* called the "Refutation Against Idealism." Beiser argues that Kant turns to a more realist understanding of space to overcome the idealism implicit in Descartes. He comments: "It is here that Kant's break with the subjectivist tradition becomes most explicit and extreme, and it is here that he makes his strongest case yet against the problematic idealism of Descartes." See Beiser, *German Idealism,* 104.

Kant represents an important step, but it is his spatiality which is suspect, because space could no longer function as a medium between subject and object. Kant correctly illuminated the importance of the role of the human mind in epistemology; however, his fateful misstep was to turn space into an ideal transcendental contained within, and thus making space dependent on, the human mind. The problem with Kant is not his turn to the subject, but the severance of the subject from space. This turned the human mind inwards instead of outwards to a reality which was independent of the human mind.

BIBLICAL TRAJECTORIES: A THEOLOGY OF MEDIATION

The main topological issues can be restated succinctly: in theology, an overdependence upon the hierarchical world created a crisis for theology when Hume attacked that system. This attack threatened the *analogia entis* that was so vital to Aquinas's system. The weakness of the medieval approach was that the cosmos did more philosophical and theological lifting than it was capable of supporting. The result was an artificial system more reliant upon Aristotelian categories than the God of the Old Testament.

This loss of the hierarchical world also threatened metaphysics. Kant's failed response to Hume was to baptize the categories of Newton as the *a priori* structures of the human mind to save them from Hume's critique. Kant's error was not in turning to human subjectivity, but in making space an ideal component of the human mind and not a means of mediation between subject and object. He severed the relationship between subject and the world by opposing them to each other. The problem with both Kant and Aquinas is at core a similar spatial problem.

Christianity cannot go back to the hierarchical world of Dante, nor should it wish to, even if that door was not forever closed. That world has been lost irrevocably. However, the way forward is to understand the way in which the old cosmos functioned, as a medium between humans and God. Hume's attack was so lethal because it undercut a strong thread of mediation and a particular way of understanding how the contingency of the world related to God. He made it more difficult, but not impossible.

Theology does not need to go back to a cosmos or to hold onto unmodified classical categories, but it does need a new theology of mediation in which to understand God's relationship to the world. Creating such a theology of mediation was central to Gunton's project. In chapter four of

Act & Being, Gunton argues that such a theology is found in the Old Testament and in the incarnation:

> The interaction of God with the world in Christ, with its implicit affirmation of the goodness of the created world, "material" as well as "spiritual," implies a radical critique of the dualism, the way of ascent becomes impossible, cut off by the "descent" of Christ—and all its anticipations in the pages of the Old Testament—who makes God known *in* the world, within the structures of space and time, not *by abstraction from* them.[35]

For Gunton, space and time are not problematic, but essential, because they mediate God's actions to humans. Whereas in the system of Aquinas, which Gunton attacks so vehemently, the task was to abstract the necessary and timeless from the earthly and the contingent, the direction he proposes is the opposite. This difference cannot be understated. The entering of God into space and time is not problematic, but affirms the created world.

Gunton argued for what he called "open transcendentals."[36] What Gunton meant by these transcendentals was a trinitarian framework where God's action in the world created a unified, but open, understanding of the world. Language for Gunton is also a form of mediation. This understanding of language is shared by continental philosophy, which understands that language, as Gadamer said, is a "medium of the hermeneutic experience."[37] Citing Coleridge, Gunton argues:

> Words, all words, are created realities. None of them is from the outset qualified to describe divine being, even, or rather especially, abstract words like "being." Words are therefore things, so that it is worth citing Coleridge: "I would endeavour[sic] to destroy the

---

35. Gunton, *Act & Being*, 65 (emphasis original).

36. See Gunton, *The One, the Three and the Many*, 141–48.

37. There is not room here to treat the relationship between theology and Gadamer's understanding of language as the medium of the hermeneutic experience at length. However, continental philosophy shares a similar understanding of language as a medium of experience and the world, which has parallels with Gunton. As an example, Gadamer says "[t]he subordination of the natural concept formation that occurs in language to the structure of logic, as taught by Aristotle and, following him, Thomas, thus has only a relative truth. *Rather, when the Greek idea of logic is penetrated by Christian theology, something new is born: the medium of language, in which the mediation of the incarnation event achieves its full truth.* Christology prepares the way for a new philosophy of man, which mediates in a new way between the mind of man in its finitude and the divine infinity" (Gadamer, *Truth and Method*, 427, emphasis original).

old antithesis of *Words and Things,* elevating, as it were, words into Things, & living Things, too."[38]

Torrance would agree. Space is also an open transcendental for him.[39] *Divine and Contingent Order* can be understood as searching for something similar to Gunton's open transcendentals. Torrance argues in his work that divine order and contingency work together.[40] The theologian looks back to see how the world depends upon God, while the scientist looks forward to how the world is properly independent from God. For him, the scientist has to presuppose an order and logic to the universe, even though that logic or system cannot be axiomatically proven.

In *The Ground and Grammar of Theology,* Torrance argued for a unitary and realist understanding of creation.[41] Torrance meant that, because the world was created by a benevolent divine will, there was a unity to it. However, this unity could not be found in the world itself. Contingency for Torrance created a proper space away *from* God for the world to have independence; however, this contingency was ultimately dependent *upon* God for its ultimate order.

Torrance wrote with a strong hope that theology stands at a great transition point:

> The future thus seems to be full of promise and excitement. Certainly at no time for nearly a millennium and a half has the opportunity for genuine theology been greater, since the ground has been cleared in the most remarkable way of the old dualist and atomistic modes of thought that have plagued theology for centuries.[42]

This paper shares that conviction. The value of Torrance and Gunton is not that they solved the issues facing philosophy and theology, but that they pointed the way forward to finding a solution in rediscovering how

---

38. Gunton, *Act & Being,* 72, emphasis added.

39. On the idea of space as an open transcendental, Torrance says: "In this kind of coordination, space and time are given a sort of transworldly aspect in which they are open to the transcendent ground of the order they bear within nature. This means that the concept of space which we use in the Nicene Creed is one that is relatively closed, so to speak, on our side where it has to do with physical existence, but one which is infinitely open on God's side" (Torrance, *Space, Time and Incarnation,* 18).

40. Torrance, *Divine and Contingent Order,* 40.

41. Torrance, *The Ground and Grammar of Theology,* ix.

42. Ibid., 178.

place and space function relationally and dynamically. In particular, what they both advocated was a turn back to understanding how place and space function relationally and dynamically. They both held to an open view of space, in that space was dynamic and relational. What this essay has tried to demonstrate is that neglect of space, and the Hebraic affirmation of place and contingency, has created problems for the theological tradition.

If common dialogue is to be found between theology, philosophy, and biblical studies, new spatial categories will be needed. From the philosophical side, there has been significant work by scholars such as Edward Casey and Jeff Malpas[43] in developing a new account of human agency, in which spatiality and a world are essential for human agency. Theologically, Gunton and Torrance have opened up broad fields of new thought. Torrance in particular is invaluable for showing how the thrust of Protestant theology "has attempted to detach the message of the Christian from any essential relation to the structures of space and time."[44] Additionally, exceptional work has been done on Kant and Hegel by Frederick Beiser and also Nicholas Adams[45] to show how the central problem is the *opposition* between subject and object and how a turn to space is a way to overcome some of those dualisms.

The loss of the cosmos removed the firm ground upon which theology and philosophy once stood. But there are other ways to speak confidently of reality and the subject matter of theology. The change they both must make is to understand the world and word as created realities which mediate between the individual, society, and God. This remains a deeply ontological project, because theology and philosophy can hold onto the reality of God and the world. However, it may look different than traditional metaphysics. The exciting thing is that the genuine possibility of renewed thought and fresh categories lies before theology. But the central task is to connect both the message of the gospel and a philosophical anthropology back to actual space and time.

Here the Old Testament has much to say about the world, creation from nothing, the value of contingency, individuality, and the notion of covenant where God and humans meet. The hope is that an awareness

---

43. Malpas's clearest account of such agency is in *Place and Experience*.

44. Torrance, *Space, Time and Incarnation*, v.

45. Adam's *Eclipse of Grace* is an excellent introduction of Hegel for theology students which elucidates the modern opposition of subject to object in Kant and how Hegel offers categories to overcome that problem.

of the philosophical issues at stake in causality, hierarchy, topology, and metaphysics may make Old Testament scholars more aware of the need for sophistication with their own methods *and* also the rich nature of the text they study. The ultimate hope, in the spirit of this volume, is to foster dialogue between theology, philosophy, and the Old Testament to think more deeply about a theology of mediation, so that we may better understand ourselves, our world, and the God who actively comes down to encounter us in space and time. To do that, theology needs to rethink its spatial categories and find more suitable categories to explain adequately the open, yet ordered, reality God discloses in revealing himself towards us in Jesus Christ.

BIBLIOGRAPHY

Adams, Nicholas. *Eclipse of Grace: Divine and Human Action in Hegel.* West Sussex, UK: Wiley-Blackwell, 2013.
Aristotle. *Aristotle: Categories and On Interpretation.* Clarendon Aristotle, edited by J. L. Ackrill and Lindsay Judson, translated by J. L. Ackrill. Oxford University Press. 1975.
———. *Prior Analytics.* Translated by Robin Smith. Indianapolis: Hackett, 1989.
Auerbach, Erich. *Mimesis: The Representation of Reality in Western Literature.* Translated by Willard R. Trask. Princeton: Princeton University Press, 1953.
Casey, Edward. *The Fate of Place: A Philosophical History.* Berkeley: University of California Press, 1997.
Cox, Harvey. *The Secular City.* New York: The MacMillan Company, 1965.
Beiser, Frederick C. *The German Historicist Tradition.* Oxford: Oxford University Press, 2011.
———. *German Idealism: The Struggle Against Subjectivism.* Cambridge: Harvard University Press, 2002.
Gadamer, Hans-Georg. *Truth and Method.* Translated by Joes Weinsheimer and Donald G. Marshall. New York: Continuum, 2004.
Gilkey, Langdon. "Cosmology, Ontology and the Travail of Biblical Language." *Concordia Theological Monthly* 33, no. 3 (March 1962) 143–154.
Gunton, Colin. *Act & Being: Towards a Theology of the Divine Attributes.* Grand Rapids, MI: Eerdmans, 2002.
———. *The One, the Three and the Many.* Cambridge: Cambridge University Press, 1993.
———. *Becoming and Being.* Oxford: Oxford University Press, 1978.
Illich, Ivan. *Rivers North of the Future: The Testament of Ivan Illich as Told to David Cayley.* Edited by David Cayley. Toronto: House of Anansi, 2005.
Kant, Immanuel. *Prolegomena to Any Future Metaphysics.* Translated by Lewis White Beck. New York: The Liberal Arts Press, 1950.
Koyré, Alendadre. *From the Closed World to the Infinite Universe.* Baltimore: Johns Hopkins University Press: 1964.
Lessing, Gotthold. "On the Proof of the Spirit and of Power." In *Lessing's Theological Writings*, translated by Henry Chadwick. Stanford: Stanford University Press, 1957.

Maplas, Jeff. *Place and Experience: A Philosophical Topography*. Cambridge: Cambridge University Press, 1999.
Milosz, Czeslaw. "The Importance of Simone Weil." In *To Begin Where I Am*. New York: Farrar, Straus and Giroux, 2001.
Provan, Iain. "Knowing and Believing: Faith in the Past." In *"Behind" the Text: History and Biblical Interpretation*, edited by Craig Bartholomew, C. Stephen Evans, Mary Healy, and Murray Rae. Vol, 4 of *Scripture and Hermeneutics Series*, edited by Craig Bartholomew. Grand Rapids, MI: Zondervan, 2003.
Taylor, Charles. *Sources of the Self*. Cambridge, MA: Harvard University Press, 1989.
Torrance, Thomas F. *Divine and Contingent Order*. Oxford: Oxford University Press, 1981.
———. *The Ground and Grammar of Theology*. Edinburgh: T&T Clark, 1980.
———. *Space, Time and Incarnation*. Edinburgh: T&T Clark, 1969.
Vanhoozer, Kevin J. "On the Very Idea of a Theological System: An Essay in Aid of Triangulating Scripture, Church and World." In *Always Reforming*, edited by A. T. B. McGowan. Downers Grove: InterVarsity, 2006.
Weber, Max. *The Protestant Ethic and the Spirit of Capitalism*. Translated by Richard Swedberg. New York: W. W. Norton & Company, 2008.
Zakai, Avihu, and David Weinstein, "Erich Auerbach and His 'Figura': An Apology for the Old Testament in an Age of Aryan Philology." *Religions* 3 (2012) 320–338.

6

GOSPEL ETHICS

ALAN P. STANLEY

INTRODUCTION

It was Augustine who said, "The true philosopher is the lover of God."[1] If that is true, then ancient philosophy has something to teach us. But what, exactly? Just how close are philosophy and God? This chapter will attempt to answer these questions by exploring the intersection between two of the most prominent Greek philosophical schools of the ancient world, and Jesus. The two schools are the Epicureans and the Stoics, which will not be completely unfamiliar to readers of the Bible.[2] They appear in Acts 17 in the Greek city of Athens debating the apostle Paul. Athens was the hub of the ancient world for anyone drawn to Greek philosophy, where locals and foreigners alike reveled, according to Acts 17:21, in "doing nothing but talking about and listening to the latest ideas." Both schools had theories about life and the universe. Academic as this sounds, such theories ultimately had to have a bearing on one's life and conduct. This is the subject of ethics and the topic of this chapter.

1. Augustine, City of God, VIII, 1; cited in Tyson, *Returning to Reality*, 114.

2. For more detail on the Stoics and Epicureans, see Long and Sedley, *The Hellenistic Philosophers*. Unless otherwise stated, all Epicurean and Stoic references will be from here.

While there are certainly differences between the two schools with respect to ethics, our focus will be on the Epicureans. We will only look at the Stoics at certain points, or where they converge with the Epicureans. But our interest is not the points of intersection between the Epicureans and Stoics. Our interest is how Epicureanism, and to a lesser extent Stoicism, intersects with Jesus's view on ethics. How compatible are they? When people heard Jesus, would they have recognized some Epicurean teaching? It is to this subject we now turn.

UNDERSTANDING THE HEART

The Heart is Foundational to Ethics

Jesus thought of the heart as fundamental to the ethical life. For it is "from the *heart*" that every conceivable vice arises (Matt 15:19; Mark 7:21–22, emphasis added). Therefore, because the heart is "that place from which we feel and think and determine our actions,"[3] the heart is foundational to Jesus's ethics.[4] Thus, Dallas Willard writes: "Wrong action, [Jesus] well knew, is not the problem in human existence, though it is constantly taken to be so. It is only a *symptom*." The problem is the heart.[5]

This explains why Jesus regularly focuses on people's hearts. He often criticizes the Pharisees for things he knows originated in their hearts (e.g., Matt 9:4; 12:34). The Synoptic Gospels emphasize the same thing (9:4; Mark 2:8; 3:5; 7:6; Luke 16:15); the hearts of Israel's leaders have become resistant to truth (Matt 13:15). Even the disciples do not escape Jesus's warnings (e.g., Mark 8:17). Jesus's command to his disciples to "[p]ay close attention to yourselves, lest your *hearts* be weighed down by dissipation and drunkenness and anxieties pertaining to daily life" (Luke 21:34),[6] indicates the susceptibility of the heart to be ruled by "the intoxicating attractions of the sinful world."[7] Presumably, this is why when people hear the gospel "the evil one comes and snatches away what was sown in the *heart*" (Matt 13:19). This not only suggests that Satan attacks where it matters, but also

---

3. Nolland, *Gospel of Matthew*, 205.
4. Elliott, *Faithful Feelings*.
5. Willard, *Divine Conspiracy*, 156 (emphasis added).
6. All biblical quotations are my own translation unless otherwise stated.
7. Marshall, *Gospel of Luke*, 782.

that the kingdom message must take root in the heart to produce "fruit" (Mark 13:23).

So what makes the heart such an ethical control center? Jesus answers in Matthew: "For where your treasure is, there your heart will be also" (Matt 6:21). The heart may be the inner person where one thinks, feels, and wills, but this verse highlights how easily influenced the heart is (see Jer 17:9). Don Carson writes: "The things most highly treasured occupy the 'heart,' the center of the personality, embracing mind, emotions, and will . . . and thus the most cherished treasure subtly but infallibly controls the whole person's direction and values."[8] Treasure never fails because it effortlessly moves the heart; or in Epicurean thought: "the body follows the mind's desire."[9]

But treasure comes in two forms: one earthly, temporal visible, and evil, the other heavenly, eternal, hidden, and good (Matt 6:19–20; 12:35). The fundamental point is that the heart in its natural state has the capacity to be influenced only by the first type of treasure. Jesus's discussion on divorce explains why. Divorce, permitted because of Israel's hard hearts, was not this way from creation (19:8). If divorce did not exist in the beginning, *neither did hard hearts.* Jesus is alluding to the fall, where sin entered the world (Gen 3; Rom 5:12).

Human Beings Have Taken God's Place

In Genesis 1, the phrase "And God *saw* that it was *good*" (Gen 1:10, 12, 18, 21, 25, emphasis added; with variation in vv. 4, 31) is repeated for emphasis. God knows what is good, and thus not good, for the people he has created (also 2:9, 18). In other words, God is King (e.g., Ps 93:1–2; 95:1–5; Isa 43:15). So, we can understand the dynamics of Eve's decision in Genesis 3 when she "*saw* that the fruit of the tree was *good* for food and . . . *took* some" for herself and Adam (Gen 3:6, emphasis added). The implication is clear: *they have become like God,* knowing good and evil, which the serpent predicted (3:5) and God confirmed (3:22).

There is more than one interpretation concerning knowing "good and evil" but the most convincing is that Adam and Eve, and their progeny, would now determine for themselves "what is right and wrong independently of

---

8. Carson, "Matthew," 177. Jonathan Edwards made a similar point in his work on religious affections. See Edwards, *Works,* 1:236–44.

9. Summarizing Lucretius: O'Keefe, "Action and Responsibility," 144, 149.

God."[10] Human beings would think it their natural "right to *define for oneself* good and evil" and in doing so would "usurp the prerogative of God in rebellious moral autonomy."[11] And this is precisely what happens, not only in the lives of individuals (Gen 6:2; Josh 7:21; 2 Sam 11:2–4)[12] but the whole world (e.g., Gen 11:1–4). Israel's history is so punctuated by idolatry (1 Chr 5:25; 2 Chr 29:6) that one commentator suggests that the law's emphasis on idolatry is driven by the reality that "human beings have a proclivity compelling them to worship idols."[13]

Ancient philosophers recognized a similar problem within humanity,[14] observing that "irrational stretching, or pursuit of an expected good", typically characterized human desire.[15] When that good is not attained, the heart becomes "sick with fear" or exhausted "with cares,"[16] resulting in "depression, irascibility, malevolence, quick temper" or "theft, adultery, and violence"[17] (see Matt 15:19). This "sickness" arises because people's desires have not been satiated. Therefore, the human heart is ruled by a "belief that what should not be pursued is intensely worth pursuing, such as the passion for women, wine[sic] and money."[18] The Gospels refer to this sickness as sin. But the key point here is that sin is when we—in God's place—presume to know what is good (and evil) for us, which was never God's intention.

According to Genesis, humanity was created to "rule" over the created things in this world rather than be ruled by them (Gen 1:26–28).[19] Hence, God's role for humanity is to rule the created universe, under himself, the ultimate ruler. Consider God's intent for humanity in light of Moses's injunction to Israel:

---

10. Gentry and Wellum, *Kingdom Through Covenant*, 217.

11. Wright, *The Mission of God*, 164 (emphasis original).

12. The three references given here include the same pattern of Hebrew words as Gen 3:6: *saw . . . good . . . took*.

13. Hamilton, *Handbook on the Pentateuch*, 192.

14. See Lucretius, 5.1105–57.

15. Andronicus, *On Passions*, 1.

16. Lucretius, 3.806–29[2].

17. Stobaeus, 2.93.1–13[1].

18. Ibid., 2.93.1–13[2].

19. See Gentry, *Kingdom Through Covenant*, 181–210, especially 196, for the point that follows. See also Middleton, *Liberating Image*, 27–28, 32, 50–55, 60, 88–90, 204–12, 236, 295.

> Then God said, "Let us make mankind in our image, in our likeness, so that they may rule over the *fish* in the sea and the *birds in the sky*, over the livestock and all the wild animals, and over all the *creatures* that move along the ground." So God created mankind in his own image . . . *male* and *female*, he created them. (Gen 1:26–27, NIV, emphasis added)

> Therefore, watch yourselves very carefully, so that you do not become corrupt and make for yourselves an idol, an image of any shape, whether formed like a *man* or a *woman*, or like any *animal* on earth or any *bird* that flies *in the air*, or like any *creature* that moves along the ground or any *fish* in the waters below. (Deut 4:15–18, NIV, emphasis added)

This shows that God intended humanity to worship him. They were not to turn the things of this world into idols.[20] But God's intent was overturned by the serpent—one of "the wild animals the Lord God had made" (Gen 3:1; see 1:28)—and, therefore, rather than humanity ruling under God, the serpent now rules. Cain's inability to "rule" over sin (Gen 4:7)—because he is ruled by "the evil one" (1 John 3:12)—illustrates this point. Soon every human heart is inclined toward "evil all of the time" (Gen 6:5). One question that arises is as follows: does the human heart have any capacity to do anything except evil?

John: The World is in Darkness

In answering this question, the philosophers argued that it was indeed possible for people to exert "total charge of where their life is going and indulge their emotions and appetites only to the extent that they themselves determine."[21] Socrates spoke of "ruling the pleasures and passions within himself."[22] Stoics taught that people must not allow worldly things to rule them. They instead must rule over their desires and emotions.[23] Both Epicureans and Stoics believed this "innate potential" to rule resided in everyone.[24] According to Epicurus: "Humans can control their own

---

20. As to how Gen 1:26 plays out in Scripture, see Beale, *The Temple and the Church's Mission*.
21. Long, *From Epicurus to Epictetus*, 7.
22. Plato, *Gorg.* 491d4; cited in ibid., 8.
23. E.g., Seneca, *Letters* 95.10–12, 61, 63–64.
24. The phrase "innate potential" occurs in both Bobzien, "Epicurus' Philosophy,"

development."²⁵ For there is "something in our chest capable of fighting and resisting" unruly desires called "volition."²⁶ Admittedly it is a "narrow path" rarely chosen, but it is still possible to "strive" to rule over our desires and "press on towards [the highest good]."²⁷

However, the Gospels paint a different picture. Every human being is "tragically flawed, both morally and spiritually,"²⁸ and needs saving (Matt 1:21; Mark 10:45; Luke 2:30–31). The only innate potential is toward sin. According to John, the world is enslaved to sin (John 1:29) and in darkness (12:46). Darkness is a pre-creation image (Gen 1:2) suggesting that the world is without God and life. Not surprisingly then, darkness is linked to idolatry. Idols lack the human senses including *sight* (Ps 115:5–7), which is why those who trust in them are, among other things, blind and in darkness (Isa 44:9; Ps 82:5). But it is not just sight that is affected. Idols lack every sense common to humanity, making those who trust in them "less than human"²⁹ (Ps 115:8). Presumably this is why Scripture likens idolaters to animals (e.g., Jer 2:23–24; 2 Pet 2:12; Jude 10). Furthermore, the difference between animals and humans, according to Genesis 1, is that only the latter are made in the image of God. Idolatry then is "a regression from the adult to the infantile level" so that "[i]f all societies lived and moved on this level, human existence would hardly be distinguishable from that of the wild beasts that live by instinct without discourse of reason."³⁰ Such a depiction only makes sense when we realize that idolatry, rather than giving life and freedom to humanity, actually removes it.

This explains why Jesus comes to a world in darkness that needs "life" (John 3:16; 20:31). Humanity is in the grip of idolatry, blindly wandering about by the world's light (12:35); blind to what will satisfy their appetites (6:35); blind to the true God. Thus, Carson defines sin in John as an "evil and enslaving devotion to created things at the expense of worship of the Creator"³¹—in other words, idolatry (see Rom 1:21–35).³² What is more,

---

217 and Stough, "Stoic Determinism," 212–13.

25. O'Keefe, "Action and Responsibility," 149.
26. Lucretius, 2.251–93[3].
27. Ibid., 6.1–28[3].
28. Groothuis, *On Jesus*, 42.
29. Watts, *Isaiah*, 34–66, 688.
30. Neill, *A Genuinely Human Existence*, 258.
31. Carson, *Gospel According to John*, 350.
32. See also Stobaeus, 2.93.1–13[2].

humanity loves it this way (John 3:19).³³ Lucretius observed a similar phenomenon. He observed that despite power, wealth, social status, fame, and good name, still "at home no one's heart was any less troubled, and that they were constantly wrecking their life, despite their intentions." Such things may be "beneficial" but there are "leaks and holes" which make it "impossible" for us "ever to be filled up."³⁴

Understanding the Relationship between the Heart and Treasure

Jesus's encounter with the rich young ruler in Matthew demonstrates humanity's problem. He claims to have kept the commandments "You shall not murder, you shall not commit adultery, you shall not steal, you shall not give false testimony" (Matt 19:18). But (in Matthew 15:19) Jesus knows that to keep or break these commandments is a commentary on the heart. This then is quite a claim. Furthermore, Jesus claims that anger in the heart is tantamount to murder and lust to adultery (Matt 5:21–22, 28). Therefore, to get to the heart, "Jesus said to him, 'If you want to be *perfect*, go sell your possessions and give to the poor, and you will have treasure in heaven, and come follow me.' But when the young man heard this he went away grieving, for he had many possessions" (19:21–22, emphasis added). Hence, what this man lacks is a heart that treasures God more than wealth.

The term "perfect" (*teleios*) recalls the main body of Jesus's ethical teaching, the Sermon on the Mount. The point of the Sermon is in Matthew 5:48: "Therefore, be perfect (*teleios*) as your heavenly Father is perfect." Greek philosophers commonly used *telos*, a derivative of *teleios*, to refer to the goal or completion of life. For Epicurus, the *telos* of life is "pleasure" ("happiness," "happy life," "blessed life," "pleasant life").³⁵ Happiness is "the final and ultimate good."³⁶ We typically think of happiness as the satisfied feeling that arises from the fulfillment of our desires for what we think is "good" (see Gen 3:6). But Epicurus called these "empty" desires that will never lead to *telos*.³⁷ As long as people depend upon factors outside

---

33. See Conzelmann, "sko/toß," 7:443–44.

34. Lucretius, 6.1–28[2–3].

35. All these expressions can be found in Cicero, *On Moral Ends,* 1.29–32, 37–9 and Epicurus, *Letter to Menoeceus,* 127–132.

36. Cicero, *On Moral Ends,* 1.29–32, 37–9[1].

37. Epicurus, *Letter to Menoeceus,* 127–132[1]. Cf. also Epicurus, Vatican sayings 21; Scholion on Epicurus, Key doctrines 29; Woolf, "Pleasure and Desire," 158–78.

themselves for happiness, they will always lack something, because things like wealth are not secure (see Matt 6:19). It is just as Lucretius explained: wealth will not set the heart free because there are "leaks and holes" which can never be filled up by money.[38] But one has reached *telos* when they have reached "contentment" irrespective of circumstances.[39]

This provides helpful understanding into Matthew's use of *teleios*, which commentators rightly point out, concerns morality and holiness. If one is to be perfect (*teleios*) one must not trust in things like wealth. Matthew 5:48 follows Jesus's instruction to love one's enemies (5:43–47). Jesus himself is the quintessential example of someone who loved his enemies. But he did so because he himself was *teleios*. In Gethsemane, Jesus became so consumed with sorrow it nearly killed him (26:38). Why the "meltdown"?[40] Nothing exposes our idols more than our reaction to suffering. Thus, Jesus's reaction to the prospect of being separated from his Father (27:46) reveals the treasure of his heart. So when a Roman centurion witnesses Jesus's death, he exclaims, "Truly this was the Son of God" (27:54). He recognized Jesus's "exclusive relationship to God."[41] In Jesus, he was seeing the *true image of God* (Gen 1:26) being lived out, a picture of humanity as it was always intended to be.[42] At the cross, therefore, "human nature reaches its own most authentic greatness."[43]

Jesus's death (and life) reveals God's intention for humanity by the fact that in Jesus we see someone who for the first time ruled over every sphere of creation (e.g., in his miracles), including the serpent (Matt 4:1–11); *and* we see someone who exclusively treasured God. This relationship to both creation and the Father is foundational to Jesus's own ethical life. Because Jesus trusts in the Father he does not need to lash out at his enemies (1 Pet 2:22–23)—which brings us back to Matthew 5:43–48. Jesus embodies *teleios,* and in doing so opens up "the new way of being human so that all who follow him can discover it."[44] This leads to two conclusions: 1) the

---

38. Lucretius, 6.1–28[2–3].

39. Diogenes Laertius, 9.60. Cf. Aristocles (*Eusebius*, 14.18.1–5; *Caizzi*, 53).

40. Wright, *Matthew For Everyone*, 2:160.

41. Quarles, *Jesus Revealed*, 152.

42. Neill, *A Genuinely Human Existence*, 66: "the manner in which Jesus meets suffering is a perfect expression of the attitude of the full-grown man."

43. Ibid.

44. Wright, *Matthew For Everyone*, 1:52–53. Neill, *A Genuinely Human Existence*, 150: "if we are to become genuinely human, the path that we must follow is the one that [Jesus] has traced for us."

way of ethics in the Gospels is to follow Jesus (discipleship); 2) Jesus's ethical teachings show God's original intent for humanity.[45] In other words, to obey Jesus is to resist making anything in creation an idol. Only then comes *teleios*.

Douglas Groothuis observes a connection between Jesus's teaching on virtue and Aristotle's teaching on virtue and *telos* "where proper conduct is conducive to human flourishing."[46] Jesus gives the rich young ruler an opportunity to flourish as a human being. But for that to happen, he needs to be completely devoted to God—as we have seen Jesus was. Only then can he let go of what is ruling him in exchange for Jesus's rule. Once again, the Sermon on the Mount provides an apt summary of what is required: "No one is able to serve two masters, for he will hate the one and love the other. Or he will be devoted to the one and will despise the other. You cannot serve both God and wealth" (Matt 6:24). If this young man wants to be *teleios* (19:21), he must worship God and not money.[47] The Old Testament use of *teleios* confirms this. Moses commands Israel to refrain from idolatry (Deut 18:9–12) and follows it up with "[y]ou shall be *perfect* (*teleios*) before the LORD your God" (Deut 18:13, LXX; see also 1 Kgs 8:61; 11:4; 1 Chr 28:9). Thus, *teleios* is grounded in worship of the true God.

People are often troubled by Jesus's commands concerning wealth. But, not unlike Epicurus, Jesus is simply trying to set this man free. He is not calling him "to obey a comprehensive system of rules."[48] He is offering him the opportunity to be whole, rather than needing money to be complete. He is offering him true treasure; that is, the opportunity to be ruled by God rather than money. But his failure to let go of his wealth reveals the nature of his ethical problem. He is not complete without possessions. However, his wealth produces, in Epicurus's words, "great poverty."[49] The Epicureans may well have sympathized with this aspect of Jesus's teaching. They themselves realized that wealth could never lead to *telos*.[50] It could buy "social status"[51] and "a peaceful life"[52] but it could never set the soul

---

45. Cf. Wright, *Virtue Reborn*.
46. Groothuis, *On Jesus*, 66.
47. Cf. Wright, *Jesus and the Victory of God*, 302–3.
48. Hayes, *Moral Vision*, 98.
49. Epicurus, *Vatican Sayings*, 25.
50. Lucretius, 2.1–61[5].
51. Ibid., 6.1–28[3].
52. Ibid., 5.1105–57.

free. For the Epicurean it was necessary to detach oneself from whatever hindered *telos*. Short-term pain is better than pleasure if the "endurance of pains is followed by a greater and long-lasting pleasure," namely, the "soul's freedom"[53] and "worth while joy."[54]

Of course, neither Epicurus nor Jesus limited their ethical instructions to wealth. The subject could be power, social status, fame, a good name,[55] murder, lust, marriage, prayer, or fasting (Matt 5:21–6:18). When Jesus encountered individuals like the rich young ruler, he could be specific (see e.g., Luke 10:25–37), but when he spoke to the crowds he generalized, calling people to deny themselves (Mark 8:34).[56] The term "deny" (*aparneomai*) occurs only once in the Septuagint to describe God's people in the last days. At that time "men will *deny* themselves" their *idols* (Isa 31:7, LXX, emphasis added). Jesus, therefore, called people to sever ties with anything that hindered them from trusting him. It might be whatever causes lust (Matt 5:29–30); it could be home (8:19–20), tradition (8:21–22), or family (10:37); anything in the "world" that one might depend on for "life" (10:39).[57] "[A] person's life does not consist in the abundance of possessions" (Luke 12:15), but neither does it consist in any of the above. Life as God intended is only found in Jesus (John 14:6; 17:3).

The radicalness of Jesus's ethics explains why the entire law and prophets hang on two commands: to love God with a *whole* heart, soul, and mind, and to "love your neighbor as yourself" (Matt 23:36–40). This twofold command then becomes "a hermeneutical filter" for understanding God's true intent concerning the law and Jesus's intent in continuing it (5:17–19; 9:13; 12:7).[58] It is akin to God seeking people to worship him in spirit and in truth (John 4:23). If Jesus's ethics are to be lived out, then people must have a heart that worships God above all else. This is the solution to which we now turn.

---

53. Epicurus, *Letter to Menoeceus* 127–32[1, 3].

54. Ibid., *Vatican Sayings* 63, 71, 73, 81.

55. Lucretius, 6.1–28[2].

56. Stanley, *Did Jesus Teach Salvation By Works?*, 228–35.

57. Ibid., 233–34.

58. Hayes, *Moral Vision*, 99–101. See also Groothuis, *On Jesus*, 69; Stassen and Gushee, *Kingdom Ethics*, 103–05; Stanley, *Did Jesus Teach Salvation by Works?*, 171–75.

THE SOLUTION TO THE HEART PROBLEM IN THE GOSPELS

A New King: A New Treasure

If humanity's ethical problem is being ruled by the desires of the heart, then the solution is to have a new ruler. The Epicureans and Stoics believed the potential to rule is available within. But, in Epicurean teaching, "people's hearts must first be purged with truth."[59] Only truth can penetrate the heart, but this can only happen via "reason" (*logos*). Reason is to be treasured, for it "is even more precious than philosophy, and it is the natural source of all the remaining virtues."[60] Therefore, only reason can reign in the heart and gain "rational control of one's desires."[61] Reason does that by teaching "us that certain desires, temperaments and ways of life are not effective for getting us what we will ultimately desire for its own sake, pleasure."[62] Through reason, one is able to honor friends, family, and country, and overcome hatred and envy.[63] Through reason, one is able to change their nature so as to rule like the gods.[64] Stoics agree: one must "be able to rule himself"[65] but that can only happen via "divine power [which] resides in reason."[66]

In a somewhat similar vein, the Gospels emphasize *wisdom* in relation to ethics (Matt 7:24–27; 24:45–50; 25:1–13). But the difference between the Gospels and the philosophical schools is that wisdom is personified in Jesus (11:19).[67] The wise person is ruled, not by wisdom per se, but by Jesus. Furthermore, unlike philosophy, the Gospels say that rule must come from the outside since humanity is incapable of ruling themselves. The arrival of God's rule means the promises of Israel's prophets are coming to fruition. But the world is not going to end and become utopian. Rather, heaven (at least a slice of it) is going to come into the daily grind of life (12:28). Israel *will* be God's holy people (e.g., Isa 4:2–3; Joel 3:17; Obad 17; Zeph 3:13),

---

59. Lucretius, 6.1–28[3].
60. Epicurus, *Letter to Menoeceus,* 127–132[6].
61. Long, *From Epicurus to Epictetus,* 20.
62. O'Keefe, "Action and Responsibility," 149.
63. Diogenes Laertius, 7.108–9[2].
64. Lucretius, 3.262–322[5]; see Epicurus, *Letter to Menoeceus,* 135; Diogenes Laertius, 10.121.
65. Seneca, *Letters,* 94.2, 31, 50–1[3].
66. Cicero, *On the Nature of the Gods,* 1.39.
67. Hagner, *Matthew 1–13,* 310–311.

CONVERGENCE

for the kingdom's arrival will make it possible to exchange the serpent's rule for God's rule, and therefore live out a kingdom ethic, as opposed to the serpent's ethic. This explains why the Gospel writers use ethical terms to describe those in God's kingdom: righteous (Matt 5:20; 25:46), good (John 5:29), fruit (Matt 3:8; John 15:1–6), doing the Father's will (Matt 7:22; 12:50), and obedience (Luke 11:28; John 8:51). Conversely, those outside the kingdom are "evil" (Matt 13:49; John 5:29) and "lawless" (Matt 7:21; 13:41). The point is that God's rule changes people.[68]

The kingdom brings us into contact with true treasure. Whatever rules the heart is what the heart treasures. It exerts itself as a power[69] and it is therefore inconceivable that rule—whether it be wealth or anything else—and treasure could ever be separated. Hence, Jesus compares the kingdom to treasure (Matt 13:44), which means that God's rule is not something to be dutifully submitted to, but rather a state to be joyfully experienced (25:21, 23). Furthermore, the kingdom is synonymous with Jesus's presence (Luke 17:20–21). So to come under Jesus's rule *is to treasure him*! Similarly in John, to have "eternal life" is synonymous with knowing Jesus (John 14:6; 17:3).

Thus, the solution to the heart problem does not reside with philosophy's reason (*logos*), but a person, John's *logos* (John 1:1) and Matthew's Immanuel (Matt 1:23). Jesus is the only treasure powerful enough to turn the human heart away from its idols. This explains why there is *power* in Jesus's name[70] (e.g., Acts 4:7; Rom 9:17). Name is synonymous with rule.[71] So one who is baptized "in the name of the Father and of the Son and of the Holy Spirit" (Matt 28:19) is *"ruled* by, Father, Son, and Holy Spirit."[72] The expressions "on account of me" and "for my name's sake" function similarly. In hard times disciples are to rejoice (5:11), not worry (10:19), persevere (10:22), and witness (Luke 21:12–13)—all on account of Jesus/ for his name's sake. These scenarios say something momentous about the worth of Jesus. Jesus is worth losing everything for (Matt 19:29; see Phil 3:8), even one's life (Matt 10:39).

---

68. Chilton, "Kingdom of God," 452; Hauerwas, *The Peaceable Kingdom*, 85. See Stassen, *Kingdom Ethics*; Stanley, *Did Jesus Teach Salvation by Works?*

69. See e.g., Philo, *Allegories of the Laws* 1.30.

70. Talbert, *Reading the Sermon on the Mount*, 36–38. Cf. Chilton, "Kingdom of God," 455: the power behind the kingdom of God is Jesus himself.

71. Bietenhard, "Name," 649.

72. Hagner, *Matthew 14–28*, 888 (emphasis added).

In sum, the arrival of God's powerful rule in Jesus means that human nature can "be delivered from its servitude. The lost image of God in man can be restored."[73] But the heart still needs a new capacity to treasure God.

A New Covenant: A New Heart

Reason in ancient philosophy cannot be limited to one's mental capacity—just as knowledge in Scripture cannot be restricted to the mind—but Epicurus's emphasis is on "the use of one's intellect."[74] Each person has the capacity to think, employ reason and judiciously weigh the "advantages and disadvantages" concerning various courses of action.[75] Not so in the Gospels where even the most astute are unable to keep the law (John 7:19).[76] The only way that one can gain a new mind is by gaining a new heart, which ultimately means a heart that has the capacity to treasure God. This is the crux of the new covenant, which Jesus institutes through the cross (Matt 26:28).

The new covenant promises new minds and hearts capable of obeying God's law (Jer 31:33). In particular, God's people will be characterized by "one heart" (32:39), meaning an undivided heart (NIV "singleness of heart"; see Ps 86:11). Likewise, Ezekiel anticipates a "new heart" cleansed from "idols" and indwelt by the Spirit with the ability to obey God's law (Ezek 36:26–27). Thus, Jesus declares that those in the kingdom are "pure in heart" (*katharoi tē kardią*) (Matt 5:8). The phrase "pure in heart" also occurs in Psalm 24 to describe the person who "does not trust in an idol or swear by a false god" (Ps 24:4, NIV). Similarly, David asks God to create in him "a pure heart" (*kardian katharan*) (Ps 51:10) so that he might again *worship* God (51:14–15).

In sum, the new covenant addresses the problem of human nature mentioned by Lucretius by dealing with the heart/idolatry problem (see also Isa 2:20; Hos 2:16–23; Zech 13:2). It provides people in the kingdom with a new capacity to treasure God. God's people will "know" the LORD (Jer 24:7; 31:34), which for Jeremiah means treating people with "justice and righteousness" and attending to "the poor and needy" (22:15–16).[77]

---

73. Neill, *A Genuinely Human Existence*, 70.
74. Bobzien, "Epicurus' Philosophy," 221.
75. Epicurus, *Letter to Menoeceus*, 127–32[3, 5]; see Seneca, *Letters* 92.3.
76. Groothuis, *On Jesus*, 42.
77. Keown et al., *Jeremiah 26–52*, 135.

Thus, knowing God is foundational to Jesus's ethics,[78] which explains why bearing fruit is impossible apart from knowing Jesus (John 15:5). It also explains why the Gospel writers are more optimistic than Epicureans concerning people's ability to change.[79]

PUTTING JESUS'S ETHICS INTO PRACTICE

The Power of Faith is in "Seeing"

For the Epicurean reason is the power that is able to rule the heart. However, reason can always be deceived by irrational desires. One must therefore fortify reason against the onslaught of such desires. In Epicureanism this is achieved through "belief." Incorrect beliefs lead to irrational desires, which in turn lead to a warped ethic. Therefore, one is able to curtail these desires by correcting false beliefs.[80] "Moral improvement will then consist mainly of restructuring a person's system of concepts and beliefs. False and empty beliefs will have to be first identified, and then measures will have to be taken so that the person gives them up and replaces them by true beliefs."[81] Thus, ultimately our choices and actions are "dependent on beliefs of our own making."[82]

The same is true in the Gospels: faith is foundational to ethics[83] (e.g., John 12:46; see esp. Jas 2:14–26). For example, Jesus promises that, "your Father in heaven will give good gifts to those who ask him" (Matt 7:11). Verse 12 follows with the Golden Rule but begins with *oun* ("therefore"), indicating that what follows is based on the immediately preceding promise of God's fatherly care.[84] This means that "the source of *power* for living the

---

78. Groothuis, *On Jesus*, 58.

79. See Lucretius, 6.1–28[3]. Cf. Carson, "Reflections on Christian Assurance," 80.

80. Elliott, *Faithful Feelings*, 72.

81. Bobzien, "Epicurus' Philosophy," 223.

82. Epicurus, *On Nature*, 34.26–30[1]; see also Cicero, *On Fate*, 21–5.

83. Cf. Stassen, *Kingdom Ethics*, 453–58.

84. Piper, *What Jesus Demands*, 252; Willard, *Divine Conspiracy*, 258–59. Not all commentators see it this way, taking the *oun* to refer back to Matt 5:17. See e.g., Davies and Allison, *Matthew*, 1:688–89. Certainly the "law and the prophets" takes us back to 5:17, but Piper and Willard, in my opinion, rightly recognize that the promises in 7:7–11 are providing the foundation of how to live out the ethical instructions in the intervening material. Seen this way, *oun* merely establishes the connection and explains the dynamic between faith and works.

Golden Rule" is faith in God's promise that he will always give his children good gifts.[85] Therefore, Dallas Willard writes, "*Our confidence in God is the only thing that makes it possible to treat others as they should be treated.*"[86] We could easily multiply similar examples (see e.g., Luke 12:32–34; 14:12–14). The point is that faith produces obedience to the Golden Rule. And because the Golden Rule "sums up the law and the prophets" (Matt. 7:12) the person "*who observes this basic principle will fulfill all the basic principles of the law the way God intended them.*"[87] The "good gifts" Jesus speaks of are nothing less than God's rule, as seen, for example, in the beatitude promises at the outset of the Sermon (5:3–10).

But not all will believe such promises. The reason goes right back to the nature of the two types of treasure. In Matthew, earthly treasure is appreciated through the natural senses (see 6:19), whereas the treasure of the kingdom is "hidden" and therefore must be found (13:44). It is heavenly (6:20) and contains "mysteries" (13:11) that can only be understood by those with eyes and ears to see and hear (13:12). Thus, "God makes himself known in the heart,"[88] which explains why the kingdom remains "hidden" to the wise (11:25) and those who trust earthly treasures (19:24). Idolatry has blinded their heart. What this means is that inherent to faith is the act of treasuring, as opposed to mere intellectual belief.[89] Thus, according to Matthew Elliott: "[F]aith takes root in both mind *and* emotion."[90] It is through faith that one sees what is hidden. Actually the principle here is rather simple: one must see Jesus in order to know, trust, and treasure him. But because this is often associated with Platonism, mysticism, or even Roman Catholicism, it is often frowned upon by many evangelicals.[91] However, its significance for ethics can hardly be overstated (see 2 Cor 3:18)[92]

---

85. Piper, *What Jesus Demands*, 252 (emphasis added).

86. Willard, *Divine Conspiracy*, 258 (emphasis original).

87. Keener, *Gospel of Matthew*, 249 (emphasis original).

88. Elliott, *Faithful Feelings*, 131.

89. Cf. Bock, "Embracing Jesus in a First Century Context," 128–39.

90. Elliott, *Faithful Feelings*, 131 (emphasis added). Cf. Tyson, *Returning to Reality*, 106. For an extended discussion, see Stanley, *Salvation is More Complicated*, 35–45.

91. See Schwanda, "'To Gaze on the Beauty of the Lord,'" 62–84. Jonathan Edwards is perhaps the most well known Christian example in support of this practice, see e.g., Edwards, *Works*, 1:281–88.

92. Cf. Talbert, "Indicative and Imperative in Matthean Soteriology," 114: God's people will only be "transformed by their vision of God-with-us." For a practical outworking of this, see Chester, *Captured by a Better Vision*; see also idem, *You Can Change*.

and Scripture does not lack examples (e.g., Gen 32:22–32; Exod 34; Isa 6). If the heart is to treasure the true God—rather than false gods—it follows that the heart must also see (gaze at) the true God, and see him as treasure! This then is the purpose of the incarnation, to reveal the true face of Israel's God (Matt 1:23; John 1:18; 14:9).[93]

In John it is the Spirit that enables one to see God (John 9:39) and deliver them from darkness (12:46). But it is the cross, the place of divine glorification (12:23), where the Father is seen (see e.g., 3:28). This explains Jesus's declaration to Thomas: "From now on, you do *know* [my Father] and have seen him" (14:7), which is most likely a proleptic reference to the cross.[94] This also explains Jesus's enigmatic response to the Greeks who wanted to *see* him: "The hour has come for the Son of Man to be glorified" (12:23). In other words, "they could not yet 'see' him" until his hour had come (12:20–32).[95]

In Mark, commentators sometimes point out that the two stage healing of the blind man of Bethsaida in chapter 8 serves to illustrate what must happen to the disciples whose hard hearts and inability to see, hear, and understand are inhibiting their faith (Mark 8:17–21).[96] It is not enough for them to trust in Jesus as "Messiah" (8:29), they must trust him as the Messiah who came "to serve and to give his life as a ransom for many" (10:45). The two-stage healing symbolizes what is needed. They must move from partial sight (8:24) to seeing "everything clearly" (8:25). "Only at the cross and resurrection will they, like the man at Bethsaida, see 'everything clearly.'"[97] Stage two sight has ethical implications. To follow Jesus requires knowing who he is, the one who will go to the cross and lose his life (8:34–35). This explains why Mark spends the next two chapters on ethical issues, but occasionally interrupts the narrative with predictions of Jesus's death

---

93. Neill, *A Genuinely Human Existence*, 70. This is the point of Taylor, *Christlike God*. Cf. Talbert, "Indicative and Imperative in Matthean Soteriology," 105, 114. Green, *Who Is This Jesus*, 10: Jesus "made God real."

94. Cf. Carson, *Gospel According to John*, 493.

95. Ibid., 438.

96. E.g., Edwards, *Gospel According to Mark*, 237–245. This view is rejected by Gundry, *Mark*, 420–25, but note Hayes, *Moral Vision*, 77: "In light of the heavy emphasis placed on 'not seeing' in the immediately preceding dialogue in the boat ([Mark] 8:14–21), we would be singularly myopic readers if we failed to see the symbolic implications of this story."

97. Edwards, *Gospel According to Mark*, 245.

(9:12, 31; 10:33–34).[98] As he comes to the end of chapter 10, Mark shows again what is needed and surely expects his readers to get the point.

James and John	**A Blind Man**
Jesus: "What do you want me to do for you? (10:36)	Jesus: "What do you want me to do for you? (10:51a)
And they said to him, "Give to us, in order that one may sit at your right hand and one at your left in your glory." (10:37)	And the blind man said to him: "Rabbi, I want to receive *sight*." And Jesus said to him, "Go, your *faith* has saved you." And immediately he received his sight and he *followed* [Jesus] on the way (10:51b–52).

Faith entails seeing the suffering Messiah, which in Mark is highlighted by the Roman centurion at the cross (15:39). "This centurion had doubtlessly seen other men die by crucifixion. But something in this crucifixion—in the very weakness and suffering of Jesus's death—becomes *revelatory*. The suffering of Jesus on the cross . . . becomes, by an act of God, the *window* into the heart and meaning of Jesus."[99]

We see a similar theme in Luke. Just as the first human couple ate and their eyes were opened (Gen 3:7), so too the couple on the road to Emmaus ate with Jesus and had their eyes opened to the identity of Jesus (Luke 24:31), indicating that in Jesus the effects of the curse are being reversed and God's original intent for humanity is being realized.[100] Thus, the disciples' minds remain closed to what Jesus is doing unless he opens them (cf. 18:34 with 24:45).

The concept of reality being hidden to one's physical sense may appear strange to twenty-first-century minds, but it would not have been unfamiliar to people in the first century. Plato is most well known for it,[101] and his teaching had widespread effect. For instance, Lucretius demonstrates platonic influence in observing that our physical "eyes cannot discover the

---

98. For a full treatment of what I have presented here, see Hayes, *Moral Vision*, 75–85.

99. Edwards, *Gospel According to Mark*, 479–480 (the first emphasis is added, the second is original).

100. Ortlund, "And Their Eyes Were Opened," 717–28.

101. See e.g., Plato, *Allegory of the Cave*.

nature of things"; "this falls to the mind's reason to discern."[102] In order to see "sharply" one must strain to see with the "mind."[103]

The Power of Grace is in "Treasure"

The Epicureans sought to bring ethical change. But in the end, they simply exchanged many of the more overt gods for their own idea of what is "good." The Pharisees similarly thought of themselves as experts in ethics, and yet they could only heap "burdens" on people (Matt 23:4). Jesus, however, demanded an ethic far greater (see e.g., 5:20–48) and yet his ethic liberates (17:26; John 8:32, 36) because Jesus is grace personified. His invitation to those who are "burdened" in Matthew 11:28–30 illustrates the point: "Take my yoke upon you and learn from me, *because* I am gentle and humble in heart (11:29, emphasis added)." This verse shows a connection between Jesus's character and ethics. It is Jesus's gracious character that *causes* discipleship. Jesus is the only treasure that will change the heart and thus change lives.[104] No worldly treasure can claim to be "gentle and humble." Worldly treasures prosper the strong. And yet it is *only* the weak that can treasure Jesus. Children best exemplify this point (11:25; 18:1–4). They, of all human beings, are the most helpless and powerless, for they have no significant influence on a world run and governed by adults. So Jesus holds up "the weakest, most-vulnerable, least-significant human being you can think of [as] the clearest possible signpost to" those he has come to rule.[105] They know they are lacking. And yet here is someone who died for them. He forgives, sympathizes, encourages, and strengthens them. The cross shows them that it is not *their* ethics that bring them to God but *his*. He comforts them when they mourn their sin, satisfies them when they hunger and thirst for righteousness, draws near to them when they repent, and completes them when they are broken. He loves them as much as the Father loves the Son (John 17:23), and by that love transforms them (17:26). Now, having found what is good, this Treasure of Grace[106] has free reign to change them into people characterized by life, freedom, and sacrificial and selfless love.

102. Lucretius, 4.379–86.
103. Ibid., 4.722–822[8].
104. See Piper, *What Jesus Demands*.
105. Wright, *Matthew For Everyone*, 2:27.
106. Cf. Edwards, *Works*, 1:314.

CONCLUSION

Our look at the intersection between ancient philosophical ethics and the Gospels is by no means comprehensive. But we have sought to get to the core. It is remarkable just how compatible the two are in many ways. This, of course, does not take away from the fact that there are profound differences. But it must be said that someone like Epicurus, for instance, demonstrates a level of insight and understanding on the subject of ethics and human nature that many Christians would do well to ponder. Too often, Jesus's commands are viewed as what we should do, but with no indication of how to do it. We see them as like the tip of an iceberg. We know there is something going on below the surface, but if we want to see below the surface we need to go to someone like the apostle Paul. But that is not the case. Rather, the Gospels reveal the intricate connection between the heart, treasure, and ethics. We have seen this same connection in Epicureanism, though it exists in other philosophical schools as well. The philosophers provide a rich source of illustrative material for those wanting to bring out these connections.

Evidently, after Epicurus died his followers would celebrate his birthday each year, honoring him as a generous savior.[107] But despite the fact that Epicurus may have indeed set people free from many of the world's treasures, he could never give them true freedom. Since we become like what we worship, the best that Epicureanism can achieve is replicas of Epicurus, whereas the best that Christianity can achieve is replicas of Jesus.[108]

BIBLIOGRAPHY

Asmis, Elizabeth. "Epicureanism." Vol. 2 of The Anchor Bible Dictionary, edited by D. N. Freedman, 559–61. New York. Doubleday, 1992.
Beale, G. K. *The Temple and the Church's Mission: A Biblical Theology of The Dwelling Place of God*. NSBT 17. Downers Grove: InterVarsity, 2005.
Bietenhard, H., F. F. Bruce. "Name." *New International Dictionary of New Testament Theology*, vol. 2. Edited by Colin Brown, 648–56. Rev. ed. Grand Rapids, MI: Zondervan, 1986.
Blomberg, Craig L. *Matthew*. NAC. Nashville: Broadman, 1992.
Bobzien, Susanne. "Moral Responsibility and Moral Development in Epicurus' Philosophy." In *The Virtuous Life in Greek Ethics*, edited by Burkhard Reis, 206–29. Cambridge: Cambridge University Press, 2006.

---

107. Asmis, "Epicureanism," 2:560.
108. I am very grateful to Dr. Paul Tyson for his help and feedback on this essay.

Bock, Darrell L. "Embracing Jesus in a First Century Context: What Can It Teach Us about Spiritual Commitment?" *Journal of Spiritual Formation & Soul Care* 3/2 (2010) 128–39.

Carson, D. A. *The Gospel According to John*. PNTC. Grand Rapids, MI: Eerdmans, 1991.

———. "Matthew." In *The Expositor's Bible Commentary*, edited by Frank E. Gaebelein. Vol. 8. Grand Rapids, MI: Zondervan, 1984.

———. "Reflections on Christian Assurance." *Westminster Theological Journal* 54 (1992) 1–29.

Chester, Tim. *Captured by a Better Vision: Living Porn-Free*. Nottingham: InterVarsity, 2010.

———. *You Can Change: God's Transforming Power For Our Sinful Behaviour and Negative Emotions*. Nottingham: InterVarsity, 2008.

Chilton, Bruce. "Kingdom of God." In *Dictionary of Scripture and Ethics* 452–56.

Conzelmann, H. "sko/toß." In *Theological Dictionary of the New Testament* 7:443–44.

Davies, W. D., and D. C. Allison Jr. *A Critical and Exegetical Commentary on The Gospel According to Saint Matthew: Introduction and Commentary on Matthew I–VII*. ICC 1. Edinburgh: T & T Clark, 1988.

Edwards, James R. *The Gospel According to Mark*. PNTC. Grand Rapids, MI: Eerdmans, 2002.

Edwards, Jonathan. *The Works of Jonathan Edwards*. 2 vols. Peabody: Hendrickson, 2005.

Elliott, Matthew. *Faithful Feelings: Emotion in the New Testament*. Leicester: InterVarsity, 2005.

Gentry, Peter J., and Stephen J. Wellum. *Kingdom Through Covenant: A Biblical-Theological Understanding of the Covenants*. Wheaton: Crossway, 2012.

Green, Michael. *Who Is This Jesus?* Nashville: Thomas Nelson, 1990.

Groothuis, Douglas. *On Jesus*. Belmont, CA: Wadsworth, 2003.

Gundry, Robert H. *Mark: A Commentary on His Apology for the Cross*. Grand Rapids, MI: Eerdmans, 1993.

Hagner, Donald A. *Matthew 1–13*. WBC 33A. Dallas: Word, 1993.

———. *Matthew 14–28*. WBC 33B. Dallas: Word, 1995.

Hamilton, Victor P. *Handbook on the Pentateuch: Genesis, Exodus, Leviticus, Numbers, Deuteronomy*. Grand Rapids, MI: Baker, 2005.

Hauerwas, Stanley. *The Peaceable Kingdom: A Primer in Christian Ethics*. London: SCM, 2003.

Hayes, Richard B. *The Moral Vision of the New Testament: A Contemporary Introduction to New Testament Ethics*. New York: HarperOne, 1996.

Keener, Craig S. *The Gospel of Matthew: A Socio-Rhetorical Commentary*. Grand Rapids, MI: Eerdmans, 2009.

Keown, Gerald L., et al. *Jeremiah 26–52*. WBC 27. Waco: Word, 1995.

Long, A. A., and D. N. Sedley, eds. *The Hellenistic Philosophers: Volume 1, Translations of the Principal Sources with Philosophical Commentary*. Cambridge: Cambridge University Press, 1987.

———. *From Epicurus to Epictetus: Studies in Hellenistic and Roman Philosophy*. Oxford: Clarendon, 2006.

Marshall, I. Howard. *The Gospel of Luke: a Commentary on the Greek Text*. New International Greek Testament Commentary. Grand Rapids, MI: Eerdmans, 1978.

Middleton, J. Richard. *The Liberating Image: The Imago Dei in Genesis 1*. Grand Rapids, MI: Brazos, 2005.

Neill, Stephen. *A Genuinely Human Existence: Towards A Christian Psychology*. New York: Doubleday, 1959.

Nolland, John. *The Gospel of Matthew: a Commentary on the Greek Text*. New International Greek Testament Commentary. Grand Rapids, MI: Eerdmans, 2005.

O'Keefe, Tim. "Action and Responsibility," in *The Cambridge Companion to Epicureanism*, edited by James Warren, 142–57. Cambridge: Cambridge University, 2009.

Ortlund, Dane C. "'And Their Eyes Were Opened, And They Knew': An Inter-Canonical Note On Luke 24:31." *JETS* 53/4 (2010) 717–28.

Piper, John. *What Jesus Demands from the World*. Wheaton: Crossway, 2006.

Plato. *Republic, Volume II: Books 6-10*. Loeb Classical Library 276. Edited and translated by Christopher Emlyn-Jones, William Preddy. Cambridge, MA: Harvard University Press, 2013.

Quarles, Charles L. *Jesus Revealed as Deliverer, King, and Incarnate Creator. Explorations in Biblical Theology*. Phillipsburg, NJ: P&R, 2013.

Schwanda, Tom. "'To Gaze on the Beauty of the Lord': The Evangelical Resistance and Retrieval of Contemplation." *Journal of Spiritual Formation & Soul Care* 7/1 (2014) 62–84.

Stanley, Alan P. *Did Jesus Teach Salvation By Works? The Relationship Between Works and Salvation in the Synoptic Gospels*. ETSMS 4. Eugene, OR: Pickwick, 2006.

———. *Salvation is More Complicated Than You Think: A Study on the Teachings of Jesus*. Colorado Springs, CO: Paternoster, 2007.

Stassen, Glen H., and David P. Gushee. *Kingdom Ethics: Following Jesus in Contemporary Context*. Downers Grove: InterVarsity, 2003.

Stough, Charlotte. "Stoic Determinism and Moral Responsibility." In *The Stoics*, edited by John M, Rist, 203–30. Berkeley: University of California Press, 1978.

Talbert, Charles H. "Indicative and Imperative in Matthean Soteriology" in *Getting Saved: The Whole Story of Salvation in the New Testament*, 95–118. Grand Rapids, MI: Eerdmans, 2011.

———. *Reading the Sermon on the Mount: Character Formation and Decision Making in Matthew 5-7*. Grand Rapids, MI: Baker, 2004.

Taylor, John V. *The Christlike God*. London: SCM, 1992.

Tyson, Paul. *Returning to Reality: Christian Platonism for our Times*. Kalos 2. Eugene, OR: Cascade, 2014.

Watts, John D. W. *Isaiah 34-66*. WBC 25. Waco: Word, 2005.

Willard, Dallas. *The Divine Conspiracy: Rediscovering Our Hidden Life In God*. London: Fount, 1998.

Woolf, Raphael. "Pleasure and Desire." In *The Cambridge Companion to Epicureanism*, edited by James Warren, 158–78. Cambridge: Cambridge University Press, 2009.

Wright, Christopher J. H. *The Mission of God: Unlocking the Bible's Grand Narrative*. Nottingham: InterVarsity, 2006.

Wright, N. T. *Jesus and the Victory of God. Christian Origins and the Question of God* 2. Minneapolis: Fortress, 1996.

———. *Matthew For Everyone, Part 1: Chapters 1-15*. London: SPCK, 2002.

———. *Matthew For Everyone, Part 2: Chapters 16-28*. London: SPCK, 2002.

———. *Virtue Reborn*. London: SPCK, 2010.

7

THE LOGIC OF PAUL

Philip D. Burggraff

Writing a chapter on Paul's relationship to philosophy presents a daunting task. Should one seek to understand Paul from the philosophical milieu of his day, or begin with a twenty-first-century philosophical position and search for strands of it within his writings and thought? Further, do the findings of either of these approaches help us better interpret his individual letters? Rather than attempting to tell the history of Greco-Roman philosophy and locating Paul's place in it or opposed to it, I seek to address one aspect of ancient philosophy, logic, by beginning with a discussion of a recent interpretation of Paul in relationship to logic and then focusing on the logical flow of a written text, Galatians. Hopefully, this attempt will demonstrate the need for understanding the logic of epistolary discourse and aid in the interpretation of Paul's letters as a whole.

N. T. WRIGHT AND THE RELATION OF PAUL TO PHILOSOPHY

In his recent two-volume tome *Paul and the Faithfulness of God*, N. T. Wright discusses Paul's worldview from the perspective of religion, politics, and philosophy, which ultimately shape the way Paul viewed the narrative of God's work in salvation. For the purposes of this chapter, I only examine his helpful discussion of ancient philosophy, focusing primarily on Wright's interaction with logic.

After briefly defining physics and ethics,[1] Wright comments that the ancient understanding of logic denoted a wider understanding than the mathematical formulae (symbolic logic) that we think of today. For the ancients it represented the entire process of reasoning, working through the issue at hand (dialectic), and the way one organized their thought or presentation so that one's entire argument was consistent rather than simply filled with emotion or lofty rhetoric.[2] Growing up in Tarsus, Paul would have been exposed to the philosophical practices and schools of his day.[3] While not deriving the central themes of his message from pagan thought, Wright argues that Paul engaged the philosophies of his day through direct confrontation and adaptation. He confronted pagan polytheism through his own defense of Jewish and Christian monotheism and pagan sexual practices through a Jewish-style sexual ethic. He could adapt any ideas that would have reflected aspects of truth, since ultimately all truth belongs to Jesus, and use them to help explain or point to the gospel.[4] Further, Paul and Christians after him engaged in practices that more aligned with philosophy than they did religion in their day: 1) they presented a case for a different, divine order of reality; 2) they argued for a different way of life that would have been noticed by the surrounding community; and 3) they created communities not tied to ethnic, gender, or class similarity, which eventually led to persecution from those in authority.[5] Wright spends the rest of his introductory chapter on Paul's worldview in relation to philosophy describing the philosophical climate of Paul's day and key figures and schools of philosophical thought prevalent in the first century. He concludes that one cannot perfectly place Paul in any of the schools of thought circulating in his day, but he utilizes concepts and tools found

---

1. According to Wright, *physics* for the ancients represented nature and "everything that is," including metaphysics and the understanding of the gods. *Ethics* dealt with what one ought to do and how to behave (Wright, *Paul and the Faithfulness of God*, 198).

2. Ibid., 198.

3. Ibid., 199. Porter, "Paul of Tarsus," 534–5, briefly discusses Paul's upbringing and training and argues that Paul would probably have not spent enough time in Tarsus to receive the full educational experience that city could have offered.

4. Wright, *Paul and the Faithfulness of God*, 201. He utilizes 2 Corinthians 10:5 as proof that Paul would have adapted the tools of philosophy to build an argument.

5. Ibid., 202–203.

in Stoic thought, especially when compared to Epictetus.[6] The Stoic perspective prevalent in the Greco-Roman world highlighted the immanence of the divine within nature, so that one should live a virtuous life, able to withstand the constant waves of change, both positive and negative, that life brings. Further, Paul would have assumed that his Gentile readers would be interpreting concepts that he raised in his letters from a Stoic perspective of Plato's thought.[7]

In his later chapter dealing with Paul's actual engagement with the philosophy of his day, Wright demonstrates how Paul transformed the idea of wisdom and the epistemology of knowing through his letters. While some may not accept the idea that Paul interacted with and used philosophy because of his statements in 1 Corinthians 1:18–25 and Colossians 2:8–10, where Paul dismisses human wisdom and philosophy, Wright points out the balance that Paul brings in the same contexts of introducing God's wisdom (1 Cor 2:6–16) and its new emphasis on Jesus as the object of wisdom and knowledge with love as its primary action.[8] Paul still engaged the philosophical investigative categories of physics, ethics, and logic, but now he understands them "in the light of the one God and of the new creation ushered in by the risen Messiah."[9] In regards to logic, Paul began with the premise that God had revealed himself within creation, but human ability to grasp God was lost due to our darkened minds, an effect of their sin and rebellion against God.[10] In contrast to the logic of his day, Paul maintained that wisdom could not come simply by learning how to see in this darkness, but rather through a direct revelation from the one God shedding the light of new creation into this darkened world and opening the eyes of those blinded to this light (Rom 12:2; 1 Cor 2:10–16).[11]

Once the true source of wisdom was revealed and understood, Paul engaged in the kinds of logical arguments that characterized his day. Wright finds evidence for this in Paul's use of diatribe (e.g., Rom 2) and the way in which Paul challenged his readers by taking certain known truths

---

6. Ibid., 213–27. Wright discusses similarities and differences between Stoic and Pauline thought in areas such as *spirit (pneuma)*, *logos*, the use of diatribe, and prayer to god/gods.

7. Ibid., 232.

8. Ibid., 1355–56.

9. Ibid., 1362.

10. Ibid., 1362–63.

11. Ibid., 1363–64.

The Logic of Paul

or premises and convincing them to embrace further truths and actions.[12] 1 Corinthians 15 serves as an example of the latter, as Paul moves from foundational beliefs in the gospel and resurrection of Christ (1 Cor 15:1–11), which Wright calls basic truths for Paul that don't need arguing,[13] to a case for the general resurrection from the dead (1 Cor 15:12–57). Wright concludes that Paul did not simply confront the philosophy of his day and dismiss it, but rather recognized in it a genuine striving after clear reasoning (logic), a true description of the world (physics), and virtuous living (ethics). Romans 6:1–14 provides a succinct example. Paul uses clear reasoning to draw a number of conclusions (baptism into Christ's death; unity of believers in Christ's death and resurrection) for a true description of the world from the perspective of the gospel (believers have died to sin). He concludes with a strong call to live out this reality (believers must live like they are dead to sin; they must stop allowing sin to reign and offering any part of themselves as instruments of wickedness). In summing up Paul's approach to logic, physics, and ethics, Wright adds,

> With these, Paul has no quarrel. His quarrel is with the fact that the aspiration always fails to meet its goal—and that he believes that the one God, the creator, who has made himself known through Jesus the Messiah, has opened eyes and minds, has unveiled his complex but coherent truth in a way never before imagined and has given a quite new *pneuma* into the hearts of his people so that, in fulfilling his ancient promises of covenant renewal, he would also fulfil[sic] the deepest and highest aspirations of all human hearts.[14]

Wright's discussion of Paul's engagement with philosophy and use of logic demonstrates the necessity for understanding these disciplines within his context in order to properly interpret his writings. One should not simply dismiss such a concerted effort to understand how Paul unfolded his argument within his letters as superfluous to supposedly more important disciplines, such as Paul's theology. In order to properly understand theology and its application to ethics, one must first comprehend how Paul arrived at the conclusions he makes, utilizing various aspects of these other disciplines. While Wright engages and discusses the logical progression of certain key passages that contribute to an understanding of Paul's thought,

12. Ibid., 1366.
13. Ibid.
14. Ibid., 1381.

CONVERGENCE

he does not provide a detailed explanation of the logical flow of an entire Pauline letter.

THE LOGIC OF A PAULINE LETTER

In what follows, I provide a description and critique of a popular attempt in current New Testament studies to explain the logic of Paul's letters through rhetorical criticism. Due to the attention rhetorical critics have given it, Paul's letter to the Galatians serves as the test case. Then I present an analysis of this letter, explaining and utilizing a proposal from linguistic theory to describe the logical flow of hortatory discourse, a text that attempts to change behavior.

Rhetorical Criticism of Galatians

With the explosion in the discovery of papyri documents over the past century from the Greco-Roman world, scholars have attempted to describe the structure of the typical letter and compare it with biblical letters. The description of letter structure using grammatical and syntactical features found at the word, phrase, and sentence levels (the strategy of traditional grammars) reveals key structural indicators at the beginning and end of letters; yet, such analysis has not revealed easily recognized and agreed upon features that deal with the structure of the much larger body of the letter, where the logical flow of the letter's message or argument is found. This has proven frustrating for scholars, and some have abandoned epistolary descriptions of the letter body for rhetorical approaches.[15] That New Testament letters were read aloud in the congregation provides the impetus for

---

15. Even individuals who have made significant contributions to understanding the epistolary nature of ancient letters have embraced rhetorical approaches. In his more recent work, J. White ("Apostolic Mission," 148–49) has shifted his focus in relation to letter body material. He writes, "My earlier analyses of Paul's letters were overly formalistic and the choice of comparative materials too narrow. I tried to understand the entirety of Paul's letters in terms of conventions found in nonliterary papyrus letters. It is still feasible to delineate the beginning and the end of Paul's letters by such means but, for the large intermediate part of the letter's body, we need to look to the literary letter tradition for our model." He argues that rhetorical analysis, especially chiastic patterns and classical argumentation may provide a way forward (153–59). Similarly, H. Klauck, *Ancient Letters*, 206–10, cautions against a wholesale acceptance of rhetorical analysis for ancient letter writing, but maintains that ancient letter writers used rhetoric in their letter writing and thus letters can and should be analyzed rhetorically.

The Logic of Paul

rhetorical approaches, since ancient rhetoric pertained to oral presentation and argumentation. Rhetorical critics seek to demonstrate that the author of a particular letter utilized one of the three species of Greco-Roman rhetoric: 1) judicial (forensic), which seeks to persuade an audience to make a judgment, most likely a judgment of blame or innocence, for a past action; 2) deliberative, which seeks to persuade an audience to take some course of action in the future; or 3) epideictic, which seeks to persuade an audience to hold to a value in the present.[16]

With the work done in the 1970s by Hans Dieter Betz, culminating in his commentary on Galatians, a new era of rhetorical criticism began. Due to its history in relation to rhetorical criticism, Galatians serves as a perfect example of the rhetorical investigations that have flourished in New Testament and Pauline studies. Betz argued that Galatians could be analyzed according to both Greco-Roman epistolography (letter writing) and rhetoric, which from his analysis revealed that it belongs to the genre of the apologetic letter[17] and represents the judicial (forensic) form of rhetoric.[18] Discussing the overall purpose of the letter, Betz maintained that through this rhetorical approach Paul presented an apologetic for his gospel by defending the gift of the Spirit to the Galatians.[19] Subsequently, others have critiqued Betz's approach, and maintain that he forced the letter into a rhetorical mold it does not fit and interpreted Paul's use of rhetoric too scholasticly and rigidly.[20] The conclusions reached by others reveal a lack of unanimity as to the type of rhetoric utilized by Paul in Galatians, with scholars proposing that Galatians is best understood in terms of deliberative rhetoric,[21] epideictic rhetoric,[22] or a mixture of the categories.[23]

---

16. Kennedy, *New Testament Interpretation*, 19.

17. Betz, *Galatians*, 14–15.

18. Ibid., 24–25.

19. Ibid., 28. He outlined Paul's rhetorical approach as follows (16–23): Epistolary Prescript (Gal 1:1–5); *Exordium* (1:6–11); *Narratio* (1:12–2:14); *Propositio* (2:15–21); *Probatio* (3:1–4:31); *Exhortatio* (5:1–6:10); Epistolary Postscript, *Conclusio* (6:11–18).

20. For a brief critique, see Longenecker, *Galatians*, cxi–cxiii, who explains these and other criticisms of Betz's approach.

21. Kennedy, *New Testament Interpretation*, 145–47; Witherington, *Grace in Galatia*, 27–36.

22. Hester, "Epideictic Rhetoric," 181–96.

23. Longenecker, *Galatians*, cxi. He maintains that the judicial/forensic categorization fits Galatians 1–2, but fails in relation to 5–6, which are deliberative.

CONVERGENCE

This lack of consensus on the categorization of Galatians according to the forms of rhetoric demonstrates the problem inherent in trying to find the solution through rhetorical criticism to Paul's logic and argument in the main body of his letters. Even though functional parallels exist between epistolary types and the genre or species of rhetoric (judicial, deliberative, and epideictic), these parallels do not mean that letter writers patterned entire letters according to the rules or rhetoric found in the rhetorical handbooks.[24] Rather, parallels between rhetoric and letter writing simply show that certain norms for argumentation are universally accepted.[25] Of greater significance for maintaining the distinction between rhetoric and epistolography is that the epistolary theorists and letter writers say nothing about structuring letters according to rhetorical categories.[26] Further, Reed points out that letters showing significant rhetorical influence typically lack many of the epistolary formulas and conventions found in personal letters.[27] Paul's letters contain the standard and added epistolary formulas, which would seem to indicate that an analysis done solely along rhetorical lines is wrong. While an understanding of rhetoric can help clarify the arguments that Paul used within his letters, the identification and interpretation of his letters according to the genre or species of rhetoric and a description of them according the arrangement of oratorical parts will most likely lead to faulty conclusions and does not provide the ultimate solution to the logic of Paul.[28] Thus strategies that analyze discourse and the flow of argument may prove more beneficial in seeking to understand Paul's logic.

---

24. Both Stowers, *Letter Writing*, 52, and Reed, *A Discourse Analysis of Philippians*, 444, make this similar point, although Reed argues more strongly for the separation of rhetoric and letter writing.

25. Reed, *A Discourse Analysis of Philippians*, 444.

26. Ibid., 450.

27. Ibid., 454.

28. Porter, "Paul of Tarsus," 584–85, comes to a similar conclusion in his discussion of the applicability of ancient rhetoric to the interpretation of Pauline letters. He maintains that formal rhetorical analysis of letters finds little support from ancient witness in either the rhetorical or epistolary handbooks or the early interpretation of letters such as Paul's. Yet he recognizes that functional correlation (arrangement, invention, and style) to rhetorical categories can be found in parts of Paul's letters.

Longacre's Approach to Discourse Analysis

Representing a subset of the larger discipline of discourse analysis, Robert Longacre has developed a strategy through which discourses can be analyzed according to their particular type. According to Longacre, monologue discourse contains a hierarchy constituent structure of the following eight items in ascending order: morpheme, stem, word, phrase, clause, sentence, paragraph, and discourse.[29] In attempting to use such a system to interpret a discourse, one must start with the last constituent in the list and work backwards. As Longacre notes, "Characteristics of individual discourses cannot be described, predicted, nor analyzed without resorting to a classification of discourse types. It is pointless to look in a discourse for a feature which is not characteristic of the type to which that discourse belongs."[30] For Longacre, an understanding of what type of discourse one is interpreting is of utmost importance in analyzing any elements within the text itself.

Discourse Typology

Discourses can be classified by the establishment of two parameters,[31] contingent temporal succession (*cts*), which refers to a basic temporal sequencing of events within the discourse, and agent orientation (*ao*), indicated by individuals participating in or being addressed by the discourse.[32] When brought together, these result in producing four discourse types (pluses indicating presence of parameter; minuses indicating absence of parameter): narrative (+*cts* +*ao*), procedural (+*cts* –*ao*), behavioral (–*cts* +*ao*), and expository (–*cts* –*ao*).[33] While these four types broadly make up all monologue discourses in communication, adding the further parameter of

---

29. Longacre, "Paragraph," 116.

30. Longacre, *Grammar of Discourse*, 7.

31. In his classification, Longacre (ibid., 8) differentiates *etic* notional structures (deep or semantic structures), such as these two parameters, from *emic* surface structures. The notional structure of a discourse relates to the overall purpose of the discourse, while surface structures deal with a discourse's formal characteristics.

32. According to Longacre (ibid., 8–9), "contingent temporal succession refers to a framework of temporal succession in which some (often most) of the events or doings are contingent on previous events or doings" while "agent orientation refers to orientation towards agents with at least a partial identity of agent reference running through the discourse."

33. Ibid., 9.

projection,[34] the anticipation of an action or event, subdivides these into eight types. In behavioral discourse, projection distinguishes hortatory texts (+projection) from a eulogy (−projection).[35] In analyzing discourses, a couple of relevant areas call for discussion: main line versus supportive material and notional structure.

Main Line Versus Supportive Material

When trying to analyze a discourse, one is confronted with the question as to what is the main line material of a discourse and what is supportive. A key distinction between main line and supportive material is that of verb tense/aspect and mood. Longacre notes,

> In the great majority of the world's languages, the main line or event line of a narrative discourse is commonly marked by some sort of past, perfective, or completive tense aspect . . . For other types of discourse, we find the main line of a procedural discourse marked by a present or habitual tense; the main line of hortatory discourse, by imperative or surrogates for imperatives; and the main line of expository discourse, by clauses that feature existential, equational, and descriptive verbs.[36]

In the Greek of the New Testament, the main line verbs in narrative, such as the Gospels and Acts, consist of the perfective aspect and aorist tense. In behavioral (hortatory) texts, commands primarily in the form of imperatives will be present in the main line. When other verb forms appear other than the ones that dominate the main line, this material often is supportive within that discourse type.

Another key to following the surface structure of discourse relates to the two parameters, contingent temporal succession and agent orientation. These become concretely evident on the surface structure through chronological linkage (the linking together of successive events) and participant reference (the characters in a narrative or author/addressees in a letter) in a given text.[37] While chronological linkage characterizes narrative and procedural texts, it does not carry along the primary argument in either be-

---

34. Longacre (ibid.) defines projection as having "to do with a situation or action which is contemplated, enjoined, or anticipated, but not realized."

35. Ibid., 9.

36. Longacre, "Discourse Peak," 83.

37. Longacre, *Grammar of Discourse*, 11.

havioral or expository discourse; instead, it gives way to logical or thematic linkage with hortatory discourse, a subset of behavioral, depending heavily on linkage through conditional, causal, and purpose relationships evidenced explicitly by conjunction.[38] In regards to participant reference, narrative and behavioral discourse strongly evidence the use of it. Of necessity, hortatory texts depend on the presence of second person reference, which can be softened through inclusive first person plural or third person examples, because it addresses behavior in the life of the reader.[39]

In following these key indicators, Galatians belongs to the behavioral discourse type, specifically hortatory discourse. It contains strong second person participant reference throughout the letter, and possesses imperative verb forms sparingly at the beginning of the letter body (Gal 1:8–9 and 3:7) but more pronounced toward the end (4:12ff.). While chronological linkage appears in a narrative subsection within the letter body (1:11–2:14), this section is subsumed within the larger logical sequencing found throughout the rest of the letter body. These elements suggest that a proper understanding of the logic of Galatians will be in line with the way in which behavioral, specifically hortatory, discourses work.

Notional Structure

Longacre argues that notional structures, basic distinct patterns, form the backbone of all discourse types, with each possessing their own unique characteristics.[40] He describes hortatory discourse as a "text whose purpose is to modify the conduct of the receivers of the text" and states that it possesses the following notional structure: 1) establishment of the authority/credibility of the text producer; 2) presentation of a problem/situation; 3)

---

38. Ibid., 11, 13.

39. Ibid., 12.

40. Much of Longacre's discussion pertains to the notional structure of narrative as emplotment along a schema moving towards climax/peak (ibid., 35–36). Climactic narratives are moving towards a peak, which usually is preceded with rising action towards the peak and followed by falling action toward resolution. In Longacre's typology, locating peak is critical to following the flow of the text. Thus, he has listed several elements that highlight the zone of turbulence, which marks peak within a discourse (Ibid., 33–50). While this works well in narrative, the question arises as to whether or not the other three discourse types contain emplotment and peak. Longacre suggests that each discourse type has its own notional structure peculiar to it, but all four in some way identify progress towards peak.

issuing of one or more commands, which can be mitigated to suggestions of varying urgency; and 4) resort to motivation (essentially threats with predictions of undesirable results and promises with predictions of desirable results).[41] Hortatory discourse must possess the third element because the presence of commands establishes a text as hortatory. Hortatory texts also require the second element; even if the text may not explicitly state the problem/situation, the context of the discourse will imply it because something causes the author or speaker to give commands. Frequently, the fourth element will accompany the commands in order to provide reason and basis for the audience to perform these actions. All of these elements require the first element, even if the text does not specifically establish the author's credibility.[42]

While Longacre's discussion moves on to the levels of paragraphs, sentences, clauses, phrases, and words, the description and analysis of Galatians along such lines would far surpass the limits of this chapter. In what follows, I will analyze Galatians for the way in which it reflects the elements of the notional structure of a hortatory discourse at the largest level of communication according to Longacre's scheme, the discourse itself.

The Logic of Galatians

The description of the logical flow of Galatians will be presented in line with the major movements found within the discourse. These movements are based on the major sections of ancient epistolography (letter opening, body, letter closing)[43] as applied to Pauline letter structure (letter opening, thanksgiving, letter body, paraenesis,[44] and letter closing).[45] Summary

---

41. Longacre, "Discourse Strategy," 110.

42. See ibid., 110–11, for descriptions of the various elements of hortatory discourse; he provides a brief statement of them in *Grammar of Discourse*, 34n.

43. Numerous scholars have recognized a basic three-part structure to Greco-Roman letters. A standard defense and treatment of this position can be found in White, "Ancient Greek Letters," 45, and *Form and Function*, 7–9. For a more recent discussion maintaining a three-part structure, see Klauck, *Ancient Letters*, 17–41.

44. *Paraenesis* is a Greek term referring to a distinct section of moral exhortation within a letter.

45. While some interpreters view Paul's letters as displaying a three-part (Aune, *The New Testament in Its Literary Environment*, 183–91; Schnider and Stenger, *Briefformular*, vii–viii) or four-part structure (Murphy-O'Connor, *Paul the Letter-Writer*, 45–113; Weima, *Neglected Endings*, 11), a number of them recognize these five distinct parts as

statements of the argument are detailed before description is given of the notional elements present within that section.[46]

The letter opening (Gal 1:1–5) begins with typical elements of sender, recipient, and salutation. It also introduces two other key themes tied to these typical Pauline letter features: the basis of Paul's apostleship and an elaboration of Jesus Christ's work. Paul did not receive his apostolic commission from any person or by human means. Rather, Jesus Christ and God the Father, who raised him from the dead, called Paul to his ministry as an apostle (1:1). Thus, he answers to no one, not even key church leaders, for the message that he preaches and has presented to the Galatians. He answers solely to God, who has decisively acted through the sacrificial work of Jesus Christ to rescue believers in him from this present evil age (1:4). While the letter opening establishes the author and his readers, Paul opens this letter by defending his authority[47] and introducing key elements to the message that he preaches, the Father's work through the death and resurrection of his Son. According to Longacre's scheme for the notional pattern of hortatory discourse, the letter opening accomplishes the first element (authority/credibility of text producer) as Paul states from whom he receives his authority to preach the message he has delivered to them and to write what will soon be read.

The body of the letter elaborates these themes as it contrasts for the Galatians Paul's understanding of the gospel with a false view that adds works of the law as a necessary basis for right standing with God and exhorts these readers to embrace the message that Paul presents. While scholars do not fully agree on the exact segmentation of the letter body, the flow of the argument can be broadly traced as follows: Paul's reception and presentation of the gospel of Jesus Christ (Gal 1:6–2:21); his elaboration and defense of the gospel contrasted with the false teachers in Galatia

---

common to the majority of Paul's letters. See Doty, *Letters in Primitive Christianity*, 27–43; Porter, "Exegesis of the Pauline Letters," 543–50; Roetzel, *The Letters of Paul*, 29–39. A five-part letter is also defended in Porter and Adams, *Paul and the Ancient Letter Form*, as they include chapters on each of the five sections of ancient letters.

46. The summary statements and description roughly occur in relation to the paragraphs of the letter. Again, due to size constraints, argument for paragraph boundaries will not be presented. The paragraph breaks do closely align with those recognized in Schreiner, *Galatians*, 58–59, and Moo, *Galatians*, 63–64, who do come to different conclusions on some of the segmentation of the major movements in the letter and break a few paragraphs differently; yet for the most part display a great deal of similarity in their identification of paragraphs.

47. Schreiner, *Galatians*, 56.

CONVERGENCE

(3:1–4:11); his exhortation[48] to the readers to accept his message and to stand firm in their freedom by walking in the Spirit (4:12–6:10).[49]

Following the letter opening in which he highlighted God's work through the death and resurrection of Jesus, Paul dramatically challenges the Galatian readers in chapter 1, verses 6–10, about accepting any pseudo-gospel for the one that he delivered to them.[50] Paul repeatedly refers to the gospel and the presentation of the gospel within this section, revealing its importance in the letter. The section crescendos in verses 8 and 9 with the repeated command *anathema estō*, cursing anyone who would preach a gospel different than the initial one he delivered to these readers. This double imperative highlights the fact that some are presenting a distortion of the gospel that the Galatian believers are being tempted to follow. Those presenting this pseudo-gospel want to gain the approval of people. Their motivation stands in contrast to Paul's, who only wants God's approval (1:10). This paragraph primarily concerns the second and third elements in the notional structure of a hortatory text as it introduces and previews the key rationale behind the writing of this letter. It presents the problem at hand in the writing of this letter: desertion of the gospel presented by Paul

---

48. This reflects a simple three-part structuring of the letter. I argue that with 4:12 Paul begins a new letter part, distinct from the letter's body, that is marked by the onset of imperative mood verbs that call the readers to specific actions. This is reflected in the segmentation of the letter toward the end of this chapter and labeled as paraenesis. I am not advocating the notion that paraenesis should be separated from exposition since exposition grounds paraenesis in Paul's letters. Yet the presence of imperative mood verbs seem to appear within Paul's letters after a usually lengthy section of exposition and form a distinct part.

49. This proposed structure most closely resembles that of Schreiner, *Galatians*, 58–59, and to a lesser extent Longenecker, *Galatians*, cix, who points out the difficulty of segmenting 4:12–6:10. He actually divides it into two sections, 4:12–5:12 and 5:13–6:10, because he sees the first section as dealing with exhortations directed toward the Judaizing threat and the latter section focused on general exhortations against libertine tendencies. I have chosen to keep them together, because at 4:12 Paul begins to use imperatives to call the readers to specific actions for the first time in the letter, and this verbal mood remains present throughout the rest of the letter.

50. The normal pattern in the Pauline letter corpus has a thanksgiving segment here. The typical explanation for its exclusion is that this reveals the severity of the situation for Paul in that he moves directly into the problem at hand. He leaves the thanksgiving out so that the Galatian readers see how grave the situation is. In a recent article, Van Voorst, "Why Is There No Thanksgiving Period," 153–72, challenges this explanation as he shows that thanksgiving sections were not common in ancient letter writing and the Galatian readers would not have known that Paul left one out because they would not have been familiar with his practice of including one in his letters.

for a different gospel that is really no gospel (1:6–7). Further, it issues an implicit command for the Galatian readers to reject this false gospel as it explicitly curses anyone who would preach another gospel other than the one initially presented by Paul to them.

In Galatians 1:11–2:21, Paul narrates for these readers his history with the gospel. In contrast to those described in 1:6–10, Paul does not preach a gospel that stems from or tries to please people (1:11). He received his gospel by a direct revelation of Jesus Christ (1:12). He supports this over the next paragraphs by rehearsing for them his gospel ministry which God ordained, not an individual or group. Although he was advancing in Judaism, God imparted his grace to Paul and called him to preach to the Gentiles through a revelation of his Son; no apostolic authority was necessary to confirm this reality (1:13–17). While he did encounter Cephas and James during the early years of his ministry, Paul did not receive an apostolic calling from them, but only a recognition by the churches of Judea that he was proclaiming the gospel that in his earlier life he tried to destroy (1:18–24). Even at his private meeting with the leadership in the Jerusalem church, Paul simply presented the gospel message he was preaching among the Gentiles, and despite pressure from some to add enslaving elements to his gospel, the influential leaders and apostles recognized Paul's apostolic authority in his mission to the Gentiles and received him in fellowship, while not adding anything to his message (2:1–10). Further, he confronted an apostle, Peter, about his inconsistency with the gospel when he submitted to the pressure of the circumcision group to separate from Gentiles (2:11–14). In this lengthy narration,[51] Paul builds his credibility, the first aspect of hortatory texts, by showing how the gospel he preached came by direct revelation from God through an encounter with Jesus Christ (1:13–16) not by some authoritative person or group (1:17–2:10). Even the apostles simply recognized Paul's mission as valid; they did not authorize him for his mission (2:6–10). In regards to the second element of hortatory

---

51. This narrative discourse (1:11–2:21) is actually embedded within the larger hortatory discourse of the letter. As Longacre (*Grammar of Discourse*, 16) points out, discourses typically embed other discourses of the same or different discourse types. This phenomenon is actually labeled *recursion* and a good explanation of it is found in Hwang, "Recursion in the Paragraph," 461. It occurs when "a unit at any given level might be a constituent on that same level," such that a phrase may occur in a phrase, a clause in a clause, or as here a discourse within a discourse. For further explanation of this phenomenon occurring at the discourse level, see Longacre, *Grammar of Discourse*, 280–81.

texts, Paul also hints at (2:1–5) and more explicitly details (2:11–14) how he has encountered aspects of this false gospel in the past.

The narrative section ends with Paul's explanation of his gospel message in which he contrasts *Christ faith*[52] with works of the law (Gal 2:15–21).[53] As Jewish believers, people like Paul and Peter knew that a person did not receive right standing with God based on the works of the law but by Christ faith (2:16). Paul then addresses a potential inconsistency by discussing the issue of sin or breaking a law: while seeking right standing in Christ shows one to be a sinner, this does not mean that Christ promotes sin (2:17); the true transgressor is the one who would try to rebuild something that they tore down—right standing with God through law-keeping (2:18). He bases this in the reality of what happened in Christ's death (2:19–20): the believer died to law in order that they may live to God. The believer has been crucified with Christ. Subsequently, they no longer live; Christ lives in them; the life they are now living is one lived in Christ faith because of what he accomplished for them in his sacrifice. If right standing with God could come through the law, then Christ's death was for nothing (2:21).[54] In

---

52. Following the lead of Moo, *Galatians*, 23, *Christ faith* is used to translate *pisteōs Iēsou Christou*, because it shows ambivalence to the much greater discussion of how to interpret this phrase. A full review of this discussion goes beyond the scope of this paper. Highlighting the authors cited in this chapter, Hayes, *The Faith of Jesus Christ*, especially 141–62, and Wright, *Paul and the Faithfulness of God*, 836–51, argue for the phrase being read as a subjective genitive construction, referring to Christ's faith/faithfulness, while Schreiner, *Galatians*, 163–6, and Moo, *Galatians*, 38–48, argue for the phrase being read as a subjective genitive construction, referring to the believer's faith in Jesus Christ. I find the arguments for an objective genitive reading more convincing.

53. This section continues and concludes the encounter with Peter at Antioch as marked by the use of the first person plural pronoun "we" (*hēmeis*) in 2:15, the first plural verb forms in vv. 16 and 17, and the close connection of vv. 18ff. with v. 17 indicated by the conjunction "for" (*gar*). At the same time, it introduces key elements that will be discussed in Paul's continued argument throughout the rest of the letter (Moo, *Galatians*, 153). It seems to function, then, as the crux or thesis statement of his argument going forward (Betz, *Galatians*, 113–14; Witherington, *Grace in Galatia*, 38, 169–73).

54. The purpose of this embedded narrative needs to be addressed. Longacre (*Grammar of Discourse*, 35–6) posits a notional structure of narrative that involves the movement of plot through the stages of exposition, inciting moment, developing conflict, climax, denouement (the loosening of tension), final suspense, and conclusion. It goes beyond the scope of this chapter to delineate a full explanation of the notional structure of this embedded narrative, but primary to understanding narrative is locating peak, which, according to Longacre, can be overtly marked in the surface structure by a number of different features (38–48). The peak of this narrative seems to be found in the incident in 2:11–21 as the pace of the narrative slows down (an indicator of peak) to focus on one specific incident in which an apostle confronts another apostle. A further

regards to the elements found in hortatory texts, this paragraph focuses the presentation of the problem (second element) to the key elements regarding the two gospels that have been presented to the readers—right standing through works of law or through Christ faith.

In Galations 3:1–4:31, Paul supports his claim that right standing with God comes through Christ faith and not works of law, and appeals to his readers to embrace this gospel truth.[55] He begins by asking a series of questions concerning their reception of the Spirit (3:1–6). Did they receive the Spirit by faith or works of the law? Obviously, like Abraham, they responded in faith to God's message. Paul concludes that the true children of Abraham are those who believe, because the Old Testament anticipates the blessing of Abraham on the nations, curses everyone who fails to keep the law, and announces that the righteous live by faith. Christ redeemed us by becoming that curse in order that the Gentiles could receive Abraham's blessing, the promised Spirit (3:7–14). Paul bases all of this in the covenant made by God with Abraham, something the law, coming later, could not nullify (3:15–18). Paul argues that the law was necessary because of sin and transgression. The law is not opposed to the promises of God because it cannot impart life; rather it served as a guardian until the work of Jesus Christ came and could give right standing with God based on faith (3:19–25). In Jesus Christ, all, without discrimination, through faith are children of God, Abraham's seed, and heirs of promise (3:26–29). God accomplished this for all those enslaved under the forces of this world by sending his Son to redeem those under law into adoption as sons and by sending his Spirit into the hearts of believers (4:1–7). Why, now that they have come to be known by God, would they want to enslave themselves again to observance of traditions that seem to indicate they are embracing teaching contrary to the gospel Paul presented to them (4:8–11)?

---

indication is the shift from narrative to actual dialogue at 2:14, as well as the shift in participant reference from second person singular to first plural to first singular within the dialogue itself. The conflation of these indicators, typical peak markers, set these verses off as the peak of the narrative. The concluding elements of the narrative notional structure are missing in this analysis due to the way Paul incorporates this incident into the larger hortatory discourse to bring out the key problem facing these Galatian readers. Resolution is found in recognizing the problem of seeking right standing based on works of law and embracing the gospel by standing firm on the message first delivered by Paul.

55. The transition at 3:1 is marked by the use of an interjection, plus the nominative of address or vocative (*ō anoētoi galatai*) and the use of second person plurals to move the focus from Paul's past experience and understanding of the gospel to the situation in Galatia (Moo, *Galatians*, 179).

CONVERGENCE

In Galations 4:12–31, Paul makes an appeal to follow his teaching that right standing comes through faith and not works of law. He pleads with them to pattern their life after his. He is puzzled by why, after their initial reception of him and his ministry, they would become his enemy (4:12–16). He admits that he is perplexed why they would be zealous for teachers that would alienate him from them (4:17–20). Again, Paul draws from the story of Abraham in the Old Testament to ground his understanding of the present situation (4:21–31). The two women who bore children for Abraham stand for two covenants: Hagar for Mount Sinai and its covenant that bore children to be slaves; and the mother of Isaac, who is truly free and bore children of promise. Paul reassures these believers that they are children of the free woman.

In regards to the notional structure of Galatians,[56] this section primarily focuses on the second element (presentation of problem/situation) as it details the outworking of key elements of the law and the work of Christ, illustrates Paul's point from the example of Abraham, and answers a rebuttal concerning the purpose of the law (3:1–25). It concludes with Paul's appeal to the readers to follow his example and reject those who would contradict it. He intersperses positive motivation (the fourth element of the notional structure) for those who accept his gospel: they are the true seed of Abraham; heirs of his promises; sons of God; possessors of the Holy Spirit (3:26–29; 4:7). Further, he ends this section contrasting the positive outcome, freedom, of the true gospel with the negative outcome,

---

56. Using Longacre's ("Discourse Strategy," 110–1; *Grammar of Discourse*, 34) scheme for notional structure, this entire section (Gal 3:1–4:31) serves as an embedded persuasive discourse, a subset of behavioral discourse. Persuasive discourse "aims at influencing beliefs and values" and consists of the following: "1) presentation (sometimes in considerable detail) of a problem or question; 2) proposed solution or answer; 3) supporting argumentation which may or may not include appeal to the authority or experience of the text producer; and 4) an appeal to give credence or to adopt certain values" (ibid., 34). In just a cursory reading of this stretch of Galatians, the text can be explained along this notional structure as follows: 3:1–5 (element 1: question concerning their reception of Spirit by law or faith); 3:6 (element 2: proposed solution in form of Old Testament quotation of Abraham's faith); 3:7–4:11 (element 3: argumentation supporting faith as basis of right standing with God); 4:12–31 (element 4: Paul's appeal for them to follow his example and accept his teaching). Recognizing that in this stretch of text Paul seeks to persuade his audience to embrace his view of the gospel and follow his example (ultimately culminating in their faith-motivated obedience to the commands that follow in 5:1) seems to contradict those who primarily view this stretch of text as narrative (Hays, *The Faith of Jesus Christ*, 6–9; Wright, *Paul and the Faithfulness of God*, 862). The elements found throughout the whole of this embedded stretch of text align more closely with persuasive discourse than narrative discourse.

slavery, of the false teachers (4:28–31). Paul accomplishes the third element by mitigating the command criterion, something he will make explicit in what follows, through his use of rhetorical questioning (especially 4:9, 15–16, 21, and 30) and his appeal to follow him (4:12).[57]

Beginning with 5:1, Paul explicitly exhorts the Galatian readers to embrace the gospel he has presented and to stand in their freedom by walking by the Spirit.[58] Based on what he has just delineated concerning the necessity of faith and the futility of works of law, they must stand firm in their previous faith and not subject themselves again to slavery (5:1). He tells them to listen to what he is saying: if they receive circumcision and fully embrace the teaching that the law will provide right standing with God, the work of Christ will be of no benefit, and they will have fallen from grace (5:2–7). He points out that certain teachers have cut in on them and are preventing them from obeying the truth; he wishes that they would just go the whole way with their promotion of circumcision and emasculate themselves (5:7–12). In relation to notional structure, this section brings the third element (commands) to the forefront. In 5:1, Paul explicitly commands these readers to stand firm and not re-burden themselves with slavery by turning towards the law for right standing through the act of circumcision (a rehearsal of the situation being addressed, element 2, in vv. 2–4 and 7–8). He again primarily uses negative motivation through warning (element 4) in 5:2–12 to bring about acceptance of these commands, but he also expresses his confidence that they will follow his teaching (5:10).

Following the strong exhortation to stay the course with their initial faith in Jesus Christ alone, Paul details for them what freedom in Jesus Christ through the presence of his Spirit looks like in action (Gal 5:13–6:10).[59] Rather than using freedom to indulge their flesh, they should serve

---

57. Longacre, *Grammar of Discourse*, 11, points out that rhetorical questions in hortatory texts may be used by a text producer to reprimand as well as to teach. In this stretch of text, these questions also work to introduce the embedded persuasive discourse.

58. The most prominent indicator of this shift to exhortation is the use of the imperative mood that appears here and throughout the rest of the letter. Although imperatives occur earlier at Galatians 1:8–9 in Paul's curse upon anyone presenting a gospel other than the one he previously delivered and in a formulaic expression in 3:7, from here on they call the readers to specific actions (Witherington, *Grace in Galatia*, 39; Schreiner, *Galatians*, 513).

59. As Schreiner, *Galatians*, 281, points out, this section should not be seen as a new transition in Paul's thought, but rather a continuation of the same argument that runs through the entire letter; *contra* both Longenecker, *Galatians*, 187 and 235, and Moo, *Galatians*, 339, who indicate a break here.

one another through love (5:13–15). They must live their lives by the Spirit and not gratify their flesh, because the Spirit and flesh are at enmity with each other, as evidenced by the works of the flesh and the fruit that the Spirit bears (5:16–26). They are responsible to sow to the Spirit (by restoring a sinning brother or sister, carrying other's burdens, examining and performing their own responsibilities within the church, and financially supporting their teachers) rather than sowing to the flesh in order to receive eternal life as opposed to destruction (6:1–10). This section primarily displays the third and fourth notional structure elements. The numerous commands (element 3) found in this section show what gospel living, using freedom to love one another and ordering life by and through the power of the Spirit, looks like. Paul motivates the acceptance of this way of living by negative (5:15; 5:21b; 6:8a) and positive reinforcement (6:8b–9).[60]

The letter concludes (Gal 6:11–18) with typical letter closing formulae and presents a final summary of the key argument presented in the letter body. Paul notifies his readers that he is writing this final section with his own hand (6:11) before laying out one last time the contrast between the false teachers and himself. Those prompting the Galatians to be circumcised are motivated by their need to impress others and their avoidance of persecution (6:12–13). Paul boasts only in Jesus's cross because all that truly matters is the new creation ushered in by Jesus's work through his death and resurrection (6:14–15). He makes a final appeal to his readers to follow this teaching, because they are the true Israel of God, the heirs of the promises to Abraham (6:16); further, they are not to let anyone challenge his message of the true gospel, because his scars for the cross mark where his allegiances lie (6:17). In this brief conclusion, Paul reveals all four elements of hortatory texts. He establishes his authority (element 1) by mentioning the persecution he has endured for the message of Jesus. He restates the problem (element 2) that has been addressed throughout the letter in 6:12–13, and implicitly calls the readers to embrace his approach through his testimony of boasting only in the cross of Christ (6:14). He motivates them to embrace his view (element 4) by stating for them the only thing that truly matters, the new creation (6:15), which they will receive and thus prove that they truly are the Israel of God if they follow his teaching here and stop entertaining the opposing view (element 3 in 6:16–17a).

---

60. The final paragraph, 6:7–10, can be seen as a microcosm of the entire section as it serves as a summary of the central commands and motivations found throughout it.

The Logic of Paul

Standing back and looking at the larger movements of the letter, one can see that the notional structure aligns well with the major parts of the Pauline letter form. The letter opening (Gal 1:1–5) begins to establish the authority/credibility of Paul and his message. Interestingly, Paul's authority is derivative from the ultimate authority, God. The Father raised Jesus from the dead (1:1), and Jesus willingly sacrificed himself to rescue us from this evil age in accord with the Father's will (1:4). Paul as preacher of the gospel to these Gentile readers seeks to defend this message, handed to him by God, not himself. The letter body begins (1:6–10) with a brief summary, displaying elements 2–4 of hortatory discourse structure, in which Paul calls his readers to reject (mitigated command/exhortation) anyone who presents a gospel contrary to the one he first preached (presentation of problem) by condemning such false teachers (motivation through threat). Through an extended narrative, Paul establishes the authority (element 1), again stemming from a revelation of Jesus Christ, of the gospel that he has delivered (1:11–2:14). In 2:15–21, Paul bridges from his past experiences with the gospel to a presentation of the problem of requiring the addition of works of law for right standing with God. Through the use of a lengthy persuasive discourse, Paul elaborates the central problem at hand, trying to attain right standing with God through works of law rather than faith (3:1–4:11; element 2), and appeals to these readers to follow his understanding of the gospel (4:12–31; element 3). Beginning with 5:1, Paul issues direct commands (element 3) for these readers to stand firm in the gospel initially presented through the power of the Spirit (5:1–6:10). He concludes this section with both negative and positive motivation (element 4) to carry out the commands presented here (6:7–9). The letter closing presents again all four elements in one final appeal for these readers to embrace the gospel (6:11–18). In summary, the notional structure of hortatory discourse aligns with the Pauline letter structure as follows: letter opening (1:1–5)—element 1: authority of text producer; letter body (1:6–4:11)[61]—elements 1 and 2: authority of text producer and presentation of problem; paraenesis[62]

---

61. This section begins with a recitation of the central problem at hand (Gal 1:6–10) and then proceeds to establish Paul's credibility and persuade the readers to follow his understanding of the gospel through the embedded narrative (1:11–2:21) and persuasive (3:1–4:31) discourses.

62. *Paraenesis* is used here to label a section in which commanding elements come to the forefront as main verbs. This shows that the direct appeal through mitigated commands (Gal 4:12–31) in the embedded persuasive discourse (3:1–4:31), overlaps with and leads into the commands section of the larger hortatory text (4:12–6:10).

CONVERGENCE

(4:12–6:10)—elements 3 and 4: issuing of commands and motivation to keep them; letter closing (6:11–18)—summary with all four elements.

CONCLUSION

This chapter has sought to show that Paul displayed a consistent logic by analyzing one particular letter, Galatians. An analysis performed according to the criteria of Longacre's discourse typology reveals that Galatians as a whole demonstrates itself to be hortatory discourse. In this discourse, Paul attempts to affect belief and behavior by defending and arguing for his understanding of the gospel before directly commanding the Galatians to stand firm in it and not embrace false teaching that adds works of law to faith. While some rhetorical approaches have come to similar conclusions,[63] suspicion remains that Paul could have and would have done this overtly through the categories of Greco-Roman rhetoric. This chapter began with Wright's discussion of Paul's logic and its contribution to Wright's proposal that it makes up one of the three key elements of Paul's worldview through which he understood God's great salvation narrative. Wright describes Paul's logic more theologically and wholistically than what I attempted here, but the findings of what make up the heart or object of that logic are quite similar: the gospel—God's work through the death of Jesus Christ—faith rather than works of law; the presence and power of the Spirit in believers' lives, lived out in the church community.[64] There must be something to the idea of an underlying logic to Paul, if vastly different approaches can tease out the same essential core.

---

63. Longenecker (see his *Galatians* outline page at the beginning of the commentary) comes to similar conclusions concerning the main movements of the letter, but it is difficult to ascertain if he gets there using epistolary or rhetorical approaches, since his presentation and conclusions are a mixture of the two. Surprisingly, he provides little rationale for how he arrived at his outline in the introduction to the commentary.

64. Wright, *Paul and the Faithfulness of God*, 1381–83. Wright argues that Paul uses "faith" to speak of God's faithfulness, both of the Father to the covenant and the Son through his life, death, and resurrection. While these statements are true, I remain unconvinced that is what Paul was referring to when he speaks of the exercising of faith in Galatians or his other letters.

BIBLIOGRAPHY

Aune, David E. *The New Testament in Its Literary Environment.* LEC 8. Philadelphia: Westminster, 1987.

Betz, Hans D. *Galatians: A Commentary on Paul's Letter to the Churches in Galatia.* Hermeneia. Philadelphia: Fortress, 1979.

Doty, William. *Letters in Primitive Christianity.* Guides to Biblical Scholarship, New Testament Series. Philadelphia: Fortress, 1973.

Hayes, Richard B. *The Faith of Jesus Christ: The Narrative Substructure of Galatians 3:1-4:11.* 2nd ed. Grand Rapids, MI: Eerdmans, 2002.

Hester, J. D. "Epideictic Rhetoric and Persona in Galatians 1 and 2." In *The Galatians Debate: Contemporary Issues in Rhetorical and Historical Interpretation,* edited by Mark D. Nanos, 181–96. Peabody, MA: Hendrickson, 2002.

Hwang, Shin J. J. "Recursion in the Paragraph as a Unit of Discourse Development." *Discourse Processes* 12 (1989) 461–77.

Kennedy, G. A. *New Testament Interpretation through Rhetorical Criticism.* Chapel Hill: University of North Carolina Press, 1984.

Klauck, Hans-Josef. *Ancient Letters and the New Testament: A Guide to Context and Exegesis.* Waco, TX: Baylor University Press, 2006.

Longacre, Robert E. "Discourse Peak as Zone of Turbulence." In *Beyond The Sentence: Discourse and Sentential Form,* edited by Jessica R. Wirth, 81–98. Ann Arbor, MI: Karoma, 1985.

———. "The Discourse Strategy of an Appeals Letter." In *Discourse Description: Diverse Linguistic Analyses of a Fund Raising Text,* edited by W. Mann and S. Thompson, 109–30. Amsterdam: Benjamins, 1992.

———. *The Grammar of Discourse,* 2nd ed. Topics in Language and Linguistics. New York: Plenum, 1996.

———. "The Paragraph as a Grammatical Unit." In *Discourse and Syntax,* edited by T. Givon, 115–34. New York: Academic, 1979.

Longenecker, Richard N. *Galatians.* WBC. Dallas: Word, 1990.

Moo, Douglas J. *Galatians.* BECNT. Grand Rapids, MI: Baker, 2013.

Murphy-O'Connor, Jerome. *Paul the Letter-Writer: His World, His Options, His Skills.* GNS 41. Collegeville, MN: Liturgical, 1995.

Porter, Stanley E. "Exegesis of the Pauline Letters, including the Deutero-Pauline Letters." In *A Handbook to the Exegesis of the New Testament,* edited by Stanley E. Porter, 503–54. Leiden: Brill, 2002.

———. "Paul of Tarsus and His Letters." In *Handbook of Classical Rhetoric in the Hellenistic Period, 330 B.C.-A.D. 400,* edited by Stanley E. Porter, 533–85. Leiden: Brill, 2001.

Porter, Stanley E., and Sean A. Adams. *Paul and the Ancient Letter Form.* Pauline Studies 6. Leiden, Netherlands: Brill, 2010.

Reed, Jeffrey T. *A Discourse Analysis of Philippians: Method and Rhetoric in the Debate Over Literary Integrity.* JSNTSup 136. Sheffield, England: Sheffield Academic, 1997.

Roetzel, Calvin J. *The Letters of Paul: Conversations in Context.* 5th ed. Louisville: Westminster John Knox, 2009.

Schnider, Franz, and Werner Stenger. *Studien Zum Neutestamentlichen Briefformular.* NTTS 11. Leiden: E. J. Brill, 1987.

Schreiner, Thomas R. *Galatians.* ZECNT. Grand Rapids, MI: Zondervan, 2010.

Stowers, Stanley K. *Letter Writing in Greco-Roman Antiquity*. LEC 5. Philadelphia: Westminster, 1986.
Van Voorst, Robert E. "Why is There No Thanksgiving Period in Galatians? An Assessment of an Exegetical Commonplace." *JBL* 129 (2010) 153–72.
Weima, Jeffrey A. D. *Neglected Endings: The Significance of the Pauline Letter Closings*. JSNTSup 101. Sheffield, England: *JSOT*, 1994.
White, John L. "Ancient Greek Letters." In *Greco-Roman Literature and the New Testament: Selected Forms and Genres*, edited by David E. Aune, 85–105. Atlanta: Scholars, 1988.
———. "Apostolic Mission and Apostolic Message: Congruence in Paul's Epistolary Rhetoric, Structure and Imagery." In *Origins and Method: Towards a New Understanding of Judaism and Christianity*, edited by Bradley H. McLean, 145–61. Sheffield, England: Sheffield Academic, 1993.
———. *The Form and Function of the Body of the Greek Letter: A Study of the Letter-Body in the Non-Literary Papyri and in Paul the Apostle*. SBLDS 2. Missoula, MT: University of Montana Press, 1972.
Witherington, Ben. *Grace in Galatia: A Commentary on St. Paul's Letter to the Galatians*. Grand Rapids, MI: Eerdmans, 1998.
Wright. N. T. *Paul and the Faithfulness of God*. Minneapolis: Fortress, 2013.

8

PATRISTIC EPISTEMOLOGY

Ryan M. Clevenger

INTRODUCTION

In order to get a glimpse at the kinds of epistemological concerns that early Christian writers had and the solutions they proposed, I will examine the writings of the fourth-century Christian leader, thinker, and writer Gregory of Nazianzus (c. 329/330–c. 390/391). Gregory is a fitting case for seeing how early Christians thought through the intersection of theology and philosophy. He came from a wealthy land-owning family that provided him with a substantial classical education, exposing him to the best of the Greek rhetorical and philosophical traditions.[1] Yet Gregory also drank deep within his own Christian tradition, especially from the well of Scripture that profoundly shaped his theology.[2] While Gregory did not write "systematic" treatises, he found creative ways to express his ideas in orations, poems, and letters.[3] These features of Gregory's background, along with

---

1. For a summary of the type of education Gregory most likely received, see Reuther, *Rhetor and Philosopher*, 18–28.

2. While Gregory left no commentaries, Gregory's works are saturated with Scripture and show the breadth and depth of his knowledge of them. For a recent examination of Gregory's understanding and hermeneutics of Scripture, see Fulford, *Divine Eloquence*.

3. Forty-four orations (the forty-fifth is made up almost entirely from *Or.* 38), two

the fact that he is less widely known in the non-scholarly English-speaking world than someone like Augustine, justify taking a closer look at Gregory.

My examination of Gregory will first begin with his understanding of the God-given human intellect as the basis for knowledge of God. Secondly, I will look at what Gregory considers to be barriers to knowledge of God; namely, sin and the infinite ontological gap that exists between God and creation. Thirdly, I will briefly look at how Gregory's friends Basil of Caesarea and Gregory of Nyssa overcame this infinite ontological gap in the Eunomian controversy through the idea of *epinoia* (concept), an idea that Gregory of Nazianzus interestingly did not exploit. Instead, fourthly, I will show that Gregory overcomes the obstacles of the infinite ontological gap through the use of *phantasia* (mental image), a term with a rich rhetorical and philosophical tradition. By using *phantasia*, Gregory both shows how we have knowledge of God as embodied creatures and reinforces the goodness of creation despite the limitations it imposes on our knowledge of God because such mental images are used by God to draw us further on toward knowledge of God.

Before I begin, I must give a few notes of caution. First, Gregory did not explore epistemological questions in isolation from his theology. For Gregory, and for many—Christian and pagan—during this time, *theological* epistemology was an important question, more so than we may think today.[4] Gregory himself is more concerned with questions of theological epistemology than epistemology in general, so I will focus my attention there. Secondly, when discussing the intersection of theology and philosophy in the early church, the question of influence is inevitably asked: Was Gregory influenced by Platonism? How much was he influenced by Aristotelianism?

---

hundred forty-nine letters, and about seventeen thousand lines of poetry (Daley, *Gregory of Nazianzus*, 1).

4. For the similarity between pagan and Christian questions concerning theological epistemology, see Elm, *Sons of Hellenism*. In this work she compares Gregory of Nazianzus with the Emperor Julian ("the Apostate") and demonstrates how much they have in common, including questions of how political leaders were supposed to know divinity in order to lead their people to it. Mark Edwards has also pointed to the concern of Second Sophistic authors such as Dio Chrysostom, Maximus of Tyre, and Philostratus to address the issue of theological epistemology from the rhetorical tradition (*Image, Word and God*, 68–74). Gregory can be said to follow in the line of these Second Sophistic authors and rightly could be called, as Frederick Norris has described him, a philosophical rhetorician. That is, he embodied the concerns of both the philosophical and rhetorical traditions and freely drew from both to address contemporary theological issues (Norris, *Faith Gives Fullness*, 17–39).

Important as questions of influence are, it seems far easier to assert influence than actually to prove it.[5] While identifying a possible influence may help illuminate what Gregory is saying, it should not ultimately determine what Gregory means, since he was an eclectic who was able to synthesize various ideas from across the Greek philosophical traditions.[6] The question I am concerned with here is not whether Gregory *adopted* the Greek rhetorical and philosophical traditions—he most certainly did—but how Gregory *adapted* those traditions for his own purposes.

CREATED TO KNOW GOD

For Gregory, humanity was made for and implanted with the capability of knowing God. The primary locus for this discussion centers around the rational soul, or the intellect.[7] Gregory understands the intellect as the central aspect of the soul implanted by God into flesh, by which we both consider the nature of God and contemplate God in our life of prayer.[8] Coming from God the intellect naturally seeks to return to its source. When Gregory says this, it can give the impression that he disparages the created body. Is Gregory just blindly smuggling in Platonism in Christian dress? Take the following example:

> [The soul] as I regard it and as I hear from wise men, is
> a divine emanation which comes down to us from above, either
> the entire soul or its ruler and guide, the mind [*nous*].

---

5. "The difficulty with such assumptions [about influence] lies both in their unverifiability and their too-easy assumption of causality; one can certainly show similarities between one assertion and another, but with much greater difficulty does one establish that the reason for the similarity lies in influence. In part, the problem lies in our having little firm evidence about what particular patristic writers had and had not read (though of course some absorption of philosophical views may have come from *ouï-dire*). Even more importantly, however, the simple fact that writer X read writer Y does not in itself establish that X adopted view Z because it was found in Y's work." Williams, *Divine Sense*, 8.

6. McGuckin, *Saint Gregory of Nazianzus*, 57–58. For specific examples of Gregory's eclectic attitude towards philosophy, see Norris, "Of Thorns and Roses."

7. Sometimes Gregory calls the intellectual soul the image of God (*Or.* 38.11). Gregory is fluid with his terminology and so can speak of the intellect or mind (*nous*) in terms of *noeros* (*Or.* 38.11), *logikos* (*Or.* 12.1; 28.13; 30.20; 32.9), *logos* (*Or.* 16.15; 21.2; 28.16), *dianoia* (*Or.* 7.21; 28.11; 28.28), and *hegēmōn* (*Or.* 39.7) (Ellverson, "Dual Nature," 23, 100).

8. In this, Gregory is not unique; see Williams, *Divine Sense*, 238.

> Therefore its one and only and essential pursuit is to be raised aloft, to be united with God, and always and by all means to look upon that which is akin to it, the while being scarcely subjected to bodily affections.[9]

While the intellect strives to know God, it must also contend with the dynamics of the body that draw it away from its natural pursuit. Is the body bad on this account? Inasmuch as it distracts us from knowing God, it seems so. Yet Gregory's account of the body is more nuanced than this—grounded as it is in his belief in the duality of human nature between soul and body[10]—and actually plays an important role in his theological epistemology. I will discuss these things in more detail below, but for now the point to keep in mind is that for Gregory humans were made to know and be in communion with God.

One of Gregory's favorite images for the intellect is that of light. Light is a particularly apt image to convey what Gregory thinks about the intellect. First, to call the intellect of human nature "light" points to a likeness to God who is the true Light and the source of all other light (or, rational beings).[11] This likeness is important for Gregory because he holds to the principle that like is known by like: "The discovery [of the divine nature] will take place . . . when this God-like, divine thing, I mean our mind and reason, *mingles with its kin*, when the copy returns to the pattern it now longs after."[12] If God did not give humanity a likeness to God, then it would be impossible for humanity—as purely material creatures without this like-

---

9. *Carmina moralia* 1.2.10, 60–66 (PG 37, 685) (Egan, *Knowledge and Vision*, 83). That Gregory more than once refers to the soul as an "emanation" should not be understood in the Neoplatonic sense. Gregory firmly holds to an ontological distinction between creator and creation that prevents him from thinking of the soul merely quantitatively different from its source, and this distinction has ramifications for his epistemology as I will discuss below.

10. Gregory is not always terminologically consistent when describing human nature. Sometimes he emphasizes its dual nature, other times he elaborates to three (*Or.* 32.9), or four parts (*Or.* 29.8). In general, though, the distinction between the immaterial soul and material body (or whatever terms Gregory may employ) is primary; see Ellverson, "Dual Nature," 21. Thus, the intellect—whether or not it is actually a distinct *part*—should be understood in the context of the soul; see Pinault, *Le Platonisme*, 48.

11. In *Or.* 40.5, Gregory outlines three levels of "light": the first is God, the highest light, the second is the angels, and the third is human beings who are called "a light because of the power of reason" in them (Harrison, *Festal Orations*, 101).

12. *Oration* 28.17 (Williams and Wickham, *On God and Christ*, 49–50, emphasis added).

ness—to know God.[13] Secondly, light has had epistemological overtones in the Greek philosophical tradition. One of the most famous examples of this is Plato's analogy of the sun in *Republic* 508 A–B, where the Form of the Good is likened to the sun in that it illuminates all the other Forms in the *intellectual* world and makes knowledge of them possible.[14] In *Oration* 21, Gregory reworks this analogy so that God becomes the highest light by which the eyes of our mind are illumined:

> For God is to intelligible things what the sun is to the things of sense. The one lightens the visible, the other the invisible, world. The one makes our bodily eyes to see the sun, the other makes our intellectual natures to see God. And, as that, which bestows on the things which see and are seen the power of seeing and being seen, is itself the most beautiful of visible things; so God, who creates, for those who think, and that which is thought of, the power of thinking and being thought of, is himself the highest of the objects of thought, in whom every desire finds its bourne, beyond whom it can no further go.[15]

For Gregory then, humanity is made to know God through the intellect's likeness to God and through the illuminating activity of God.

THE NOETIC EFFECT OF SIN

While Gregory holds that knowledge of God is something that we were made for, something God equipped us to have, and something that is received only through the activity of God, there are two main obstacles to knowledge of God. The first obstacle I want to look at is human sin, even though Gregory actually spends little time discussing *how* sin distorts knowledge of God. It is hard to say why Gregory does this, though it cannot be that Gregory thinks lightly of sin. Sin for Gregory is something that corrupts the soul and moves one away from God, who is the goal of humanity's existence: "There is one life: to look to life," Gregory says in *Oration* 18.42, "There is one death, sin, for it is the destruction of the soul."[16] Furthermore, while humanity's created existence poses problems for knowledge of God

---

13. "Like known by like" was a common concept in Greek thought (Egan, "Mysticism of Light," 477).
14. Plato, *Republic*, 88–90.
15. *Oration* 21.1 (Gregory, "Select Orations," 269–70).
16. McCauley, *Funeral Orations*, 155.

(more on that later), those who are mired in sin are even less able to grasp with their mind divine things.[17] Knowledge of God can only be attained, then, if the soul flees sin and returns to its likeness to God.[18]

A clue as to why Gregory spends less time on the noetic effects of sin may be found in Gregory's understanding of the fall. In regards to Adam's fall, Gregory takes a view similar to Irenaeus, that Adam fell out of a premature grasp for something that he was meant one day to have (i.e., greater knowledge of God).[19] On the other hand, Lucifer's fall was greater since he was closer in nature to God than humanity—as a mixed nature—would ever be.[20] In *Or.* 28.12, Gregory seems to say that God created humanity in the flesh in order to prevent us from falling like Lucifer by making our striving for God *difficult* in order that we appreciate it more, for "[w]hat is gained by effort is usually kept; what is lightly gained is quickly spurned because it can be gained anew."[21] Thus, God creates in order to provide the opportunity to buffer the foreseen effects of sin: to prevent pride and to increase appreciation of virtue through struggle. Perhaps, then, Gregory does not discuss the noetic effects of sin in detail because he understands sin only within the larger context of our created existence.[22] That is to say, because of his understanding of created existence, sin merely exacerbates the difficulties for knowledge of God inherent in finite rational creatures.

---

17. *Oration* 28.4.

18. "Our unhealed condition arises from our evil and unsubdued nature, and from the exercise of its powers. Our repentance when we sin, is a human action, but an action which bespeaks a good man, belonging to that portion which is in the way of salvation. For if even our dust contracts somewhat of wickedness, and the earthly tabernacle presseth down the upward flight of the soul, which at least was created to fly upward, yet let the image be cleansed from filth, and raise aloft the flesh, its yoke-fellow, lifting it on the wings of reason" (*Or.* 16.15 [Gregory, "Select Orations," 252]).

19. *Oration* 38.12.

20. *Oration* 28.12. On the angelic nature being closer to the divine, see *Or.* 31.15.

21. Williams and Wickham, *On God and Christ*, 45–46. A similar statement can be found in *Or.* 38.11 where, in describing the dual nature of the first man, Gregory says that the flesh was given in order that suffering might reign in the pride that would come from having a spiritual nature.

22. For a detailed discussion of this, see Ellverson, "Dual Nature," 67–68.

INFINITE GOD AND FINITE CREATION

The second obstacle to knowledge of God, and the one about which Gregory speaks most, is the epistemological limits of created existence. How can finite, limited creatures, subject to constant change and eventual dissolution have knowledge of the infinite, unchanging, and eternal God?[23] In *Or.* 28.4, Gregory succinctly expresses his pessimism: "But mentally to grasp so great a matter is utterly beyond real possibility even so far as the very elevated and devout are concerned, never mind slack and sinking souls. This truth applies to every creature born, to all beings whose view of reality is blocked by this gloom, this gross portion of flesh."[24] Such statements by Gregory scattered throughout his corpus may give the impression that he has a negative view of the body and created existence.[25] However, Gregory balances such statements as these with an equally high estimation of humanity's dignity. Humans are the summit of creation, and their creation in the image of God would be grounds for great boasting. In *Or.* 38.11, Gregory uses antinomy to express the strange mixture of greatness and lowliness that is human nature:

> So he set upon the earth a kind of second world, great in its littleness: another kind of angel, a worshipper[sic] of mixed origins, a spectator of the visible creation and an initiate into the intelligible, king of the things on earth yet ruled from above, earthly and heavenly, subject to time yet deathless, visible and knowable, standing halfway between greatness and lowliness. He is at the same time spirit and flesh: spirit because of grace, flesh because of pride—the one, that he might always remain in being and glorify his

---

23. Gregory describes God as beyond being (*Or.* 6.12), beyond time and space (*Or.* 2.5, 76; 37.2), unapproachable (*Or.* 2.5, 74), beyond quantity (*Or.* 37.2), an ocean of being (*Or.* 28.7), the supreme nature (*Or.* 31.10) who is absolutely unique (*Or.* 28.31), whose existence is radically different from ours (*Or.* 25.17), and surpasses our ability to understand or express in language (*Or.* 30.17).

24. Williams and Wickham, *On God and Christ*, 40–41.

25. Or, take for example, Gregory's view on the utter futility of speech itself: "For all speech is by nature loose and inadequate and, because it is open to challenge, vulnerable, and speech about God all the more so as the subject is more important and the emotion runs higher and the venture is more difficult. What shall we fear? And where then place our trust? Human reason? Speech? The things we hear? We oscillate precariously between three poles: the difficulty of forming a conception of him, the near impossibility of expressing it in words, and the still greater task of finding an ear to receive it in purity" (Vinson, *Select Orations*, 201).

benefactor; the other, that he might suffer, and in suffering come to his senses, and be corrected from his ambitions of grandeur.[26]

Our created state exhibits a tension that further exacerbates the difficulty of attaining knowledge of God. How can these seemingly opposite characteristics of human nature allow for such knowledge?

As much as Gregory admits that the body inhibits knowledge of God, he is unwilling to bypass it. For Gregory, a created rational nature is bound to its created state in such a way that the intellect cannot think *anything* without some corporeality attached to the thought.[27] At times Gregory can speak of the attempt to retreat within ones mind and to block out all corporeal inclinations as one ascends to contemplation of God. In *Or.* 28.3, Gregory uses the figure of Moses and says that he will ascend the mountain to contemplate God, but a cloud and darkness (the human body) blocks his intellectual vision. His corporeality makes such endeavors futile:

> Sight cannot approach its object without the medium of light and atmosphere; fish cannot swim out of water; and no more can embodied beings keep incorporeal company with things ideal. Some corporeal factor of ours will always intrude itself, even if the mind be most fully detached from the visible world and at its most recollected when it attempts to engage with its invisible kin.[28]

Such corporeality being involved in our conception of the divine has two significant implications for his theological epistemology. First, it is therefore necessarily impossible for humans to conceive or comprehend of the divine nature in its totality. If God is by nature infinite and immaterial,

---

26. Daley, *Gregory of Nazianzus*, 122. The use of such antithesis in rhetoric was common in Gregory's time, and it is a technique that Gregory uses often. Such antinomies are employed by Gregory as a "logic" or "grammar" for his theology and theological method (see Harrison, "Illumined from All Sides by the Trinity," 16–17).

27. *Oration* 28.21.

28. *Oration* 28.12 (Williams and Wickham, *On God and Christ*, 46).

how can a materially constructed concept even come close?[29] What we do apprehend is the activity of God as it comes to us:[30]

> Peering in I saw not the nature prime, inviolate, self-apprehended (by "self" I mean the Trinity), the nature as it all abide within the first veil and is hidden by the Cherubim, but as it reaches us at its furthest remove from God, being, so far as I can understand, the grandeur, or as divine David calls it the "majesty" inherent in the created things he has brought forth and governs.[31]

Secondly, since there is nothing in principle that can contain all of the divine nature, there is freedom to use the God-given intellect to try to apprehend the divine nature. That is, since no one concept can contain the divine nature, humans are free to grasp at conceiving God with different terms/phrases or images. While Scripture itself would be a good guide on the images one uses to conceive of the Trinity—and indeed Gregory prefers to use such images—one is not restricted solely to such images.[32]

Why Gregory thinks that we have freedom to use various images and primarily know the activity (instead of the essence) of God can be seen by contrast with the Emperor Julian. The Emperor Julian was a contemporary with Gregory and is most (in)famously known for renouncing his Christian upbringing and attempting to return the Empire back to paganism. Like Gregory, Julian was concerned with appropriate modes for the knowledge

---

29. "It was better to hear the voice of praise than to be an expounder of truths beyond my power; the majesty, and the height, and the dignity, and the pure natures scarce able to contain the brightness of God, Whom the deep covers, Whose secret place is darkness, since He is the purest light, which most men cannot approach unto; Who is in all this universe, and again is beyond the universe, Who is all goodness, and beyond all goodness; Who enlightens the mind, and escapes the quickness and height of the mind, ever retiring as much as He is apprehended, and by His flight and stealing away when grasped, withdrawing to the things above one who is enamoured[sic] of Him" *Oration* 2.76 (Gregory, "Select Orations," 220).

30. It is tempting to read the later Palamite distinction between essence and activity (or energies) back into Gregory. One thing that I think Beeley has persuasively argued is that Gregory does not completely deny knowledge of the essence of God, only that any knowledge one has of God's essence is (and only ever will be) partial, indeed, a mere fraction of the essence of God (*Trinity*, 98–99). Egan (*Knowledge and Vision*) has helpfully pointed to the importance of pre- and post-resurrection knowledge in Gregory, and the importance of 1 Cor 13:12 in this regard. Any knowledge we have now pre-resurrection will pale in comparison to the knowledge of God we have in our completely purified state (Egan, *Knowledge and Vision*, 61–72).

31. *Oration* 28.3 (Williams and Wickham, *On God and Christ*, 39).

32. Norris, "Contemplating the Beautiful," 30.

of God. As the Emperor he saw himself responsible for leading the empire on towards the gods, which first required knowledge of them.[33] In order to do this Julian banned Christians from teaching the Greek classics. Julian justified the ban by making a connection between Greek language and literature and Greek religion. If one did not adhere to the Greek religion, one cannot be trusted to instruct the Greek classics which were—if one properly understood the nature of myth[34]—used to aid one in knowing the gods. Such knowledge, however, was achieved to the fullest extent in the practice of "theurgy."

For Julian, following the Neoplatonist philosopher Iamblichus, theurgy was vital to attaining knowledge of the gods. Principally, theurgy worked by conforming the participant to the inherent structures of the universe by re-enacting through symbolic rituals the activity of the gods.[35] By conforming the participant to the structures inherent in the universe, theurgy allowed all people—philosophers and the uneducated—to ascend the chain of being up to the gods.[36] Corporeal nature is the end product of a series of causes going back to the gods, and to which our soul (preexisting the body in the ethereal realm and there having knowledge of the Forms) is united.[37] For Julian, there was no creator/creation gap as there was for Gregory. Instead, practitioners of theurgy naturally had ontological access to the divine nature.

Gregory, on the other hand, denied this type of an ontological connection, so he must somehow overcome the gap that exists between the infinite God and finite creation.[38] Since the intellect was for Gregory the means by which humans have knowledge of God, I will examine *how* Gregory thinks the intellect can leap the gap. Gregory saw human reason (*logos*) as a gift given by God to all people, and in reality, a gift from the true *Logos*—Christ—which is why he argued so vehemently against Julian's program to kick Christian teachers out of the schools.[39] For Gregory, the role of the

---

33. Elm, *Sons of Hellenism*, 105.
34. Ibid., 113–114.
35. Shaw, *Theurgy*, 45–57.
36. Elm, *Sons of Hellenism*, 128–129.
37. Ibid., 129n135.
38. This difference is also why Gregory's understanding of *theōsis* (a term he coined in *Or.* 4, his first invective against Julian) cannot be said to be platonic; see Maslov, "Limits of Platonism," 447–52.
39. Ibid., 395–96.

reason was twofold: 1) the investigation of impressions left by the sense on the intellect, which are stored in the memory, and 2) expression through speech.[40] My investigation will primarily be concerned with the first role and what Gregory thinks about the cognitive process.

GREGORY'S USE OF *EPINOIA* (CONCEPT)

Before I look at Gregory, however, I want to briefly look at how some other Christians approached the human cognitive process in their theological epistemology. The fourth-century Arian bishop Eunomius of Cyzicus viewed the human cognitive process for knowledge of God as completely futile.[41] Eunomius instead placed a significant burden for knowledge of God on the divine name revealing God's nature. Anything else was merely a human concept (*epinoia*) that could give us no access to the divine nature. Contrary to this, the other two "Cappadocians," Basil of Caesarea and Gregory of Nyssa, made positive use of the idea of concepts and the whole process of conceptualization for knowing and speaking about God in their debates with Eunomius.[42] *Epinoia* has a long history in Greek philosophy

---

40. *Carmina moralia*, 1.2.34, 28–32.

41. Recent scholarship on the Arian controversy has challenged the older idea of a monolithic Arian tradition (see Gregg and Groh, *Early Arianism*; Hanson, *Search*; Ayres, *Nicaea and Its Legacy*; Behr, *Way to Nicaea*, and *Nicene Faith*; and Anatolios, *Retrieving Nicaea*). I used the term here only because it would be more recognizable than *heterousian* or *anomoen*, as Eunomius is sometimes called in the scholarly literature. Eunomius was engaged in a different context than Arius or his associates in the decades following the Council of Nicaea in 325 CE, and his arguments and conclusions bear his own unique stamp. Indeed, there has been recent work that has significantly changed the scholarly understanding of Eunomius. Previously, and in no small part due to the rhetoric of the Cappadocians, Eunomius was seen merely as a rationalist logic-chopper. Recent works by Vaggione (*Eunomius of Cyzicus*), Wiles ("Hair Splitting Dialectician"), and DelCogliano (*Anti-Eunomian*) have shown this not to be the case. A summary of this recent scholarship can be found in Hildebrand, *Basil of Caesarea*, 72–76.

42. Related to *epinoia* is the term *ennoia* (notion), which was important to Stoic and Epicurean epistemology (sometimes qualified as common [*koinē*] or natural [*phusikē*]) and helped them overcome the epistemological objections of skeptics. *Ennoia* "was any ordinary, naturally well-founded concept that is available to the mind as a '"preconception' (*prolēpsis*)" (DelCogliano, *Anti-Eunomian*, 155). A search through *TLG* shows that Gregory uses it only sixteen times, three of which follow the idea of common or natural notion: *Or* 29.16; 31.33; and 34.36. While it may be interesting to look at how Gregory uses this idea, there are two reasons I do not. First, Mark DelCogliano has already thoroughly explored the importance of *ennoia* in Basil of Caesarea, which need not be repeated for Gregory. Secondly, the scarcity of this term and the related idea of *epinoia* in

prior to Gregory, especially under the Stoics, and is put to good use by them to show that, *contra* Eunomius, the names of God could be understood as human conceptions without doing insult to the divine nature.[43]

Gregory of Nazianzus, however, makes little use of the term in the same way that they did. A search of *Thesaurus Linguae Graecae* reveals only twenty-five occurrences of the term in Gregory's corpus, only four of which are relevant here:

1. *Oration* 18.16: For, since every quality of the Godhead is incomprehensible and beyond our power of intellect (*epinoian*), how can the transcendence therein be either conceived or defined?[44]

2. *Oration* 29.13: Thus too there is a single substance, nature, and appellation of God, even though the names are distinguished along with the distinct ideas (*epinoiais*) about him.[45]

3. *Oration* 30.8: Which means that when the natures are distinguished, the titles are differentiated along with the ideas (*epinoiais*).[46]

4. *Oration* 31.15: Yes, but in these cases the universal is only a unity for speculative thought (*epinoia*).[47]

In *Or.* 29.13 and 30.8, Gregory is arguing that the divine names do not apply to the divine nature, and so the nature of the Father and Son cannot be separated (as Eunomius argued). Instead, arguing along the lines of Basil in *Eun.* 1.5–1.9, the names apply to the ideas or concepts that humans have.[48] In *Or.* 18.16, Gregory uses the term to express the limits of our intellectual ability to grasp the infinite divine nature. As for *Or.* 31.15, Gregory is responding to his opponents' argument about seeing the divine nature

---

Gregory leads me to look elsewhere for Gregory's solution to this theological epistemological problem, namely in Gregory's use of *phantasia* (see below).

43. For a detailed description of *epinoia* in Basil, see DelCogliano, *Anti-Eunomian*, 163–71. For a brief history and significance of *epinoia* and Gregory of Nyssa's particular use of it, see Kobusch, "Die Epinoia," 3–20.

44. McCauley, *Funeral Orations*, 132.

45. Williams and Wickham, *On God and Christ*, 81.

46. Ibid., 99.

47. Ibid., 128.

48. DelCogliano and Radde-Gallwitz, *Against Eunomius*, 96–104. For Basil, *epinoia* can refer both to the process of conceptualizing and the end result (i.e., the concept), but Gregory here seems to speak only of the idea and not so much the process of conceptualization.

as a universal in the same way that "humanity" is the universal category of individual people, which would make Gregory a polytheist. Gregory denies the analogy, since the divine nature does not relate to the Trinity in the same way that "humanity" (a mere "speculative thought") relates to individual humans.[49]

Gregory's favorable (yet limited) use of *epinoia* can further be compared to that of Eunomius. Like Gregory, and against Julian, Eunomius did believe in a gap between Creator and creation, but the question was where to draw the line. Gregory and the pro-Nicene party emphatically drew the line between the Trinity and creation. Eunomius, on the other hand, drew the line between the Father and the Son. It is because the Son is created—the highest of all created things and the means through which all other things were brought into being—that knowledge of God was possible, because he reveals the true essence of the divine nature: *unbegotten*.[50] By giving his name, God brings real knowledge of the divine essence, as opposed to concepts (*epinoia*) which Eunomius views as being nothing more than fleeting and vain imaginings of creatures.[51] If there is an infinite gap between Creator and creation, then it would be impossible for creatures to come close to conceptually constructing the divine nature, so God must reveal his nature to humankind, and this God did through God's name.

GREGORY'S USE OF *PHANTASIA*

Instead of bridging the epistemological gap through the idea of *epinoia*, Gregory interestingly employs another term that is revealing for his theological epistemology: *phantasia*.[52] For Gregory,

49. Norris, *Faith Gives Fullness*, 199–200. In this, Gregory is no Social Trinitarian.

50. Unbegotten was a description of God used beginning in the second century and growing in importance up to the fourth (DelCogliano, *Anti-Eunomian*, 97–124).

51. "To say, then, that names are 'tools' in that context is to say that, when they tell us what things are, they do so by putting us *in actual contact* with the essence. What is true in general is true also of God: to know God's Name is to acknowledge the presence in our minds of the Essence it represents. Our knowledge is thus 'real' because in this, as in other instances, the name brings us into contact with a really existing non-material essence whose existence does not depend upon whether or not we are thinking it. To know the name, therefore, is to gain 'real' access to an intelligible reality that really exists independently of ourselves" (Vaggione, *Eunomius of Cyzicus*, 254).

52. I was prompted to look into *phantasia* in Gregory, in part because of Ben Fulford's article "Divine Names." He does a good job of showing how *phantasia* works in Gregory's *Theological Orations*. My analysis of Gregory's use of *phantasia* in his entire

> Our starting-point must be the fact that God cannot be named...
> No man has yet breathed all the air; no mind has yet contained or language embraced God's substance in its fullness. No, we use facts connected with him to outline qualities that correspond, collecting a faint and feeble mental image (*phantasia*) from various quarters. Our noblest theologian is not one who has discovered the whole—our earthly shackles do not permit us the whole—but one whose mental image (*phantasthē*) is by comparison fuller, who has gathered in his mind a richer picture, outline, or whatever we call it, of the truth.[53]

Instead of naming, Gregory says the closest one can get to the divine nature is to construct a mental image (*phantasia*) of God in one's mind.[54]

That Gregory would use this term in this way is particularly interesting for two reasons: 1) *phantasia* has a long philosophical and rhetorical pedigree going back to Plato, and 2) contemporaneous Christians like Evagrius of Pontus—who was an associate of Gregory for a short time—are very suspicious of mental images of the divine.[55] In order to understand the significance of Gregory's position, it will be important to examine first, the background of the term in Greek philosophy and rhetoric and then how Gregory employs it.

Phantasia first appears in the writings of Plato—specifically in the *Republic*, *Theaetetus*, and *Sophist*—and is defined by him as the combination of belief (*doxa*) and perception (*aisthēsis*).[56] Plato makes little use of the term, but it survived to be used extensively by Aristotle. In criticizing Plato's definition, Aristotle constructed his own theory of *phantasia* that placed the faculty of *phantasia* as an intermediary between *aisthēsis* and the various forms of *noēsis* (thought/understanding). This intermediary role ascribed

---

corpus coheres with his analysis of the *Theological Orations*. However, I am most interested in the philosophical and rhetoric background of the term, which he discusses to some extent (226–28), though mostly as it relates to the important shift detailed by Watson (Phantasia *in Classical Thought*) for the term in the works of Philostratus.

53. *Oration* 30.17 (Williams and Wickham, *On God and Christ*, 107–108).

54. Gregory goes on in 30.18 to say that "He who is" and "God" are special names that are probably the best one can do, "He who is" being the best since it is the name God revealed to Moses (i.e., Yahweh).

55. See, for example, Evagrius's *Prayer* 66: "When you pray do not form images of the divine within yourself, nor allow your mind to be impressed with any form, but approach the Immaterial immaterially and you will come to understanding" (Sinkewicz, *Evagrius of Pontus*, 199).

56. Watson, Phantasia *in Classical Thought*, 1, 4.

to *phantasia* is important for Aristotle because it allows him to explain how thought arises from *aisthēsis* while maintaining the deliberative faculty of the intellect. In *On the Soul* 3.3 428a1–2, Aristotle defines *phantasia* as "the process by which we say that an image (*phantasma*) is presented to us, it is one of those faculties or states of mind by which we judge and are either right or wrong."[57] For Aristotle, *aisthēsis* gives rise to *phantasma* in the soul, which can be thought of as a vestige of the object that was perceived. These *phantasmata* are not always noticed if the perceptible (that which is perceived) is still being perceived, but if one is aware of the *phantasmata* when the perceptible is absent, then he/she is exercising the faculty of *phantasia*.[58] *Phantasia* retains the form of the perceptible as well as the value content, and can be stored in the memory for later deliberation when the perceptible is no longer immediately present.[59] Aristotle goes so far as to say that "for this reason as no one could even learn or understand anything without the exercise of perception, so even when we think speculatively, we must have some mental picture of which to think; for mental images are similar to objects perceived except that they are without matter."[60] That a *phantasia* exists without the perceptible opens up the possibility for hallucinations and dreams being considered under this same faculty. Nevertheless, *phantasia* remains an important part of Aristotle's cognitive theory.

With the Stoics, *phantasia* takes on a distinctive role in their philosophical system drawing on the positions of both Plato and Aristotle. For the Stoics, the event of perception can be divided into *phantasia* and *sunkaisthēsis* (assent). This means that cognitive content is not added to the *phantasia*, but in the event of *sunkaisthēsis* the perceiver recognizes the cognitive content that is inherent within every *phantasia*.[61] Such cognitive content can naturally be expressed in language, and this they call a *lekton* (sayable). This theory becomes the basis of Stoic logic, in which all objects that are perceived can become "signs" with propositional content.[62] With their particular understanding of *phantasia*, the Stoics are able to then con-

---

57. Aristotle, *On the Soul*, 159.

58. Moss, *Aristotle on the Apparent Good*, 51–52.

59. Ibid., 63–65.

60. *On the Soul*, 432a7–11 (*On the Soul*, 181).

61. As Julia Annas (*Hellenistic Philosophy of Mind*, 75) points out, only *phantasiai* experienced in rational animals can be expressed in language even though they also believe that non-rational animals can have *phantasiai*.

62. Imbert, "Stoic Logic and Alexandrian Poetics," 187.

nect *phantasia* with the rhetorical practice of *ekphrasis* in which the orator presents a mental image through words in the mind of the audience.[63]

Phantasia continues to develop under Plotinus and later Neoplatonic writers, and as the philosophical schools debated and interacted with each other, they gave rise to a synthesis that would be characteristic of philosophy in late antiquity. While there is much to examine about *phantasia* in this period, I will highlight three relevant features. First, Plotinus distinguishes two types of *phantasia* in the soul, one corresponding to the sensible world (like Plato, Aristotle, and the Stoics), and one corresponding to the intelligible world.[64] Positing two faculties of *phantasia* allows Plotinus to reason "imaginatively" about the intelligible world with images of the material: "For both have come together into one and the better soul is on top of the other. The other soul, then, sees everything, and takes some things with it which belong to the other when it goes out [of the body] but rejects others."[65] Secondly, *phantasia* is the faculty of the soul that allows one to have visions of the gods.[66] The gods, Iamblichus thinks, appear to humans by illuminating the luminous part of the soul, and this is often in the Neoplatonic tradition (save the objections of Porphyry) necessarily facilitated by *theurgy* for both the philosopher and laity alike.[67] Finally, *phantasia* functions as the creative and linguistic imagination. The paradigmatic figure here is Philostratus's account in the *Life of Apollinarius* in which Apollinarius explains Pheidias's statue of Zeus. Pheidias did not sculpt his statue constructed by imitation (*mimēsis*), which requires something to be *seen*, but he did so in relation to the *unseen* reality itself.[68] Writing in the fifth century CE, Proclus criticizes

---

63. Ibid., 200.

64. Sorabji, *The Commentators*, 63–64.

65. *Ennead* 4.3.31 15–18 (Armstrong, *Plotinus: Enneads IV*, 133). This is different from Aristotle, who works by abstracting forms—which are real universals—from sensible objects. Plotinus, like Plato, thinks one can have direct knowledge of the forms (the higher *phantasia*), but discursive reasoning in our present embodied state requires the use of both *phantasia* in concert.

66. "*Phantasia* was instrumental in attaching the soul to a mortal body through its attraction to sensate images and, again, *phantasia* was instrumental in leading the soul back to its union with the gods in *phōtagōgia* [drawing in the light]. For Iamblichus, *phantasia* has a dual function: it mirrors sensate phenomena and our concepts about it, and it is the medium for the appearances (*phantasma*) of the gods" (Shaw, "The Role of Aethesis in Theurgy," 99).

67. Sorabji, *The Commentators*, 70–71.

68. Ibid., 81.

Pheidias for not making his statue according to the Form (*eidos*), but to the concept (*ennoia*) of Zeus found in Homer.[69]

By the time one gets to the fourth century, it is difficult to completely separate the philosophical tradition from the rhetorical one, and so examining *phantasia* in the rhetorical tradition would overlap with much of what has been summarized so far, so I want to highlight some of the distinctive features. The first thing to be noticed is that for the rhetorical tradition, *phantasia* was approached in more general terms. The focus was not so much epistemological or psychological, but functional; *phantasia* was a tool of persuasion. Thus, ps-Longinus can say:

> For the term *phantasia* is applied in general to an idea which enters the mind from any source and engenders speech, but the word has now come to be used predominantly of passages where, inspired by strong emotion, you seem to see what you describe and bring it vividly before the eyes of your audience.[70]

Secondly, note that ps-Longinus explains *phantasia* in terms of a mental image appearing in the mind of the orator *first*, and then being transferred to the mind of the audience. This transfer is accomplished through the use of language and the rhetorical device of *enargeia*. Through vivid description (*enargeia*), the orator uses language to call to mind *phantasia* stored in the memory of the audience, and this process the rhetoricians called *ekphrasis*.[71] Lastly, ps-Longinus's definition points to the effectual aspect of *phantasia*. The image itself is not the point of the *ekphrasis*, but the *effect* that the image has on the listener.[72] Again, the goal is not epistemology *per se*, but persuasion. Thus, one can see how orators were able to adopt and adapt philosophical reflection on *phantasia* within the context of the persuasive arts.

Gregory uses *phantasia*, *phantazomai*, and *phantasma* in a variety of ways. God is the object—that which appears—of these terms (except *phantasma*) twenty-nine out of the total fifty-four occurrences.[73] The fol-

---

69. Ibid., 81

70. *On the Sublime*, 15.1 (Longinus, *On the Sublime*, 215–16).

71. Webb, *Ekphrasis*, 110–13.

72. Ibid., 127.

73. *Oration* 18.14; *Or.* 20.4; *Or.* 28.6, 11, 13, 18, 19 (three times); *Or.* 29.8; *Or.* 30.17 (twice); *Or.* 31.3, 5, 12, 14, 33; *Or.* 32.16; *Or.* 38.7, 8; *Or.* 39.9; *Or.* 40.5 (twice), 6 (twice), 41; *Or.* 41.11; *Or.* 45.4, 11. It is interesting that Gregory never uses *phantasma* to speak of God's appearance since, as I mentioned in footnote 64, *phantasma* could be used by

CONVERGENCE

lowing persons see God: those who have been purified (*Or.* 40.5), the Old Testament Patriarchs (*Or.* 41.11), Paul on the road to Damascus (*Or.* 40.6), Moses (*Or.* 18.14; *Or.* 32.16; *Or.* 40.6), Manoah (*Or.* 20.4; *Or.* 28.19; *Or.* 39.9), Ezekiel (*Or.* 28.19), David (*Or.* 31.3), Gregory himself (*Or.* 31.33.7; *Or.* 40.41.19), a true theologian (*Or.* 30.17.13), the Jews at Mt. Sinai (*Or.* 45.11, referred to vaguely as "human beings"), and once as the theologically minded pagans (31.5).[74]

I want to make two observations about Gregory's use of *phantasia*. First, one of the qualifications that Gregory makes for God's appearance is that one must be purified. Purification is an important concept in Gregory's theological epistemology.[75] For Gregory, there is a direct correlation between one's purification and knowledge of God. The more one is purified, the more one knows God; the more one knows God, the more one is purified.[76] Conversely, not to be purified, to sin and mar one's soul, to turn away from God, means one will know God less. One is purified, first and foremost, in baptism, but also through ascetic practices, such as constant meditation, prayer, witness, praise, a contrite heart, hospitality, brotherly love, conjugal affection, chastity, feeding the poor, singing psalms, nightly vigils, penitence, fasting, meditation on death, mastery of passions, fasts, sleeping on the ground, tears, and alms giving.[77] *Phantasiai* help in this regard because they simultaneously reveal and hide God.[78] That is, *phanta-*

Iamblichus to speak of the image of the divine that appeared in theurgy.

74. For theologically minded pagans, Gregory may have in mind Platonists and Aristotelians (Norris, *Faith Gives Fullness*, 188). Other objects that are "seen" are: beauty (*Or.* 37.11; *Or.* 43.19; *Carm.* I.II.10.79), belief/*doxa* (*Carm.* I.II.34.99), the body of Christ (*Epist.* 102.15), demons (*Or.* 39.7), vain human desires (*Or.* 16.18) and fantasies (*Or.* 18.26), temporary government of Julian (*Or.* 4.75), Gregory himself (*Or.* 18.31; *De vita sua* 1529, 1772), heavenly bliss (*Or.* 7.21), knowledge of the future (*Or.* 4.31), Maximus the Cynic (referred to as a phantom from Egypt) (*De vita sua* 751), nothing higher than the demons (*Or.* 4.44), pagan myths (*Or.* 4.119), paradise (*Or.* 43.34), God's providence (*Or.* 17.4), the deeper meaning of Scripture (*Or.* 2.48), the reasons for human suffering (*Or.* 14.32), divine warnings (*Or.* 5.2), and other "things" (*Carm.* I.II.28.130; 33.211).

75. Christopher Beeley has given extensive treatment to the idea of purification in Gregory that need not be reproduced here. See in particular chapter 1 of his book, *Gregory of Nazianzus on the Trinity and the Knowledge of God*, 63–113.

76. Oration 40.5.

77. Oration 16.2; 27.4, 7; 40.31.

78. "But, as we have seen, images were the necessary way in which the memory received perceptions from outside itself; they played a positive role: first of all in the creation, recording, and storing of what came to mind from the sense; secondly, in the recollection and retrieval of what had formed the memory in the past, so that they conveyed

siai—by being an explicitly corporeal concept—force one to recognize one's own limits as well as the constant need for purification. Indeed, *God* uses *phantasia* as a means by which he entices us to come to him and purifies us.[79]

Secondly, and perhaps most interestingly, Gregory uses *phantasia* and *phantazomai* frequently to speak of (the immaterial!) God appearing. I noted above that Iamblichus used *phantasia* to speak of the images of the gods in *theurgy* that lead practitioners back up to them. In that sense, what Gregory is doing with the term is not unique, but if he denies the ontological chain leading back up to God that I discussed under Julian, it seems plausible that Gregory is doing something unique. *Phantasiai* function in two ways: as a necessary form of cognition and as a means of persuasion. For Gregory, we only ever think in corporeal terms, so any knowledge of God must be mediated in this way. Thus, Gregory overcomes the ontological gap between the infinite Creator and finite creation, not by ascending an ontological chain, nor by having direct knowledge of God's essence through a name. Instead, God leaps the gap, unites himself to our nature, purifies our minds, and spurs us on through a variegated array of corporeal images we learn primarily through Scripture that point us to, simultaneously revealing and hiding, God.[80] Gregory draws this all together, including his favorite image of light, in *Or.* 32.15:

> God is light, light the most sublime, of which all our light is but a momentary emanation or radiance penetrating the regions below, dazzling though it may appear. As you see, he tramples the gloom

and contained within themselves an identity which had been shaped by habit, custom, and tradition; finally, they were instrumental in ensuring that the memory never became fixed, or took anything as an end in itself, but was aware that what it knew it knew in and through images and signs—that the truth lay beyond it. In other words, images—precisely because they are images and not the reality itself—point beyond themselves, resist idolatry, maintain a sense of openness, and thus, as in the activity of *cogitatio*, invite not so much rational, logical reflection, as exploration, creative improvisation, and the allusive, playful extemporization—in short, imagination—reaching towards their archetypes" (Harrison, *The Art of Listening*, 249).

79. Fulford, "Divine Names," 228–30.

80. *Oration* 38.7. Beeley expresses this same idea but in slightly different terms: "Yet paradoxically—as our discussion here already indicates—God's absolute transcendence can only be understood and expressed *through* the categories of greatness, magnitude, and loftiness (*Or.* 37.2). It is crucial to see that, for Gregory, the pure logic of transcendence serves to characterize a real epistemic ascent through *created concepts* of greatness, which themselves depend on and reflect the nature of the transcendent Creator" (*Trinity*, 95–96, emphasis added).

that surrounds us and made darkness his covering around him, putting it between himself and us, just as Moses also once put a veil between himself and Israel's hardness of heart so that dark nature might not win an easy glimpse of that secret beauty of which only a few are worthy and just as easily reject it because it was effortlessly acquired; and that light might commune with light, drawing it ever upward with desire, and that a mind made pure might approach the most pure and a portion of that light reveal itself now and a portion in the time to come as a reward of virtue and of our inclination or assimilation to it while on this earth. For, says Scripture, now we see in a mirror dimly, but then face to face. Now I know in part; then I shall understand fully, even as I have been fully understood.[81]

CONCLUSION

This study of Gregory has given a snapshot of the types of theological and epistemological issues with which early Christian thinkers wrestled. For Gregory, and for the Patristic authors in general, human beings were created to know God, and even if their articulation of this knowledge differed from author to author, this fundamental principle did not. Moreover, I have shown with Gregory that the two fundamental obstacles to knowledge of God are sin and creation, but that creation itself is strongly affirmed as a good gift of God. Indeed, God uses creation to make himself known to his creatures primarily in the incarnation of Jesus Christ.[82] Yet, despite his positive estimation of the role of creation, and his use of *phantasia* for his theological epistemology, Gregory retains some reticence. He warns that any image is but a small glimpse of the divine, a swift fleeting flash of lighting that is gone as soon as it appears.[83] As helpful as images are—and here would be a fitting place to conclude—they must also be held cautiously as ultimately inadequate:

> In a word, there is nothing to satisfy my mind when I try to illustrate the mental picture I have, except gratefully taking part of

---

81. Vinson, *Select Orations*, 201–2.

82. This affirmation of creation is seen throughout the Christological debates as Christian thinkers struggled to articulate just how exactly Jesus could be both God and man, and their positive affirmation of created existence meant that there was no part of human nature that could be thrown out.

83. *Oration* 38.7.

the image and discarding the rest. So, in the end, I resolved that it was best to say "goodbye" to images and shadows, deceptive and utterly inadequate as they are to express the reality. I resolved to keep close to the more truly religious view and rest content with some few words, taking the Spirit as my guide and, in his company and in partnership with him, safeguarding to the end the genuine illumination I had received from him, as I strike out a path in this world.[84]

BIBLIOGRAPHY

Anatolios, Khaled. *Retrieving Nicaea: The Development and Meaning of Trinitarian Doctrine*. Grand Rapids, MI: Baker Academic, 2011.
Annas, Julia. *Hellenistic Philosophy of Mind*. Hellenistic Culture and Society 8. Berkeley: University of California Press, 1992.
Aristotle. *On the Soul. Parva Naturalia. On Breath*. Translated by W. S. Hett. LCL 288. Cambridge, MA: Harvard University Press, 1957.
Armstrong, A. H., trans. *Plotinus: Ennead IV*. LCL 443. Cambridge, MA: Harvard University Press, 1984.
Ayres, Lewis. *Nicaea and Its Legacy: An Approach to Fourth-Century Trinitarian Theology*. Oxford: Oxford University Press, 2006.
Beeley, Christopher. *Gregory of Nazianzus on the Trinity and the Knowledge of God: In Your Light We Shall See Light*. Oxford Studies in Historical Theology. Oxford: Oxford University Press, 2008.
Behr, John. *The Nicene Faith*. Vol. 2. Formation of Christian Theology. Crestview, NY: St. Vladimir's Seminary Press, 2004.
———. *The Way to Nicaea*. Vol. 1. Formation of Christian Theology. Crestview, NY: St. Vladimir's Seminary Press, 2001.
Daley, Brian E. *Gregory of Nazianzus*. The Early Church Fathers. New York: Routledge, 2006.
DelCogliano, Mark. *Basil of Caesarea's Anti-Eunomian Theory of Names: Christian Theology and Late-Antique Philosophy in the Fourth Century Trinitarian Controversy*. Supplements to Vigiliae Christianae 103. Leiden, Netherlands: Brill, 2010.
DelCogliano, Mark, and Andrew Radde-Gallwitz. *Saint Basil of Caesarea: Against Eunomius*. The Fathers of the Church, A New Translation 122. Washington, DC: The Catholic University of America Press, 2011.
Edwards, Mark. *Image, Word and God in the Early Christian Centuries*. Ashgate Studies in Philosophy & Theology in Late Antiquity. Farnham, UK: Ashgate, 2013.
Egan, John P. "The Knowledge and Vision of God according to Gregory Nazianzen: A Study of the Images of Mirror and Light." PhD diss., Institut Catholique de Paris, 1971.
———. "Towards a Mysticism of Light in Gregory Nazianzen's Oration 32.15." *Studia Patristica* 18 (1989) 473–81.

---

84. *Oration* 31.33 (Williams and Wickham, *On God and Christ*, 142–43).

Ellverson, Anna-Stina. "The Dual Nature of Man: A Study in the Theological Anthropology of Gregory of Nazianzus." PhD diss., Uppsala University, 1981.

Elm, Susanna. *Sons of Hellenism, Fathers of the Church: Emperor Julian, Gregory of Nazianzus, and the Vision of Rome*. Transformation of the Classical Heritage 49. Berkeley: University of California Press, 2012.

Fulford, Ben. *Divine Eloquence and Human Transformation: Rethinking Scripture and History through Gregory of Nazianzus and Hans Frei*. Emerging Scholars. Minneapolis, MN: Fortress, 2013.

———. "Divine Names and Embodied Intellect: Imagination and Sanctification in Gregory of Nazianzus' Account of Theological Language." *Studia Patristica* 50 (2011) 217–31.

Gregg, Robert C., and Dennis E. Groh. *Early Arianism: A View of Salvation*. Minneapolis, MN: Fortress, 1981.

Gregory of Nazianzus. "Select Orations of Saint Gregory Nazianzen." In *S. Cyril of Jerusalem, S. Gregory Nazianzen*. Nicene Post-Nicene Fathers Series 2, vol. 7, edited by Phillip Schaff and Henry Wace, translated by C. G. Browne and J. E. Swallow, 202–434. New York: Christian Literature Company, 1894.

Hanson, R. P. C. *The Search for the Christian Doctrine of God: The Arian Controversy*, 318–81. Grand Rapids, MI: Baker Academic, 1988.

Harrison, Carol. *The Art of Listening in the Early Church*. Oxford: Oxford University Press, 2013.

Harrison, Nonna Verna. *Saint Gregory of Nazianzus: Festal Orations*. Popular Patristics Series 36. Yonkers, NY: St. Vladimir's Seminary Press, 2008.

Harrison, Verna E. F. "Illumined from All Sides by the Trinity: Neglected Themes in Gregory's Trinitarian Theology." In *Re-Reading Gregory of Nazianzus: Essays on History, Theology, and Culture*, edited by Christopher Beeley, 13–30. CUA Studies in Early Christianity. Washington, DC: The Catholic University of America Press, 2012.

Hildebrand, Stephen M. *Basil of Caesarea*. Foundations of Theological Exegesis and Christian Spirituality 3. Grand Rapids, MI: Baker Academic, 2014.

Imbert, Claude. "Stoic Logic and Alexandrian Poetics." In *Doubt and Dogmatism: Studies in Hellenistic Epistemology*, edited by Malcolm Schofield, Myles Burnyeat, and Jonathan Barnes, 182–216. Oxford: Clarendon, 1980.

Kobusch, Theo. "Die Epinoia—Das Menschliche Bewusstsein in Der Antiken Philosophie." In *Gregory of Nyssa: Contra Eunomium II: An English Version with Supporting Studies Proceedings of the 10th International Colloquium on Gregory of Nyssa (Olomouc, September 15–18, 2004)*, edited by Lenka Karfíková, Scot Douglass, and Johannes Zachhuber, 3–20. Supplements to Vigiliae Christianae 82. Leiden: Brill, 2007.

Longinus. *On the Sublime*. Translated by Hamilton W. Fyfe. LCL 199. Cambridge, MA: Harvard University Press, 1995.

Maslov, Boris. "The Limits of Platonism: Gregory of Nazianzus and the Invention of *theōsis*." *Greek, Roman, and Byzantine Studies* 52, no. 3 (2012) 440–68.

McCauley, Leo P. *Funeral Orations by Saint Gregory Nazianzen and Saint Ambrose*. The Fathers of the Church, A New Translation 22. Washington, DC: The Catholic University of America Press, 1968.

McGuckin, John A. *St. Gregory of Nazianzus: An Intellectual Biography*. Crestwood, NY: St Vladimir's Seminary Press, 2001.

Moss, Jessica. *Aristotle on the Apparent Good: Perception*, Phantasia, *Thought, and Desire*. Oxford Aristotle Series. Oxford: Oxford University Press, 2012.

Norris, Frederick W. *Faith Gives Fullness to Reasoning: The Five Theological Orations of Gregory of Nazianzen*. Leiden, Netherlands: Brill, 1991.

———. "Gregory Contemplating the Beautiful: Knowing Human Misery and Divine Mystery Through and Being Persuaded by Images." In *Gregory of Nazianzus: Images and Reflections*, edited by Jostein Børtnes and Tomas Hägg, 19–36. Copenhagen, Denmark: Museum Tusculanum Press, 2006.

———. "Of Thorns and Roses: The Logic of Belief in Gregory Nazianzen." *Church History* 53, no. 4 (1984) 455–64.

Pinault, Henri. *Le Platonisme de Saint Grégoire de Nazianze: Essai Sur Les Relations Du Christianisme et de l'Hellénisme Dans Son Oeuvre Théologique*. G. Romain: La Roche-sur-Yon, France, 1925.

Plato. *Republic, Volume II: Books 6-10*. Edited and translated by Christopher Emlyn-Jones, William Preddy. Loeb Classical Library 276. Cambridge, MA: Harvard University Press, 2013.

Ruether, Rosemary Radford. *Gregory of Nazianzus: Rhetor and Philosopher*. Oxford: Clarendon, 1969.

Shaw, Gregory. "The Role of *Aesthesis* in Theurgy." In *Iamblichus and the Foundations of Late Platonism*, edited by Eugene Afonasin, John Dillon, and John F. Finamore. Studies in Platonism, Neoplatonism, and the Platonic Tradition 13. Leiden, Netherlands: Brill, 2012.

———. *Theurgy and the Soul: The Neoplatonism of Iamblichus*. University Park, PA: The Pennsylvania State University Press, 1995.

Sinkewicz, Robert E. *Evagrius of Pontus: The Greek Ascetic Corpus*. Oxford Early Christian Studies. Oxford: Oxford University Press, 2003.

Sorabji, Richard. *The Philosophy of the Commentators, 200–600 AD, A Sourcebook: Psychology (with Ethics and Religion)*. Vol. 1. Ithaca, NY: Cornell University Press, 2005.

Vaggione, Richard Paul. *Eunomius of Cyzicus and the Nicene Revolution*. Oxford Early Christian Studies. Oxford: Oxford University Press, 2000.

Vinson, Martha. *St. Gregory of Nazianzus: Select Orations*. The Fathers of the Church, A New Translation 107. Washington, DC: The Catholic University of America Press, 2004.

Watson, Gerard. *Phantasia in Classical Thought*. Galway, Ireland: Galway University Press, 1988.

Webb, Ruth. *Ekphrasis, Imagination and Persuasion in Ancient Rhetorical Theory and Practice*. Farnham: Ashgate, 2009.

Wiles, Maurice. "Eunomius: Hair-Splitting Dialectician or Defender of the Accessibility of Salvation?" In *The Making of Orthodoxy: Essays in Honour of Henry Chadwick*, edited by Rowan Williams, 157–72. Cambridge: Cambridge University Press, 2002.

Williams, A. N. *The Divine Sense: The Intellect in Patristic Theology*. Cambridge: Cambridge University Press, 2009.

Williams, Frederick, and Lionel R. Wickham. *On God and Christ: The Five Theological Orations and Two Letters to Cledonius*. Popular Patristics Series 23. Yonkers, NY: St. Vladimir's Seminary Press, 2002.